INTELLECTUAL FREEDOM MANUAL

FOURTH EDITION

Compiled by the   OFFICE FOR INTELLECTUAL FREEDOM
of the
AMERICAN LIBRARY ASSOCIATION

AMERICAN LIBRARY ASSOCIATION

Chicago and London 1992

A revision of "Intellectual Freedom and Librarianship" by Judith F. Krug and
James A. Harvey from *Encyclopedia of Library and Information Sciences*, vol.
12, appears on page xiii.

Composed by Alexander Typesetting, Inc.
in Century and Helvetica on
Datalogics System.

Printed on 50-pound Glatfelter, a pH-neutral stock, and
bound in 10-point Carolina cover stock
by Edwards Brothers Inc.

Project Editor: Kathryn P. Solt

Index: Compiled by Kathryn A. Cairns

The paper used in this publication meets the minimum requirements of
American National Standard for Information Sciences—Permanence of Paper
for Printed Library Materials, ANSI Z39.48-1984.∞

Library of Congress Cataloging-in-Publication Data

Intellectual freedom manual / compiled by the Office for Intellectual Freedom
    of the American Library Association.—4th ed.
        p.   cm.
    Includes bibliographical references and index.
    ISBN: 0-8389-3412-9
    1. Libraries—Censorship—United States—Handbooks, manuals, etc.
    2. Freedom of information—United States—Handbooks, manuals, etc.
    I. American Library Association. Office for Intellectual Freedom.
    Z711.4.I57   1992
    025.2′13—dc20   92-10699
                                                                          CIP

Printed in the United States of America.

96 95 94 93   5 4 3 2

Contents

PART II: PROTECTING THE FREEDOM TO READ

Preface

This manual is designed to answer the many practical questions that confront librarians in applying the principles of intellectual freedom to library service. It is our hope that every librarian will keep this volume close at hand as a convenient reference work. If, for example, a librarian wants to know what the American Library Association can do to help resist censorship of library materials, or how to handle complaints, or simply how to write an appropriate letter to legislators, help can be found in this volume. If the problem is complex—for example, the development of a materials selection program—practical guidelines on how to tackle the problem are offered.

The first section of the manual offers a different kind of help. ALA and Intellectual Freedom explains not only the meaning of intellectual freedom in library service, but also how today's broad concept of intellectual freedom evolved from opposition to book censorship. In parts I and II, Library Bill of Rights and Protecting the Freedom to Read, the documents and brief histories of ALA's various policies interpreting and supporting the Library Bill of Rights also give concrete examples of the kinds of problems librarians can expect to encounter; problems they should anticipate in formulating policy of their own institutions.

Application of the principles and guidelines of this manual cannot assure that the rights of librarians and library users will never be challenged, nor can it guarantee that unexpected difficulties will not arise. But their application to service in every library is absolutely essential if librarians and library users are to escape the whims of the censor and fully enjoy the benefits of freedom of expression under the First Amendment.

JUDITH F. KRUG, *Director*
Office for Intellectual Freedom

Acknowledgment

Special thanks and appreciation are due Andréa Gambino, consultant to the Office for Intellectual Freedom, who updated, edited, and rewrote extensive portions of this manual, and summarized major revisions in many basic policy documents. Without Andréa's detailed, thorough, and meticulous work, this fourth edition of the manual would not have come into existence.

Introduction

Censorship reflects a society's lack of confidence in itself. It is a hallmark of an authoritarian regime...
—JUSTICE POTTER STEWART, dissenting
Ginzberg v. United States, 383 U.S. 463 (1966)

In basic terms, intellectual freedom requires the fulfillment of two essential conditions: first, that all individuals have the right to hold any belief on any subject and to convey ideas in any form the individual deems appropriate; second, that society makes an equal commitment to the right of unrestricted access to information and ideas regardless of the communication medium used, the content of the work, and the viewpoints of both the author and receiver of information. Without the ability of all people to have access to information without restriction, the freedom to express oneself through a chosen mode of communication becomes virtually meaningless. The right of intellectual freedom implies a circle, and that circle is broken if either freedom of expression or access to ideas is stifled.

Intellectual freedom is freedom of the mind, and as such, it is not only a personal liberty, but also a prerequisite for all freedoms leading to action. Moreover, as manifested in the freedoms of speech and press dictates of the First Amendment, intellectual freedom forms the bulwark of our constitutional republic. It is an essential part of the mechanism of government by the people. The right to vote is alone not sufficient to give citizens effective control of official actions and policies. They must also be able to take part in the formation of public opinion by engaging in vigorous and wide-ranging debate on controversial matters. Censorship can only stifle this debate, thus weakening government by the people. In the words of Thomas Paine:

He that would make his own liberty secure, must guard even his
enemy from opposition; for if he violates this duty he establishes a
precedent that will reach to himself.[1]

Intellectual freedom is not only the bulwark of our own constitutional republic, but the rallying cry of those who struggle for democracy from Czechoslovakia to China. The metaphorical circle of
intellectual freedom has expanded to global proportions over the past
two decades with the advent of potent new communications technologies and the growing international recognition of the Universal Declaration of Human Rights, of which article 19 embodies the right of all
people to freedom of expression. As the free flow of information tran-
scends national boundaries, it becomes increasingly clear that prohibitions on the freedom of expression in one country will inhibit the
freedom of those in many other countries around the world. In an age of
multinational media corporations, international computer links, and
global telecommunications, we can no longer think simply in local
terms. Promoting and defending intellectual freedom requires "thinking globally, and acting locally."

The ALA has recognized the importance of global thinking in a new
interpretation of the Library Bill of Rights, entitled The Universal
Right to Free Expression. Recognizing the crucial role which free access to information plays in the international arena, and the international effects of restrictions imposed on the creation, distribution, and
receipt of information and expression, this interpretation acknowledges free expression as a basic human right. The ALA has also recognized for many years the right of individuals to be free from
governmental intimidation in the exercise of their right to free expression. The Policy on Government Intimidation was adopted February 2,
1973, and amended July 1, 1981.

In the realm of local action, all those concerned with preserving
First Amendment rights must work together to counter a multitude of
new challenges to intellectual freedom in the United States. Significant
changes in political, social, and economic conditions in the 1980s and
early 1990s already are having a powerful effect on librarians' ability to
defend intellectual freedom.

The resignation of Supreme Court Justice William Brennan, a
staunch defender of First Amendment rights for many decades, and
Thurgood Marshall, a champion of civil rights, marked the end of an era
of protecting and expanding free expression and individual liberty. The
new court has issued several decisions which narrow considerably the
interpretation of First Amendment protections. First amendment ad-

---

1. Thomas Paine, *Dissertation on First Principles of Government*, p. 242.

vocates must now to turn to the states, where consistency of protection is far from certain. These developments correspond to and are aggravated by a politically conservative climate in which campaigns against free expression can reap political capital for their leaders—e.g., Jesse Helms' crusade against NEA funding for "obscene" art, or President Bush's campaign against flag burning.

A declining economy has given rise to greater social tensions among different racial, ethnic, religious, and class-based groups, engendering calls for restrictions on speech in a misguided effort to curb the harassment or violence that often erupts as a result of real or perceived inequities and unaddressed frustrations. Unstable economic conditions also lead to budget cuts for libraries, schools, and academic institutions, making it easier to eliminate controversial materials and limit the diversity of collections under the guise of economic necessity, thus further limiting access to information for those who are least able to afford it.

In these turbulent times, intellectual freedom is challenged by groups of all descriptions—from right wing conservatives to left wing liberals—and untraditional methods are being used to silence critics or suppress materials deemed objectionable for a variety of reasons. Included among these approaches to censorship are: the use of the federal Racketeer Influenced and Corrupt Organizations (RICO) Act and similar state statutes to prosecute booksellers, newspaper editors, and others for selling allegedly obscene materials (sometimes resulting in confiscation of inventories composed largely of nonobscene constitutionally protected material); the use of Strategic Lawsuits Against Public Participation (SLAPPs) by developers, businesses, or public officials to intimidate critics and quell locally organized opposition to their projects or public policies; the use of zoning laws to restrict booksellers or movie theaters who allegedly sell obscene materials or show obscene films; attempts by law enforcement officials and others to gain access to confidential patron records; labeling campaigns—voluntary or not—to "warn" consumers about the content of books, videos, or musical lyrics; "political correctness" campaigns to purge library collections of works deemed offensive due to racist, sexist, homophobic, ethnic, or religious stereotyping or themes; and perhaps the most insidious and difficult to combat—the trend toward self-censorship to avoid legal battles, negative economic results, emotional duress, or any number of other deleterious consequences which may befall the writer or purveyor of a controversial work.

Now more than ever, librarians need to be mindful of the special role libraries play as centers for uninhibited intellectual inquiry. Librarians have taken upon themselves the responsibility to provide, through their institutions, all points of view on all questions and issues of our times, and to make these ideas and opinions available to anyone who needs or wants them, regardless of age, background, and views. These statements should sound familiar; they are basic principles outlined in the Library Bill of Rights, which serves as the library profession's interpretation of the First Amendment to the United States Constitution.

The freedom of expression guaranteed by the First Amendment and article 19, and the corollary to that freedom, the freedom to read, are uniquely fulfilled by the library. Any person, regardless of station, can have access to materials and information. Of course, libraries are widely recognized as the repositories of civilization, but in order to guarantee that the freedom to read has substance, libraries must also acquire and provide information without prejudice or restriction. It is this latter point which gives the Library Bill of Rights and its guidance of professional librarianship special importance.

But intellectual freedom cannot bring itself into existence. Librarians must apply the principles of intellectual freedom to activities undertaken daily—materials selection, reference service, reevaluation, protection of confidential patron information, and most important, collection building. It is in collection activities and their product, the collection, that intellectual freedom must be reflected.

The role of the library as governed by the Library Bill of Rights cannot be filled by any other societal institution. Newspapers provide information, but it is perforce abridged and can reflect the prejudices of an editor or publisher. Schools educate, but according to a program designed to fit the many, and one attends schools on the conditions of administrators and educators. It is in the library, and in the library alone, that one can learn to the limits of one's abilities and to the limits of what is known.

No one—least of all the librarian—should underestimate the importance of this role. If the significance of this role has been overlooked by many, including librarians, perhaps it is because some librarians have been neither vigorous in the application of these principles nor imaginative in the provision of library services. With the application of the principles of intellectual freedom, with vision and imagination, librarians can, and do, measure up to their unique task.

ALA and Intellectual Freedom: A Historical Overview

Judith F. Krug and James A. Harvey

At the outset, two myths can be dispelled, namely, that intellectual freedom in libraries is a tradition, and that intellectual freedom has always been a major, if not the major, part of the foundation of library service in the United States. Both myths, assumed by many librarians, are grounded in the belief that librarians support a static concept of intellectual freedom. Nothing, however, could be further from the truth.

The attitude of librarians toward intellectual freedom has undergone continual change since the late 1800s when, through the American Library Association (ALA), the profession first began to approach such issues with the semblance of a unified voice. However, ALA has never endorsed a uniform definition of "intellectual freedom." Instead, through the Council, ALA's governing body, the Intellectual Freedom Committee (IFC), and the Office for Intellectual Freedom (OIF), ALA has promoted a variety of principles aimed at fostering a favorable climate for intellectual freedom, but without the limits imposed by a rigid definition. In effect, this approach has allowed a broad definition capable of meeting the needs of librarians as they arise.

A thrust against censorship of published materials initiated the general definition of intellectual freedom, but from this main trunk numerous branches have continued to spring. One concerns the library user's access to all the materials in a library collection. Another pertains to the librarian's professional practice, particularly selecting and making available all published materials to all library users, and *protecting the confidentiality of patron records to ensure that every individual may use the library freely and without fear of reprisals*. At stake also is the librarian's personal intellectual freedom: participation in the democratic process, the right to free expression and to pursue a chosen life-style without fear of professional reprisal. Yet another aspect of intellectual freedom encompasses the library as an institution and its role in social change and education. Of particular importance is the question of "advocacy" versus "neutrality." Can a library committed to intellectual freedom and to providing materials that represent all points of view also support one point of view?

Each of these main branches has sprouted a plethora of twigs, and viewed in its entirety the tree makes anything other than an issue-oriented approach nearly impossible. Consequently, the profession's stance on intellectual freedom has sometimes lagged behind society at large; most often it has paralleled public opinion; and, occasionally, it has anticipated changes in taste, mores, and social issues and has taken positions in advance of the rest of the citizenry.

Censorship of Published Materials

The catalyst spurring librarians to take initial steps toward supporting intellectual freedom was the censorship of specific publications. "Censorship" in this context means not only deletion or excision of parts of published materials, but also efforts to ban, prohibit, suppress, proscribe, remove, label, or restrict materials. Opposition to these activities emanated from the belief that freedom of the mind is basic to the functioning and maintenance of democracy as practiced in the United States. Such democracy assumes that educated, free individuals possess powers of discrimination and are to be trusted to determine their own actions. It assumes further that the best guarantee of effective and continuing self-government is a thoroughly informed electorate capable of making real choices. Denying the opportunity of choice, for fear it may be used unwisely, destroys freedom itself. Opposition to censorship derives naturally from the library's historical role as an educational institution providing materials that develop individuals' abilities, interests, and knowledge. Censorship denies the opportunity to choose from all possible alternatives, and thereby violates intellectual freedom. The library profession has aimed to ensure every individual's freedom of the mind so that society as a whole benefits. Even in this central area, however, the professional position has fluctuated, being influenced by such factors as taste, quality, responsibility, morality, legality, and purpose.

One early incident concerning censorship, one involving a substantial number of librarians, occurred in 1924 when the Librarians' Union of the American Federation of Labor reported that Carnegie libraries fostered "a system under which only books approved in a certain manner may be placed on Carnegie Library shelves and that amounts to censorship and is so intended."[1] The ALA Executive Board considered

---

1. American Library Association, "Minutes of Executive Board Meetings," mimeographed, 3:20 (Sept. 29, 1924).

the union's charges and offered to enlist volunteers to investigate the claims. Apparently, however, the union did not act upon the offer, and the matter was not considered further by the Executive Board.

In 1929, the Association indicated its future approach to censorship when the ALA Executive Board studied a proposed federal tariff bill and opposed prohibition of importing materials "advocating or urging treason, insurrection, or forcible resistance to any law of the U.S. . . . or any obscene book, paper, etc." The board's opposition was based

> on the grounds that this clause creates an effective censorship over foreign literature; will ban many of the classics on modern economics; will keep out material relating to revolution in foreign countries; will indirectly stop the reprinting of such books by our own publishers; and is a reflection upon the intelligence of the American people by implying that they are so stupid and untrustworthy that they cannot read about revolutions without immediately becoming traitors and revolutionaries themselves; and because the question of social policy is withdrawn from the ordinary courts and placed in the hands of officials primarily chosen for their special qualifications in dealing with the administrative details of tariff laws.[2]

Ironically, just four years later, when the Executive Board received a letter requesting that the Association "take some action in regard to the burning of books in Germany by the Hitler regime," the matter was "considered briefly but it was the sense of the meeting that no action should be taken."[3]

In 1934, the Association recorded its first protest against the banning of a specific publication, *You and Machines*, a pamphlet by William Ogburn. Prepared for use in Civilian Conservation Corps camps under a grant from the American Council on Education, the pamphlet was denied circulation by the camps' director, who believed it would induce a philosophy of despair and a desire to destroy existing economic and political structures. Initially, the ALA president and executive secretary wrote a joint letter to President Roosevelt stating that "[governmental] censorship on a publication of this character written by a man of recognized authority is unthinkable."[4] Later the board discussed the banning further and appointed a committee to draft another letter for approval by the ALA Council. The result was a formal request that President Roosevelt "make it possible for the U.S. Commissioner of Education and the Education Director of the Civilian Conservation Corps to direct the educational policies to be operative in

---

2. Ibid., 5:11 (Jan. 1, 1930).
3. Ibid., 6:214 (Oct. 15, 1933).
4. Ibid., 7:89 (Dec. 27, 1934).

these camps and to make available the reading matter essential in a modern program of education."[5]

These examples illustrate the Association's wavering position and reflect the ambivalent attitude of the profession as a whole regarding censorship. A review of library literature reveals relatively few articles on intellectual freedom prior to the 1930s, and many of the articles that did appear supported censorship and only quibbled over the degree and nature of it. Typical was the opinion of ALA President Arthur E. Bostwick, whose inaugural address at the 1908 Annual Conference included these remarks:

> "Some are born great; some achieve greatness; some have greatness thrust upon them." It is in this way that the librarian has become a censor of literature. . . . Books that distinctly commend what is wrong, that teach how to sin and how pleasant sin is, sometimes with and sometimes without the added sauce of impropriety, are increasingly popular, tempting the author to imitate them, the publishers to produce, the bookseller to exploit. Thank Heaven they do not tempt the librarian.[6]

Given the multiplicity of professional attitudes toward censorship of print materials, it is not surprising that censorship of nonprint media was once viewed as completely outside the concerns of the profession. For example, as late as 1938, the ALA Executive Board believed it was inappropriate to protest when the Federal Communications Commission forced a radio station to defend its broadcast of Eugene O'Neill's *Beyond the Horizon*.[7]

The Association's basic position in opposition to censorship finally emerged in the late 1930s when John Steinbeck's *The Grapes of Wrath* became the target of censorship pressures around the country. It was banned from libraries in East St. Louis, Illinois; Camden, New Jersey; Bakersfield, California; and other localities. While some objected to the "immorality" of the work, most opposed the social views advanced by the author.

ALA's initial response to the pressures against *The Grapes of Wrath* was the adoption in 1939 of the Library's Bill of Rights, the precusor of the present Library Bill of Rights, the profession's basic policy statement on intellectual freedom involving library materials. (*See* Library Bill of Rights, in part I.)

---

5. Ibid., 7:48–49 (Dec. 27, 1934).

6. Arthur E. Bostwick, "The Librarian as Censor," *ALA Bulletin* 2:113 (Sept. 1908).

7. American Library Association, "Minutes of Executive Board Meetings," mimeographed, 10:48 (Oct. 5, 1938).

In 1940, one year after adoption of the Library's Bill of Rights, the Association established the Intellectual Freedom Committee. (Originally called the Committee on Intellectual Freedom to Safeguard the Rights of Library Users to Freedom of Inquiry, the committee's name was shortened by Council action in 1948 to Committee on Intellectual Freedom and inverted through usage to Intellectual Freedom Committee.) The 1940 charge to the IFC was "to recommend such steps as may be necessary to safeguard the rights of library users in accordance with the Bill of Rights and the 'Library's Bill of Rights' as adopted by Council."[8] Although the IFC's role has varied, its main function has been to recommend policies concerning intellectual freedom, especially—but not limited to—matters involving violations of the Library Bill of Rights. Although its original statement of authority referred only to library users, in reality the IFC became active in promoting intellectual freedom for librarians and patrons as well. Its diversified role was recognized and formalized in 1970 when the Council approved a revised statement of authority:

> To recommend such steps as may be necessary to safeguard the rights of library users, libraries, and librarians, in accordance with the First Amendment to the United States Constitution and the *Library Bill of Rights* as adopted by the ALA Council. To work closely with the Office for Intellectual Freedom and with other units and officers of the Association in matters touching intellectual freedom and censorship.[9]

The original Library's Bill of Rights focused on unbiased book selection, a balanced collection, and open meeting rooms. It did not mention censorship or removal of materials at the behest of groups or individuals. Over the years, however, the document has been revised, amended and interpreted, often in response to specific situations with general implications. The first change, a 1944 amendment against banning materials considered "factually correct," was occasioned by attacks on *Under Cover*, an exposé of Nazi organizations in the United States, and *Strange Fruit*, a novel about interracial love. Reference to "factually correct" was later dropped, but the directive against removal of materials remained. Opposition to censorship of nonprint media was amended to the document in 1951 because of attacks on films alleged to promote communism. To combat suppression of communist materials or other allegedly "subversive" publications, the Association

---

8. "Cincinnati Proceedings—Council," *ALA Bulletin* 34:P-37 (Aug. 1940).

9. American Library Association, *Handbook of Organization, 1971–1972* (Chicago: ALA, n.d.), p.13.

issued its Statement on Labeling (*see* in part I), which stated that designating materials "subversive" is subtle censorship, because such a label predisposes readers against the materials. Responding to pressures against materials about civil rights activities, a 1967 amendment to the Library Bill of Rights warned against excluding materials because of the social views of the authors. In its 1971 Resolution on Challenged Materials, the Association counseled libraries not to remove challenged materials unless, after an adversary hearing in a court of law, the materials are judged to be outside the protection of the First Amendment. (*See* Challenged Materials, part I.)

The present Library Bill of Rights, as revised in 1980, with its interpretive documents, which were sytematically reviewed and updated in 1980, 1981, 1982, and most recently in a process which began in 1989 and was completed in 1991, recognizes that censorship of any materials, in any guise, eventually affects the library. The bill therefore provides principles for libraries to support, in the broadest sense, in order to oppose censorship and promote intellectual freedom. Referring directly to censorship practices, the bill states that no library materials should be "excluded because of the origin, background, or views of those contributing to their creation," and that materials should not be proscribed or removed because of partisan or doctrinal disapproval" (also in part I).

On its face, the profession's view of intellectual freedom is a pure one, based on a strict reading of the First Amendment to the U.S. Constitution, which states that "Congress shall make no law . . . abridging freedom of speech, or of the press." Within certain limits, for example, laws governing libel and "fighting words," the position relies on the extension of First Amendment rights, through the Fourteenth Amendment, to all library services governed by public agencies. In actual practice, the purist position sometimes gives way to compromises by individual librarians, resulting in removal, labeling, or covert nonselection of certain materials. Changing circumstances necessitate constant review of the Library Bill of Rights and often result in position statements to clarify the document's application. (*See* Interpretations of the Library Bill of Rights in part I.)

If followed by librarians and governing bodies, however, the Association's policy statements provide an effective means of helping to prevent library censorship. Ideally, application of these policies to materials selection, circulation practices, and complaint handling establishes the library as an indispensable information source for individuals exercising their freedom of inquiry.

Free Access to Library Materials

Access to library collections and services is another concern of the profession. For intellectual freedom to flourish, opposition to censorship of materials is not enough. Free access to materials for every member of the community must also be assured. ALA first recognized this in the 1939 Library's Bill of Rights, which included a proviso that library meeting rooms be available on equal terms to all groups in the community regardless of the beliefs and affiliatons of their members.

Another policy on free access emerged from a study of segregation made by the Association's Special Committee on Civil Liberties during the late 1950s. One result of the study was a 1961 amendment to the Library Bill of Rights, stating that "the rights of an individual to the use of a library should not be denied or abridged because of his race, religion, national origins, or political views." This amendment was broadened in 1967, when "social views" and "age" were incorporated to emphasize other areas of potential discrimination. "Age" was included to resolve a long-standing debate on the right of minors to have access to libraries on the same basis as adults. It should be noted that the addition of "age" illustrates one instance in which the library profession acted well in advance of public opinion.

In 1971, at the urging of the Task Force on Gay Liberation of the Social Responsibilities Round Table, the Association recommended that libraries and ALA members strenuously combat discrimination in serving any individual from a minority, whether it be an ethnic, sexual, religious, or any other kind of minority. In 1980, the Library Bill of Rights was revised to encompass all discrimination due to "origin, age, background, or views."

Another aspect of the library patron's access to materials was broached in 1970 when the Internal Revenue Service requested permission from several libraries to examine circulation records to determine the names of persons reading materials about explosives and guerilla warfare. The Association responded by developing its Policy on the Confidentiality of Library Records, urging libraries to designate such records as confidential and accessible only "pursuant to such process, order, or subpoena as may be authorized under the authority of, and pursuant to, federal, state, or local law relating to civil, criminal, or administrative discovery procedures or legislative investigatory power" (*see* part II). The rationale of the policy was that circulation records are purely circumstantial evidence that a patron has read a book, and that fear of persecution or prosecution may restrain users from borrowing any conceivably controversial materials, for whatever purpose.

The question of library records and the confidentiality of relationships between librarians and library users arose again in 1971 regarding the "use of grand jury procedure to intimidate anti-Vietnam War activists and people seeking justice for minority communities." In response, the Association asserted "the confidentiality of the professional relationships of librarians to the people they serve, that these relationships be respected in the same manner as medical doctors to their patients, lawyers to their clients, priests to the people they serve," and that "no librarian would lend himself to a role as informant, whether of voluntarily revealing circulation records or identifying patrons and their reading habits" (*see* policy in part II).

In late 1987 it was disclosed that FBI agents were visiting libraries, in what are best described as "fishing expeditions." In their approaches, agents generally first solicited information from library clerks. They requested information on the use of various library services (e.g., interlibrary loan, database searches) by "suspicious looking foreigners" and, in some instances, asked to see the library's circulation records.

A public confrontation between the IFC and the FBI eventually ensued. The IFC stressed the inextricability of First Amendment and privacy rights, as well as the fact that the Bureau was requesting that librarians violate not only their profession but also the law in 38 states and the District of Columbia. (As of this writing, there are confidentiality laws in 44 states and attorney general opinions supporting confidentiality in two additional states.) The Bureau refused to back away from what it characterized as a program to alert librarians to the possibility that libraries were being used by foreign agents as a place to recruit operatives, that librarians themselves were sometimes targeted for approach by foreign agents, and that valuable material was being stolen by these agents and their operatives. The IFC emphasized, in congressional testimony and in the media, the principle of open access to publicly available information and the central role of libraries in this society as providers of that access.

In Fall 1989, through a Freedom of Information Act (FOIA) request, the ALA obtained documents from the FBI in which 266 individuals, all of whom had in some way criticized the Library Awareness Program (LAP), were identified as subjects of "index checks." These documents also suggested that the Library Awareness Program covered parts of the country other than solely New York City, as previously claimed by the FBI.

Early in 1990, the ALA wrote to President Bush, then Director of the FBI William Sessions, and the relevant House and Senate Committees, urging that the LAP be discontinued and that the files of the 266 individuals be released to them and expunged from FBI records. Direc-

tor Sessions responded in March 1990, defending the program and denying that any investigation of the 266 had taken place, claiming that
"index checks" were administrative and not investigative in nature.
Gordon Conable, Chair of ALA's Intellectual Freedom Committee,
then published an article in *American Libraries*, urging individuals to
make their own FOIA request. To date, to the best of our knowledge,
only one person who filed such a request has received any information
from the FBI.

In addition, the ALA had filed yet another FOIA request which
was denied, as was the appeal of that denial, on the grounds that the
FBI was in litigation with the National Security Archive (NSA) over
the same issue. The FBI promised instead to give the ALA any information released to the NSA. The ALA has yet to receive any further
material form the FBI and has reserved the right to bring suit against
the FBI for denying the ALA's right of appeal and obstructing a legitimate attempt to gain information under the Freedom of Information
Act.

In early 1992, the FBI is still, to the best of our knowledge, conducting what it has termed the Library Awareness Program.

Federal agencies are not alone in attempting to make use of library
patron records. Local law enforcement officials, journalists, students,
parents, fundraisers, marketing professionals, and politicians have
been known to seek borrowing records, registration data, mailing lists,
and other information about library patrons. In 1990, a library director
in Decatur, Texas, challenged one such attempt in court and won an
important first victory for library confidentiality policies. In *Decatur
Public Library* v. *The District Attorney's Office of Wise County* [No.
90-05-192, 271st Judicial District Court; Wise and Jack Counties,
Texas; (Letter Opinion) Judge John R. Lindsey], the district attorney,
investigating a child abandonment case, subpoenaed the records of all
libraries in Wise County, requesting the names, addresses, and telephone numbers of all individuals who had checked out books on childbirth within the previous nine months, the titles they borrowed, and
the dates the materials were checked out and returned. The police had
no evidence indicating that the person who abandoned the child might
have borrowed library books or otherwise used the library. They were
simply conducting a "fishing expedition."

The director of the Decatur Public Library refused to comply with
the subpoena and, with the help of the city attorney, filed a motion to
quash it on behalf of the library's patrons. On May 9, 1990, Judge John
R. Lindsey ruled in favor of the library and quashed the subpoena. His
decision recognized the library's standing to assert a constitutional
privilege on behalf of its unnamed patrons and clients, affirmed a constitutional right of privacy available to patrons, and held that the State

was unable to demonstrate a compelling governmental objective under its police powers or other legitimate function of government to warrant intrusion of those rights.

Through the Association's various position statements, the profession has established a code of free access to services and materials for all library users. Opposed to using the library as a means of intimidating patrons, the profession strives to enhance the intellectual freedom of the library user by providing not only all materials requested, but also free and equal access to all materials without fear of recrimination for pursuing one's interests.

The Librarian and Intellectual Freedom

While the profession, through ALA, formulates policies to help ensure a climate favorable to intellectual freedom, the individual librarian is the key to achieving the end result. Adherence to the Library Bill of Rights by individual librarians is the only means of effecting the profession's goals. Consequently, the concept of intellectual freedom also considers the individual librarian's intellectual freedom, both in pursuit of professional responsibilities and in personal life. Several agencies within or closely affiliated with ALA, accordingly, encourage and protect the librarian's commitment to the principles of intellectual freedom.

From 1940 until 1967, most of such activities were centered in the Intellectual Freedom Committee. For many years it not only recommended policies but also directed a variety of educational efforts including collecting and publicizing information about censorship incidents, sponsoring censorship exhibits at conferences, conducting preconferences on intellectual freedom themes, and planning complementary programs to further the Association's goals regarding intellectual freedom.

One of these complementary programs is the Office for Intellectual Freedom, established in December 1967. OIF evolved finally from a 1965 preconference on intellectual freedom held in Washington, D.C. That meeting recommended establishing an ALA headquarters unit to conduct and coordinate the Association's intellectual freedom activities and to provide continuity for the total program. The goal of OIF is to educate librarians and the general public on the importance of intellectual freedom, relieving the IFC of this task and allowing it to concentrate on developing policy. The OIF serves as the administrative arm of the Intellectual Freedom Committee and bears the responsibility for implementing ALA policies on intellectual freedom, as approved by the Council. The philosophy of the Office for Intellectual Freedom is based on the premise that if librarians are to appreciate the importance of intellectual freedom they must first understand the concept as it relates to the individual, the institution, and the functioning of society. Believing that with understanding comes the ability to teach others, OIF maintains a broad program of informational publications, projects, and services.

The regular OIF publications are the bimonthly *Newsletter on Intellectual Freedom* and the monthly *OIF Memorandum*. In addition, the office prepares special materials, including the *Banned Books Week Resource Kit;* the *Bill of Rights Bicentennial: A Resource Book*, prepared for use during the 1991 bicentennial celebration of the Bill of Rights; issue-oriented monographs such as *Censorship and Selection: Issues and Answers for Schools;* and *Confidentiality in Libraries: An Intellectual Freedom Modular Education Program*. OIF also distributes documents, articles, and all ALA policy statements concerning intellectual freedom. As part of its information program, OIF also maintains and distributes the OIF exhibits, one, a banned books exhibit and the other, a collection of materials representing the broad spectrum of social and political thought. These exhibits are available for display at national, state, and local conferences, workshops, seminars, and other meetings.

The Office for Intellectual Freedom advises and consults with librarians confronting potential or actual censorship programs. Telephone and letter requests about materials which have drawn the censorial efforts of an individual or group in the community prompt efforts to give appropriate assistance. OIF also coordinates the Intellectual Freedom Committee's relations with other agencies having similar concerns. These include the intellectual freedom committees of the ALA divisions and state library association intellectual freedom committees. Close contact with nonlibrary organizations, such as the Association of American Publishers, the American Civil Liberties Union, the National Education Association, and others, is also maintained.

As ALA's intellectual freedom program developed, the need for an organizational form through which individual ALA members could participate in intellectual freedom activities according to their varying levels of interest began to be felt. In June 1973, at the Annual Conference in Las Vegas, the Intellectual Freedom Round Table was organized as the Association's membership activity program for intellectual freedom. The activities of the round table supplement OIF's education program and offer opportunities for ALA members to become active in the Association's intellectual freedom efforts.

By joining IFRT, ALA members contribute financially to various intellectual freedom projects. In 1990, the IFRT's traditional "roll call of the states," which takes place at annual conferences, was reorganized to provide a forum, referred to as the Soap Box, for individuals to discuss the intellectual freedom questions they face daily and to learn how others resolve similar problems. The annual state intellectual freedom committee award, given by the IFRT since 1984, also was revised in 1991. Formerly presented to a state Intellectual Freedom Committee, the award has been expanded to include "state educational media association[s], intellectual freedom committee[s], or state intellectual freedom coalition[s] that ha[ve] implemented the most successful and creative state intellectual freedom project during the calendar year. The award also may be presented for on-going or multiyear projects." IFRT also established the John Philip Immroth Memorial Award for Intellectual Freedom, given annually in memory of the cofounder and first chairperson of the round table, "to honor notable contributions to intellectual freedom and demonstrations of personal courage in defense of freedom of expression." Biennially, the IFRT sponsors the Eli M. Oboler Award presented for the best published work in the area of intellectual freedom.

Soon after adoption of the Library Bill of Rights and establishment of the Intellectual Freedom Committee, the profession realized that more than just informational sources were needed to foster the practice of intellectual freedom in libraries. Some members called for a "policing" effort to publicize censorship problems and bring pressure upon authorities to correct conditions conducive to censorship. As early as the 1948 ALA Annual Conference in Atlantic City, Robert D. Leigh, director of the Public Library Inquiry, addressed the Council and recommended that "some responsible group" be created to investigate reports of library censorship, to make public reports of investigations, to give possible aid to professionals who become victims of censorship, and in extreme cases, to exercise "a professional boycott against the libraries of censoring authorities."[10] Some of Leigh's recommendations were debated for nearly twenty years before a national resolution of the problems began to emerge. As a first substantive step, in 1969 the Association adopted its Program of Action in Support of the Library Bill of Rights.

The first Program of Action, developed by the IFC and approved by the Council, created a mechanism whereby complaints about censorship incidents were reported to the Office for Intellectual Freedom and acted upon by the Intellectual Freedom Committee. Such complaints were studied by the OIF and the IFC to determine whether or not they involved intellectual freedom problems within the scope of the Library Bill of Rights. If the complaint fell under the Program of Action, the Office for Intellectual Freedom and the Intellectual Freedom Committee attempted to mediate, arbitrate, or provide appropriate assistance

---

10. Robert D. Leigh, "Intellectual Freedom," *ALA Bulletin* 42:369 (Sept. 1948).

to effect a just resolution of the problem. If these means failed, one prerogative of the committee was to establish a fact-finding team to investigate further. After such a fact-finding, the team reported its findings to the IFC for review. Further substantive action required a recommendation by the IFC to the ALA Executive Board. Under a Sanctions Policy adopted in 1971, the IFC could recommend publication of a summary of the report, it could recommend publication of the entire report, or it could recommend various other sanctions against groups or individuals violating the spirit of the Library Bill of Rights. The ALA Executive Board made the final disposition of the Intellectual Freedom Committee's recommendations.

From 1969 to 1971, in response to requests for action, three fact-findings were undertaken by the IFC. The first major case was brought by Joan Bodger. An extensive investigation explored Bodger's charge that she had been fired from the Missouri State Library because of her public support of intellectual freedom. She had written a letter to a local newspaper protesting the suppression of an underground newspaper. The IFC concluded that her allegations were correct and recommended publication of the complete report in *American Libraries*. The Executive Board approved, and the report of the Bodger fact-finding team appeared in the July/August 1970 issue of *American Libraries*, vindicating Bodger and deploring the Missouri State Library Commission's actions which resulted in her firing.

The other two requests for action also entailed fact-finding studies, after which the Intellectual Freedom Committee found it could not support charges contained in the complaints. Reports summarizing the two cases were published in *American Libraries*.[11]

The three complaints investigated under the Program of Action made it clear that cases involving intellectual freedom might also raise issues of tenure, academic status, ethical practices, and a variety of other matters. The difficulty of focusing only on intellectual freedom increased in late 1970 when a complaint was received from J. Michael McConnell, who was denied a position at the University of Minnesota Library shortly after his well-publicized application for a marriage license to marry another male. Charging the university discriminated against him because of his homosexuality, McConnell appealed to the IFC, claiming his case fell under the Program of Action. To support his claim, he cited the 1946 ALA Statement of Principles of Intellectual Freedom and Tenure for Librarians, which states: "Intellectual freedom precludes partisan political control of appointments and makes it possible for librarians to devote themselves to the practice of their

---

11. Rosichan summary, *American Libraries* 1:433 (May 1970) and Scott summary, *American Libraries* 2:316–17 (March 1971).

profession without fear of interference or of dismissal for political, religious, racial, marital or other unjust reasons."

The IFC did not dispute McConnell's claim his case fell under the scope of the 1946 policy statement. It disagreed, however, that it came within the jurisdiction of the Program of Action, because that mechanism dealt only with violations of the Library Bill of Rights. The committee attempted to resolve the problem by rewriting the Program of Action to allow jurisdiction over all ALA policies on intellectual freedom. The revision, completed during a special December 1970 meeting of the IFC, was to come before the Council for approval in January 1971. But at its Midwinter Meeting, the committee again revised the document to include all ALA policies on intellectual freedom and tenure. It was then pointed out that both the Library Administration Division (LAD) and the Association of College and Research Libraries (ACRL) claimed vested interests in investigations, particularly those involving tenure of academic librarians. The complex jurisdictional problems resulted in an appeal to ALA President Lillian Bradshaw to take steps immediately to develop a central investigatory agency for the entire Association. Moving swiftly, President Bradshaw appointed a membership group representing various interests. In June 1971, the group presented the Program of Action for Mediation, Arbitration, and Inquiry to the Council, which adopted it and rescinded the first Program of Action.

The new Program of Action established a Staff Committee on Mediation, Arbitration, and Inquiry (SCMAI), which functioned somewhat as the IFC did under the old document. In addition to intellectual freedom problems, however, the new committee handled cases involving tenure, professional status, fair employment practices, ethical practices, and due process as set forth in ALA policies. In June 1990, SCMAI was replaced by the Standing Committee on Review, Inquiry and Mediation (SCRIM). (see p. 247.) Due to lack of funding, SCRIM ceased to operate on September 1, 1992.

The Intellectual Freedom Committee, the Office for Intellectual Freedom, and the Intellectual Freedom Round Table are the primary agencies for establishing and promoting the Association's positions on questions involving intellectual freedom. The activist element in the Association's program in support and defense of intellectual freedom, however, is the Freedom to Read Foundation. The foundation was created outside the structure of ALA and, to insure its full freedom to act with vigor in the political arena, it remains legally and financially independent. But the foundation is closely affiliated with ALA through the ex officio membership of ALA officers on its board of trustees. The foundation's executive director also serves as the director of the Office for Intellectual Freedom.

Incorporation of the Freedom to Read Foundation in November 1969 was ALA's response to librarians who increasingly wanted defense machinery to protect their jobs from jeopardy when they undertook to challenge violations of intellectual freedom. Another primary objective in establishing the foundation was to have a means through which librarians and other concerned individuals and groups could begin to set legal precedents for the freedom to read.

A program of education on the importance of, and the necessity for a commitment to, the principles of intellectual freedom requires assurance that such commitment will not result in reprisals, such as legal prosecution, financial loss, or personal damage. The Freedom to Read Foundation attempts to provide that assurance through financial and legal assistance and judicial challenge of restrictive legislation, thereby helping to create a favorable climate for intellectual freedom. Through the provision of financial and legal assistance, the foundation attempts to negate the necessity for librarians to make the difficult choice between practical expediency (that is, maintaining a job) and upholding principles, such as in selecting materials for library collections. Through its various projects and grants, the foundation hopes to establish those principles enunciated in the Library Bill of Rights as legal precedents rather than mere paper policies.

Established by the Freedom to Read Foundation, but now formally independent, is the LeRoy C. Merritt Humanitarian Fund, created in 1970. The Merritt Fund was established by the Freedom to Read Foundation's board of trustees in recognition of the individual's need for subsistence and other support when his position is jeopardized or lost as a result of defending intellectual freedom. This special fund offer short-term, immediate assistance even prior to the development of all pertinent facts in a particular case, whether or not legal action has been taken.

The philosophy underlying the Freedom to Read Foundation and the Merritt Fund is perhaps best expressed in the Intellectual Freedom Statement (adopted June 1971 by the ALA Council), which states in part:

> Both as citizens and professionals, we will strive by all legitimate means open to us to be relieved of the threat of personal, economic, and legal reprisals resulting from our support and defense of the principles of intellectual freedom.
>
> Those who refuse to compromise their ideals in support of intellectual freedom have often suffered dismissals from employment, forced resignations, boycotts of products and establishments, and other invidious forms of punishment. We perceive the admirable, often lonely, refusal to succumb to threats of punitive

action as the highest form of true professionalism: dedication to the cause of intellectual freedom and the preservation of vital human and civil liberties (*see* p. 101).

In the combined forces of the Intellectual Freedom Committee, the Office for Intellectual Freedom, the Intellectual Freedom Round Table, the Staff committee on Mediation, Arbitration, and Inquiry, and the Freedom to Read Foundation, along with the LeRoy C. Merrit Humanitarian Fund, the library profession has available a complete program to support the practice of intellectual freedom. However, the profession has not yet achieved the same success in a closely related area, that of the librarian's personal rather than professional intellectual freedom. The question of what support should be given to librarians who suffer professionally because of personal beliefs and actions has been approached in individual cases but has not been fully resolved.

One of the first instances involving potential recriminations in a professional capacity due to personal beliefs occurred in the late 1940s, with the advent of "loyalty oaths" and "loyalty programs" designed to ferret out Communists and "subversives." The Intellectual Freedom Committee faced the loyalty issue with its Policy on Loyalty Programs, first adopted by the Council in 1948 and revised in 1951. When another case arose in Florida in 1969, the Policy on Loyalty Programs was reexamined and again revised. The last revision, adopted by the Council in January 1971, states, in part, that: "The American Library Association strongly protests loyalty programs which inquire into a library employee's thoughts, reading matter, associates, or membership in organizations, unless a particular person's definite actions warrant such investigation. We condemn loyalty oaths as a condition of employment and investigations which permit the discharge of an individual without a fair hearing."[12]

In 1969, another incident arose involving a librarian who lost his position because of actions, based on personal beliefs, taken in his capacity as a private citizen. T. Ellis Hodgin was fired as city librarian of Martinsville, Virginia, shortly after he joined a lawsuit challenging the constitutionality of a religious education course taught in the city school his daughter attended. He had also been active in civil rights efforts. Hodgin's situation sparked a controversy among librarians, resulting in a recommendation from the Intellectual Freedom Subcommittee of the Activities Committee on New Directions for ALA (ACONDA) that:

---

12. "Resolution on Loyalty Investigations," *American Libaries* 2:270 (March 1971).

The scope of intellectual freedom encompasses considerably more than just the freedom to read. Support must also be rendered to the librarian who is fired for sporting a beard, for engaging in civil rights activities, etc., etc. And he should not have to claim "poverty" in order to receive it.[13]

The recommendation, however, was not approved as part of the final ACONDA report.

Some concerned librarians responded to Hodgin's plight by organizing the National Freedom Fund for Librarians (NFFL) which collected several thousand dollars to aid him. (When the NFFL disbanded in 1971, its cash balance was sent to the LeRoy C. Merritt Humanitarian Fund.)

Hodgin also appealed to the Freedom to Read Foundation for assistance to defray the financial hardship he suffered due to the loss of his position. In June 1970, the foundation's executive committee awarded him $500 "for having suffered in his defense of freedom of speech as a result of which he lost his position as a librarian. Inasmuch as it is the obligation of the librarian to protect free speech and a free press through his work as a librarian, it is then particularly appropriate that, when he is deprived of his job because of his own exercise of free speech, the Freedom to Read Foundation assist him in the defense of his freedom."[14] A second grant of $500 was made to Hodgin in January 1971, for the specific purpose of perfecting an appeal of his suit for reinstatement to the U.S. Supreme Court.

The limits of intellectual freedom were again debated by the profession when the previously mentioned case of J. Michael McConnell arose in 1970. The Intellectual Freedom Committee found that McConnell's rights "under the First Amendement have been violated" because he met reprisals for freely expressing his sexual preference.[15] On that basis the LeRoy C. Merritt Humanitarian fund granted $500 to help defray financial hardship occasioned by his inability to find another job.

The question of how far librarians are willing to extend the scope of intellectual freedom for the benefit of their colleagues was raised anew in 1979 by the case of Utah librarian Jeanne Layton. In September 1979 Layton was dismissed from her position as library director in Davis County after she refused to comply with requests to remove the novel

---

13. American Library Association Activities Committee on New Directions for ALA, "Final Report and Subcommittee Reports, June 1970," mimeographed, p. 53.

14. "Hodgin Appeal Rests with U.S. Supreme Court," *Freedom to Read Foundation News* 1:5 (Fall 1971).

15. David K. Berninghausen, "Report of the Intellectual Freedom Committee to Council, Dallas, June 25, 1971," *American Libraries* 2:891 (Sept. 1971).

Americana, by Don DeLillo, from library shelves. The following month she filed suit to regain her job.

The suit was supported from the beginning by the Freedom to Read Foundation, but it soon became clear that the legal battle would be a lengthy and very costly one. Both the Intellectual Freedom Committee and the Freedom to Read Foundation designated the case a priority for 1980. The Utah Library Association rallied librarians and others statewide in support. At the 1980 ALA Annual Conference in New York, the Freedom to Read Foundation announced that it would match two dollars for every dollar contributed to Jeanne Layton's defense from June 27, 1980, to December 31, 1980, up to a limit of $10,000 in matching funds. The response was in the words of Foundation President Florence McMullin, "nothing short of overwhelming." When the challenge expired, $6,024 had been received, of which $5,000 was matched "2 for 1" by the foundation. Moreover, Jeanne Layton won her suit, regained her job, and one of her main antagonists was defeated for reelection to the county commission.

While the question of how far librarians will go to support colleagues in defense of intellectual freedom will always be resolvable only on a case-by-case and issue-by-issue basis, the response to Layton's courageous stand surely indicates that in general the library profession takes its responsibilities on this front seriously indeed.

The Library and Intellectual Freedom

Each aspect of intellectual freedom in libraries which has been discussed to this point has involved people—library users and their access to all published materials, as well as librarians and their practice of professional and/or personal intellectual freedom.

One last branch of intellectual freedom remains to be examined, that being the library as an institution and the nature of its role in social change and education. Continually debated within the profession and the American Library Association, the issue has been summarized as "neutrality versus advocacy." In essence, the question is, can libraries, as institutions, advocate social or political causes and still maintain their image as providers of views representing all sides of all questions?

Whenever the question is raised, it initiates further queries. For example, what constitutes advocating a cause—biased book selection, biased displays, prejudicial assignment of library meeting rooms? Or, what constitutes a cause—peace, ecology, democracy? If a library sponsors a display of books on peace, in order to maintain neutrality must it also sponsor a display on war? The questions are complex, and the answers have shown no uniformity whatsoever. The American Library Association itself has vacillated on the main issue, reaching only a partial resolution in the late 1960s and and the early 1970s.

At the 1969 Annual Conference in Atlantic City, the membership and the Council debated whether or not the Association should take a public stand opposing the war in Vietnam or opposing deployment of an antiballistic missile system (ABM). It was argued that because political and moral issues are so deeply entangled with education and library issues, institutions such as ALA and libraries are obligated to take such positions. Those who opposed such positions argued in favor of neutrality on questions not directly related to libraries. They argued that intellectual freedom for those librarians opposed to the majority view would be violated if the Association attempted to take stands on social and political issues. They further maintained that they had tradition on their side, since the Association had always declined to take a stand on issues not directly related to libraries. That argument, of course, was incorrect. The Association had previously taken stands in some instances and refused to do so in others.

In June 1921, for example, the ALA Council espoused a very decided position on the question of disarmament after the First World War. In a strong resolution, the Council stated:

> WHEREAS, The members of the American Library Association had full demonstration of the pain and pinch that belongs to war and the increased cost of all necessities, both personal and professional, caused thereby; and
>
> WHEREAS, The exigencies of international conditions brought about by the cost of war is appalling from every standpoint; and
>
> WHEREAS, We believe the example of the United States in this matter will be followed by the other nations—therefore be it
>
> RESOLVED, That the American Library Association urges upon the president of the United States and Congress the initiative of a movement leading to a reduction of armament at the earliest possible moment; and be it further
>
> RESOLVED, That a request be made by the members of the American Library Association to their individual congressman for such action and that a record be made of the replies.[16]

However, in 1928, when faced by a request from the American Civil Liberties Union that ALA adopt "one or more resolutions on civil liberty," the ALA Executive Board declined, saying the Association "does not take actions on questions outside the library and biblio-

---

16. *ALA Bulletin* 15:169 (July 1921).

graphic field."[17] That was similar to the philosophy which prevailed in 1969, when the Vietnam and ABM resolutions failed to pass the Council. The question arose again, though, at the 1970 and 1971 Midwinter Meetings and Annual Conferences. After a great deal of debate, the Council voted at its 1970 Annual Conference in Detroit to "define the broad social responsibilities of ALA in terms of . . . the willingness of ALA to take a position on current critical issues with the relationship to libraries and library service clearly set forth in the position statements.[18]

In line with this policy a carefully reworded resolution opposing the war in Vietnam was adopted by the Council one year later:

> WHEREAS, The stated objective of the American Library Association is the promotion and improvement of library service and librarianship; and
>
> WHEREAS, Continued and improved library service to the American public requires sustained support from the public monies: and
>
> WHEREAS, The Continuing U.S. involvement in the conflict in Southeast Asia has so distorted our national priorities as to reduce substantially the funds appropriated for educational purposes, including support for library services to the American people; and
>
> WHEREAS, Continued commitment of U.S. arms, troops, and other military support has not contributed to the solution of this conflict, be it therefore
>
> RESOLVED, That the American Library Association call upon the president of the United States to take immediately those steps necessary to terminate all U.S. military involvement in the present conflict in Southeast Asia by December 31, 1971, and to insure the reallocation of national resources to meet pressing domestic needs.[19]

With approval of the Vietnam resolution, the Association seemed to give broader interpretation to the old "library and bibliographic field." However, this more permissive interpretation still did not resolve the more basic question of whether libraries themselves should follow the course of neutrality or advocacy.

The contradiction was further focused in July 1974, when ALA endorsed the Equal Rights Amendment. ALA's support for ERA went much further than its opposition to U.S. military involvement in South-

---

17. American Library Association, *Minutes of Executive Board Meetings* 4:142 (May 29, 1928).

18. *American Libraries* 1:674 (July–Aug. 1970).

19. "Resolution on Southeast Asia Conflict," *American Libraries* 2:826 (Sept. 1971).

east Asia. In 1977, the Council voted not to hold conferences in states which had not ratified the amendment. In June 1978, the Council endorsed the ERA Extension Resolution and, at the 1979 Midwinter Meeting, established an ERA Task Force charged with assisting and consulting with "ALA Chapters in carrying out the commitment to passage of the Equal Rights Amendment in ways best suited to the individual states."[20]

The Association justified this active support of the proposed amendment, first, by noting the support already expressed by other professional associations "by reason of its beneficial implications for all persons in the American society," and, more specifically, as an outgrowth of ALA's policy requiring equal employment opportunity in libraries, adopted at the 1974 Midwinter Meeting. The resolution in support of ERA noted that "women constitute 82 percent of the library profession." Hence, it was argued, "equal employment . . . required support of equal rights for women."[21] None of the operative resolutions on ERA addressed themselves to the content of library collections. Opponents of the amendment and pro-ERA advocates of ALA neutrality, however, were quick to argue that library users "have a right to expect the library to furnish them with uncensored information on both sides of this and all other issues. Adoption of advocacy positions and participation in boycotts cannot help but strike a blow at the public's confidence in the fair-mindedness and even-handedness of librarians."[22]

Yet another aspect of the advocacy versus neutrality conundrum was addressed by the Association in 1987 at its Annual Conference in San Francisco. David Henington, director of Houston Public Library, brought to the IFC for its response and assistance an anti-apartheid ordinance passed and implemented by the City of Houston. This ordinance required that all city agencies obtain certification from suppliers of goods and services that they had no affiliates in, and did no business with, the Republic of South Africa.[23] Henington asserted that this requirement was causing serious acquisition problems for the library. Major information services such as the New York Times Company, the Wall Street Journal and leading publishers refused to sign such certificates. Some refused because they have reporters in South Africa, one religious group because it has missionaries there, and on principle, in the belief that the free flow of information both into and out of the

---

20. *News Release*, American Library Association, September 1979.

21. ALA Council Minutes, 1974, p.335.

22. Terence L. Day, Chairman, Neill Public Library Board of Trustees, Letter to the Editor, *Chicago Tribune*, January 21, 1979.

23. The Houston City Council subsequently voted to exempt both the public library and the city zoo from the requirements of the ordinance.

Republic of South Africa must be defended and enlarged for the sake of those struggling to dismantle the apartheid system there. Because it did not have a copy of the ordinance in hand and because it has received reports of similar ordinances elsewhere, the IFC voted to explore the matter further.

Two ALA members decided that the issue should be taken to the membership at that Conference, and they presented a resolution at the Membership Meeting. The resolution stressed the intellectual freedom implications of this policy and asked that ideas and information be exempted from the laudable goal of enforcing economic sanctions against the Republic of South Africa for its abhorrent apartheid system. A heated encounter ensued between the presenters and other supporters of the resolution and those who saw it as supportive of apartheid and, therefore, racist. The resolution was resoundingly defeated.

At the 1988 Annual Conference in New Orleans, the membership adopted a resolution reaffirming its commitment to article 19 of the Universal Declaration of Human Rights: "Everyone has the right to freedom of opinion and expression; this right includes freedom to hold opinions without interference and to seek, receive and impart information and ideas through any media regardless of frontiers."

Measuring the Profession's Response

The foregoing discussion illustrates that anything other than an issue-oriented definition of intellectual freedom is impossible. At the present time the profession uniformly disdains censorship of published materials, print or nonprint. The attitude toward user access is somewhat uniform, but contains a great deal of dissent on the question of access for minors to all the materials in a library collection. On the question of the librarian's professional practice of intellectual freedom, there is near agreement that every effort should be made to encourage and protect this aspect of librarianship. The librarian's personal intellectual freedom, on and off the job, presents some points of agreement, but major areas of dissent still exist. The same is true in the area of institutional neutrality versus advocacy.

One conclusion from a review of the history, status, and future of intellectual freedom in libraries is that the American Library Association's positions and programs provide one of the few gauges for measuring the profession's response to the problems of defining, promoting, and defending the concept. ALA's evolving position reflects the steady emergence of a philosophy within the entire library community. While that philosophy exhibits some loose ends, its core grows firmer, based on a history of trial and error and forced response to a changing social climate. The philosophy is young, too young to be rooted in tradition, but, gradually it has gained recognition as the substance of the total philosophy shaping library service in the United States.

At the 1990 Midwinter Meeting, the ALA was asked to review and support an Association of American Publishers (AAP) report on the effect of book boycotts in South Africa entitled, *The Starvation of Young Black Minds: The Effect of Book Boycotts in South Africa,* which recommended that the boycott on books and other educational materials be discontinued. The Intellectual Freedom Committee reported no existing ALA policy upon which to base recommendations regarding the AAP report, and at the 1990 Annual Conference proposed a new interpretation of the Library Bill of Rights, initially called The Free Flow of Information, to address free expression issues raised in the global arena. The resolution was adopted by Council at the 1991 Midwinter Meeting as, The Universal Right to Free Expression, An Interpretation of the Library Bill of Rights. At the same time, Council adopted article 19 of the Universal Declaration of Human Rights as official ALA policy. This action superseded a 1988 ALA membership resolution, reaffirming its commitment to article 19, which reads: "Everyone has the right to freedom of opinion and expression; this right includes freedom to hold opinions without interference and to seek, receive and impart information and ideas through any media regardless of frontiers."

Simultaneously with the 1990 AAP request, the Social Responsibility Round Table (SRRT) proposed Guidelines for Librarians Interacting with South Africa. The Intellectual Freedom Committee responded with a Memorandum on Guidelines for Librarians Interacting with South Africa in which the Committee recommended that the guidelines be rewritten to address, among other matters, the intellectual freedom concerns absent from the text. The ALA Council declined to adopt the guidelines as written, following which a motion carried to refer the guidelines back to the IFC, the International Relations Committee (IRC), and the Committee on Professional Ethics. At the 1991 Midwinter Meeting, these committees returned a joint recommendation that no further action be taken until the guidelines were rewritten. The Council then referred the document to the Executive Board.

As of this writing, the subject of including books and informational materials in the sanctions against South Africa has yet to be revisited in light of the new policy, The Universal Right to Free Expression. With the recent relaxation of sanctions against South Africa by many members of the European Community, the issue soon may be mooted by the rapidly changing course of events both in South Africa and around the world.

The most recent issue to raise the advocacy versus neutrality controversy was the war in the Persian Gulf. At the 1991 Midwinter Meeting, the Council passed a resolution condemning the war, an action which provoked strong protest from parts of the ALA membership, many of whom believe the Association should not involve itself in matters of public policy not directly related to library interests and concerns. Also at the 1991 Midwinter Meeting, the new policy on The Universal Right to Free Expression was inaugurated with the passage of two resolutions calling for the "exemption of publications and other informational materials from sanctions" levied by the United States and by the United Nations against Iraq and Kuwait.

The passage of the Universal Right to Free Expression opens new vistas to librarians' concerned about intellectual freedom. With the exponential growth in global communications and publications, it will be possible for American Librarians to act in support of their colleagues and counterparts in countries where intellectual freedom principles are under fire, such as China, Turkey, Israel, Syria, Saudi Arabia, Guatemala, El Salvador, Kenya, and many others. Conversely, librarians facing censorship attempts in the United States may benefit from the experience and support of those in other countries who have endured far greater challenges. Undoubtedly, as threats to free expression at home and abroad become more complex and interwoven, the line separating advocacy from neutrality will be crossed many times. Following the best of democratic traditions, a healthy debate on the library's role in the issues of the moment must be encouraged.

PART I

Library Bill
of Rights

1

LIBRARY BILL OF RIGHTS

The American Library Association affirms that all libraries are forums for information and ideas, and that the following basic policies should guide their services.

1. Books and other library resources should be provided for the interest, information, and enlightenment of all people of the community the library serves. Materials should not be excluded because of the origin, background, or views of those contributing to their creation.

2. Libraries should provide materials and information presenting all points of view on current and historical issues. Materials should not be proscribed or removed because of partisan or doctrinal disapproval.

3. Libraries should challenge censorship in the fulfillment of their responsibility to provide information and enlightenment.

4. Libraries should cooperate with all persons and groups concerned with resisting abridgment of free expression and free access to ideas.

5. A person's right to use a library should not be denied or abridged because of origin, age, background, or views.

6. Libraries which make exhibit spaces and meeting rooms available to the public they serve should make such facilities available on an equitable basis, regardless of the beliefs or affiliations of individuals or groups requesting their use.

Adopted June 18, 1948. Amended February 2, 1961, June 27, 1967, and January 23, 1980, by the ALA Council.

Library Bill of Rights: History

The Library Bill of Rights constitutes the American Library Association's basic policy on intellectual freedom. The bill derives from a statement originally developed by Forrest Spaulding, librarian of the Des Moines Public Library, and adopted by that library on November 21, 1938, as the Library's Bill of Rights.

> Now when indications in many parts of the world point to growing intolerance, suppression of free speech, and censorship, affecting the rights of minorities and individuals, the Board of Trustees of the Des Moines Public Library reaffirms these basic policies governing a free public library to serve the best interests of Des Moines and its citizens.
>
> 1. Books and other reading matter selected for purchase from public funds shall be chosen from the standpoint of value and interest to the people of Des Moines, and in no case shall selection be based on the race or nationality, political, or religious views of the writers.
>
> 2. As far as available material permits, all sides of controversial questions shall be represented equally in the selection of books on subjects about which differences of opinion exist.
>
> 3. Official publications and/or propaganda of organized religious, political, fraternal, class, or regional sects, societies, or similar groups, and of institutions controlled by such, are solicited as gifts and will be made available to library users without discrimination. This policy is made necessary because of the meager funds available for the purchase of books and reading matter. It is obviously impossible to purchase the publications of all such groups and it would be unjust discrimination to purchase those of some and not of others.

4. Library meeting rooms shall be available on equal terms to all organized nonprofit groups for open meetings to which no admission fee is charged and from which no one is excluded.

The document approved by the ALA Council at the 1939 Annual Conference in San Francisco as the Library's Bill of Rights retained the spirit of the Des Moines Public Library policy, but differed from the original in several respects. The principal differences concerned articles 2, 3, and 4 of the Des Moines policy. In article 2, reference to equal representation "in the selection of books on subjects about which differences of opinions exist" was changed to "fair and adequate" representation. This change recognized the impossibility of equal representation in terms of numbers of volumes on a particular subject. Article 3 of the Des Moines policy was completely deleted because it dealt with the invidividual budget, needs, and purposes of a specific library. As such, it was inappropriate for a document to be applied nationwide.

Article 4 of the Des Moines policy, concerning the use of library meeting rooms, was revised extensively before approval by the Council. An introductory phrase establishing the library as "an institution to educate for democratic living" was added, and references to "nonprofit groups" and "admission fee" were deleted. The resulting article broadened the sense of the original by stating that library meeting rooms be available "on equal terms to all groups in the community regardless of their beliefs or affiliations." As adopted by the ALA Council, the revised Library's Bill of Rights read as follows:

Today indications in many parts of the world point to growing intolerance, suppression of free speech, and censorship affecting the rights of minorities and individuals. Mindful of this, the Council of the American Library Association publicly affirms its belief in the following basic policies which should govern the services of free public libraries.

1. Books and other reading matter selected for purchase from the public funds should be chosen because of value and interest to people of the community, and in no case should the selection be influenced by the race or nationality or the political or religious views of the writers.

2. As far as available material permits, all sides of questions on which differences of opinion exist should be represented fairly and adequately in the books and other reading matter purchased for public use.

3. The library as an institution to educate for democratic living should especially welcome the use of its meeting rooms for socially useful and cultural activities and the discussion of current public questions. Library meeting rooms should be available on equal

terms to all groups in the community regardless of their beliefs or affiliations.

The three-point declaration approved by the Council was recommended by the Association to governing boards of individual libraries for adoption. ALA could not force individual librarians and boards to take specific action but this policy statement, as all other Association recommendations and statements, provided a guide.

For five years, the Library's Bill of Rights stood without change. In 1944 the Intellectual Freedom Committee, chaired by Leon Carnovsky, recommended that article 1 of the document be amended to include the statement, "Further, books believed to be factually correct should not be banned or removed from the library simply because they are disapproved of by some people." Approved by the ALA Council on October 14, 1944, the amendment proclaimed for the first time the Association's position regarding the banning or removal of materials. The addition, however, also introduced the phrase "factually correct," which was later to be a source of controversy, debate, and change.

Four years later, with David K. Berninghausen as chair, the Intellectual Freedom Committee recommended a broad revision of the Library's Bill of Rights and called for a considerable expansion of the document's scope. Its introductory passage was pared to a precise statement of the Association's purpose: "The Council of the American Library Association reaffirms its belief in the following basic policies which should govern the services of all libraries." By 1948, there was no longer the pre-World War II need to point out "growing intolerance, suppression of free speech, and censorship affecting the rights of minorities and individuals." In the developing cold war, those factors justifying the 1939 policy were even more evident, and it was recognized that the remedies stated in the Library's Bill of Rights were necessary to protect free library service in times of peace as well as of crisis.

Article 1 was prefaced by the phrase, "As a responsibility of library service." Intellectual freedom was thus clearly related to the process of materials selection and, moreover, highlighted by being designated as a "responsibility." Reference to purchase from the public funds was deleted, thereby extending application of the policy to all library materials, not just those acquired through purchase. Whereas the 1939 document stated that selection should not be influenced by the race, nationality, or political or religious views of writers, the revision more explicitly said that no materials by any authors should be excluded on those grounds.

The first part of article 2 was changed to effect a smoother reading, but there were no substantive alterations. However, the 1944 amendment concerning "books believed to be factually correct" was changed to "books . . . of sound factual authority" and the word "banned" was replaced by "proscribed." Despite their seeming slightness, these subtle changes in the second part of the article actually enlarged the scope of the policy.

A totally new article 3 recognized the need of libraries to challenge "censorship of books, urged or practiced by volunteer arbiters of morals or political opinion or by organizations that would establish a coercive concept of Americanism." A new article 4 recognized the libraries' responsibility to cooperate with "allied groups . . . in science, education, and book publishing in resisting all abridgment of the free access to ideas and full freedom of expression." Article 3 of the 1939 document, concerning the use of library meeting rooms, became article 5 of the new policy. Although the wording was altered, no change was made in the intent.

The entire recommended revision was adopted by the ALA Council on June 18, 1948. In effect, it was a completely different document from its predecessor, the 1939 bill. The new bill's scope and possible applications were broadly expanded, establishing its national significance. For the first time, the policy mentioned censorship, and also for the first time, the Association declared the responsibility of libraries to challenge censorship—alone and with allied organizations. As adopted by the Council, the newly entitled Library Bill of Rights read as follows:

> The Council of the American Library Association reaffirms its belief in the following basic policies which should govern the services of all libraries.
>
> 1. As a responsibility of library service, books and other reading matter selected should be chosen for values of interest, information and enlightenment of all the people of the community. In no case should any material be excluded because of race or nationality, or the political or religious views of the writer.
>
> 2. There should be the fullest practicable provision of material presenting all points of view concerning the problems and issues of our times, international, national, and local; and books or other reading matter of sound factual authority should be proscribed or removed from library shelves because of partisan or doctrinal disapproval.
>
> 3. Censorship of books, urged or practiced by volunteer arbiters of morals or political opinion or by organizations that would establish a coercive concept of Americanism, must be challenged by libraries in maintenance of their responsibility to provide public information and enlightenment through the printed word.

4. Libraries should enlist the cooperation of allied groups in the fields of science, of education, and of book publishing in resisting all abridgment of the free access to ideas and full freedom of expression that are the tradition and heritage of Americans.

5. As an institution of education for democratic living, the library should welcome the use of its meeting rooms for socially useful and cultural activities and discussion of current public questions. Such meeting places should be available on equal terms to all groups in the community regardless of the beliefs and affiliations of their members.

While the text of the 1948 document remained unchanged until 1961, its application was broadened in 1951. On the recommendation of the Intellectual Freedom Committee, with the endorsement of the Audio-Visual Board, the Council unanimously resolved that "the Library Bill of Rights shall be interpreted as applying to all materials and media of communication used or collected by libraries." The statement, appended as a footnote to all printings of the Library Bill of Rights until June 27, 1967, resulted from a Peoria, Illinois, case of attempted censorship by the American Legion and a local newspaper. The Peoria Public Library was pressured to remove the films *The Brotherhood of Man, Boundary Lines*, and *Peoples of the U.S.S.R.* All three films appeared on the ALA Audio-Visual Committee's 1947 list of films suggested for purchase by small libraries. The Educational Film Library Association urged ALA to combat censorship of library film collections, but some librarians contended that the Library Bill of Rights applied only to print on paper. The Council resolved the problem by its action of February 3, 1951.

In 1961, another major addition to the Library Bill of Rights was approved by the Council. From 1948 through February 1961, the library profession had studied the problem of segregation in libraries. A study made by the Association's Special Committee on Civil Liberties recommended that a new article be added to the Library Bill of Rights stating that "the rights of an individual to the use of a library should not be denied or abridged because of his race, religion, national origins, or political views." The recommendation was approved by the Council February 2, 1961. The new statement became article 5 and the old article 5, concerning use of meeting rooms, became article 6. The revised Library Bill of Rights read:

The Council of the American Library Association reaffirms its belief in the following basic policies which should govern the services of all libraries.

1. As a responsibility of library service, books and other reading matter selected should be chosen for values of interest, infor-

mation and enlightenment of all the people of the community. In no case should any book be excluded because of the race or nationality or the political or religious views of the writer.

2. There should be the fullest practicable provision of material presenting all points of view concerning the problems and issues of our times, international, national, and local; and books or other reading matter of sound factual authority should not be proscribed or removed from library shelves because of partisan or doctrinal disapproval.

3. Censorship of books, urged or practiced by volunteer artibers of morals or political opinion or by organizations that would establish a coercive concept of Americanism, must be challenged by libraries in maintenance of their responsibility to provide public information and enlightenment through the printed word.

4. Libraries should enlist the cooperation of allied groups in the fields of science, of education, and of book publishing in resisting all abridgment of the free access to ideas and full freedom of expression that are the tradition and heritage of Americans.

5. The rights of an individual to the use of a library should not be denied or abridged because of his race, religion, national origins or political views.

6. As an institution of education for democractic living, the library should welcome the use of its meeting rooms for socially useful and cultural activities and discussion of current public questions. Such meeting places should be available on equal terms to all groups in the community regardless of the beliefs and affiliations of their members.

By official action of the Council on February 3, 1951, the "Library Bill of Rights" shall be interpreted to apply to all materials and media of communication used or collected by libraries.

On June 27, 1967, almost thirty years after its origin, the Library Bill of Rights underwent its second thorough revision. The need for change was made explicit during a special preconference, sponsored by the Intellectual Freedom Committee with Ervin Gaines as chair, held prior to the 1965 Midwinter Meeting in Washington, D.C. The primary target in the text was the phrase "of sound factual authority," introduced into article 1 in 1944, and revised and transferred to article 2 in 1948. Criticism of the phrase arose when a librarian in Belleville, Illinois, used it to exclude a Protestant publication which he, being Catholic, described as lacking "sound factual authority."

In their discussion of the Belleville situation, the preconference participants determined that some of the most profound and influential publications in our culture lack the element of "sound factual authority," and the phrase itself could easily be abused to thwart the intent and purpose of the Library Bill of Rights. It was apparent that the phrase also could effectively hold the Association from defending fiction or any of those great works which start from philosophical premises but that have nothing to do with fact.

Along with a recommendation that the troublesome phrase be dropped, the Intellectual Freedom Committee also asked that several other textual changes be made. In articles 1 and 5, the word "social" was a suggested addition because of far-reaching results of the civil rights movement. In article 4, the committee recommended eliminating the phrase "that are the tradition and heritage of Americans" because it was both redundant and nationalistic. The committee further recommended that the reference in article 4 be expanded beyond the groups in science, education, and book publishing to reflect the wider context in which librarians and the Association actually operated.

It was also recommended that article 6, concerning the use of meeting rooms, be amended to include the phrase, "provided that the meetings be open to the public." This amendment clarified the Association's position regarding the use of library meeting rooms by private groups with restricted attendance. The enlarged scope of the text led the IFC to recommend that "library materials" be substituted for "reading matter," thus making the footnote of 1951 regarding nonprint materials unnecessary.

By the time the Intellectual Freedom Committee's proposed changes came before the Council in 1967, a preconference on Intellectual Freedom and the Teenager had recommended that young people be given free access to all books in a library collection. Accordingly, the committee included with its previous suggestions the recommendation that article 5 include the word "age."

On June 28, 1967, the Council adopted all of the Intellectual Freedom Committee's recommendations. The revision was a statement very different from its 1939 progenitor. Whereas the original document concerned itself primarily with unbiased book selection, a balanced collection, and open meeting rooms, the new version went much further. It recognized that censorship of any materials and in any guise eventually affects the library. It therefore provided libraries with principles for opposing censorship and promoting intellectual freedom, in the broadest sense. The 1967 revision of the Library Bill of Rights read:

> The Council of the American Library Association reaffirms its belief in the following basic policies which should govern the services of all libraries.
>
> 1. As a responsibility of library service, books and other library materials selected should be chosen for values of interest, information and enlightenment of all the people of the community. In no case should library materials be excluded because of the race

or nationality or the social, political, or religious views of the authors.

2. Libraries should provide books and other materials presenting all points of view concerning the problems and issues of our times; no library materials should be proscribed or removed from libraries because of partisan or doctrinal disapproval.

3. Censorship should be challenged by libraries in the maintenance of their responsibility to provide public information and enlightenment.

4. Libraries should cooperate with all persons and groups concerned with resisting abridgment of free expression and free access to ideas.

5. The rights of an individual to the use of a library should not be denied or abridged because of his age, race, religion, national origins or social or political views.

6. As an institution of education for democratic living, the library should welcome the use of its meeting rooms for socially useful and cultural activities and discussion of current public questions. Such meeting places should be available on equal terms to all groups in the community regardless of the beliefs and affiliations of their members, provided that the meetings be open to the public.

Yet the document, though thoroughly refined, was still not above criticism. During the following decade, questions were raised about its silence with respect to sex discrimination and institutional censorship in college and research libraries, while its unqualified references to "the community" and to "public" meeting rooms made it appear as a document for public libraries only. Moreover, the profound changes in American society which took place in the late 1960s and early 1970s virtually mandated further changes. Hence, in January 1980, the Library Bill of Rights underwent a third major revision, the product of nearly three years of careful review.

The initial impetus for revision came in 1977 with a request from the Committee on the Status of Women in Librarianship that the Library Bill of Rights be revised to reject sex discrimination in library services and to eliminate sex-linked pronoun usage from the document itself, which the Intellectual Freedom Committee agreed to act upon as part of an overall reassessment of the document. The subsequent review process involved unprecedentedly broad participation from all sectors of the library community.

At the 1978 Midwinter Meeting, the Intellectual Freedom Committee asked a subcommittee of its own members to prepare a new draft. At the 1978 Annual Conference, the Committee received a report from the subcommittee and conducted a membership hearing on the revision process. At the 1979 Midwinter Meeting, a draft Library Bill of Rights was approved for distribution and sent for comment to all ALA councilors, divisions, round tables, and committees, and to all chapter intellectual freedom committees, journals, and bulletins. The draft was also published in the national library press. Comments received were then reviewed at the 1979 Annual Conference, where the committee also held another open hearing. Shortly after the close of this conference, a new draft was approved by mail and circulated by the IFC to all councilors and ALA units and the library press. Final comments were reviewed by the committee at the 1980 Midwinter Meeting, where Frances C. Dean, its chair, submitted the final revision to the Council.

In addition to eliminating use of sex-linked pronouns, the committee recommended revision of the preamble to state explicitly the role of libraries in maintaining intellectual freedom. Libraries are described in the revision as "forums for information and ideas," employing the word "forum" to indicate that the library should be open to any opinion or view. During discussion of this revision, it was suggested that the library be defined as in article 6, as "an institution of education for democratic living." This formulation was rejected because it could imply support for the idea that libraries should censor all materials which are antidemocratic.

Democracy, strictly speaking, means rule by the majority. From the standpoint of intellectual freedom, the library's role in our society is not based on the principle of majority rule, but on the principle embodied in the First Amendment, that minority points of view have a right to be heard, no matter how unpopular with or even detested by the majority.

In article 1, the Intellectual Freedom Committee recommended elimination of verbiage which seemed to detract from clarity and simplicity of expression, and modification of the word "community" to read "the community the library serves," since many libraries serve a special public, such as a specific academic or school community. The committee further recommended replacing the word "author" with the phrase "those contributing to their creation" because the originators of many library materials are today referred to by other terms.

In article 2, the committee recommended adding the point that libraries have an obligation to provide information and diverse points of view on historical as well as current issues. In article 3, stylistic changes were suggested as well as elimination of the modifier "public." The meaning of that word in the article's context placed an obligation on nonpublic libraries that such libraries insist they do not have.

Revision of article 5 was marked by considerable debate as to whether a general statement affirming the rights of all individuals to library use could serve the same function as a more detailed list of all those specific conditions or factors which may lead to infringement of this right. Considering that explicitly designating one or more factors may risk excluding other grounds of discrimination that are not included, either by oversight or inability to predict the future, and judging the so-called "laundry-list approach" stylistically unwieldy, the committee recommended instead a general statement condemning discrimination according to origin, background, or views. The committee recommended, however, retaining specific reference to age, because a suitable generic term which readily would be recognized as inclusive of this factor could not be found.

Finally, article 6 was revised to take into account differences among types of libraries and to eliminate any implication that libraries may censor materials and exclude programs on the grounds that they contain antidemocratic ideas or are not socially useful. The revision laid firm emphasis on the principle of equitable and nondiscriminatory application of rules and regulations governing meeting rooms and exhibit space, while permitting libraries broad flexibility in formulating these according to the dictates of their widely varied situations.

On January 23, 1980, the Council adopted the recommendations of the Intellectual Freedom Committee. The resulting document constitutes the present Library Bill of Rights. At the 1988 Annual Conference, the Minority Concerns Committee recommended, and Council approved that "the Library Bill of Rights be reviewed to include the concepts of freedom of access to information and libraries without limitation by language or economic status." During its initial review of this Council action at the 1989 Midwinter Meeting, the Intellectual Freedom Committee suggested that a revision of the interpretations be undertaken first to address explicitly and immediately the issues raised by the Minority Concerns Committee. The Library Bill of Rights would then be reassessed in light of the revised interpretations. Thus began a review process which resulted in the reworking of all but one of the then-extant interpretations, the addition of a new interpretation on the Universal Right to Free Expression, and a proposal for a new interpretation on fees for library services. Reconsideration of the Library Bill of Rights, in light of the revised interpretations, will begin in 1992. While there can be little doubt that future unforeseen developments will mandate yet further revision, the document is by no means a product of hasty work, and, as its history proves, remains a viable statement of principle and a useful guide to action. The Library Bill of Rights is one of the American Library Association's most basic policies.

Interpretations of the Library Bill of Rights

Although the articles of the Library Bill of Rights are unambiguous statements of basic principles which should govern the service of all libraries, questions do arise concerning application of these principles to specific library practices. For example, a 1951 Peoria, Illinois, case involving certain films in the public library required the Association to clarify the application of the Library Bill of Rights to nonprint materials. A recommendation by the Intellectual Freedom Committee and the Audio-Visual Board resulted in the ALA Council's adding an interpretive footnote, explaining that the Library Bill of Rights applies to all materials and media of communication used or collected by libraries.

During the 1971 Annual Conference in Dallas, the Intellectual Freedom Committee considered censorship cases which clearly called for interpretations of the Library Bill of Rights to define its application to certain practices. Believing that frequent revisions, amendments, or additions of footnotes weaken the document's effectiveness, the committee resolved instead to develop statements to be called interpretations of the Library Bill of Rights. The committee said further that certain documents already in existence should be designated as interpretations of the Library Bill of Rights.

After the Council adopted the 1980 revision of the Library Bill of Rights, the Intellectual Freedom Committee undertook the first systematic review of all the interpretations. The initial purpose of this review was to make all policies consistent with both the letter and the spirit of the revised Library Bill of Rights. As the process developed, however, the goals became more sweeping. Important gaps in policy were filled, and, taken as a group, the interpretations were remolded into a unified general guide to application of the Library Bill of Rights. Not only were most policies thoroughly rewritten or amended, but new interpretations were also formulated, and outdated or inadequate material eliminated. As with the 1980 revision of the Library Bill of Rights, the IFC sought and received extensive input from ALA councilors, units, and chapters to whom all drafts were circulated in advance for comment. The process of revision was completed at the 1982 Annual Conference in Philadelphia.

In response to a 1988 Minority Concerns Committee report, recommending a revision of the Library Bill of Rights to ensure protection against discrimination in library services based on language or economic status, the Intellectual Freedom Committee began the second comprehensive review of the interpretations. The IFC agreed that each interpretation would be considered separately and recommended to the Council for adoption upon completion of any necessary revisions. The process resulted in the revision of all but one interpretation, the addition of one new interpretation on the Universal Right to Free Expression, a proposal for a new interpretation regarding fees for library services, and the recision of an interpretation no longer deemed relevant. The committee plans to reconsider the Library Bill of Rights in 1992.

Following are those documents designated by the Intellectual Freedom Committee as interpretations of the Library Bill of Rights and background statements detailing the philosophy and history of each. These documents are policies of the American Library Association, having been adopted by the ALA Council.

2.1

FREE ACCESS TO LIBRARIES FOR MINORS

An Interpretation of the Library Bill of Rights

Library policies and procedures which effectively deny minors equal access to all library resources available to other users violate the Library Bill of Rights. The American Library Association opposes all attempts to restrict access to library services, materials, and facilities based on the age of library users.

Article 5 of the Library Bill of Rights states, "A person's right to use a library should not be denied or abridged because of origin, age, background, or views." The "right to use a library" includes free access to, and unrestricted use of, all the services, materials, and facilities the library has to offer. Every restriction on access to, and use of, library resources, based solely on the chronological age, educational level, or legal emancipation of users violates article 5.

Libraries are charged with the mission of developing resources to meet the diverse information needs and interests of the communities they serve. Services, materials, and facilities which fulfill the needs and interests of library users at different stages in their personal development are a necessary part of library resources. The needs and interests of each library user, and resources appropriate to meet those needs and interests, must be determined on an individual basis. Librarians cannot predict what resources will best fulfill the needs and interests of any individual user based on a single criterion such as chronological age, level of education, or legal emancipation.

The selection and development of library resources should not be diluted because of minors having the same access to library resources as adult users. Institutional self-censorship diminishes the credibility of the library in the community, and restricts access for all library users.

Librarians and governing bodies should not resort to age restrictions on access to library resources in an effort to avoid actual or anticipated objections from parents or anyone else. The mission, goals, and objectives of libraries do not authorize librarians or governing bodies to assume, abrogate, or overrule the rights and responsibilities of parents or legal guardians. Librarians and governing bodies should maintain that parents—and only parents—have the right and the responsibility to restrict the access of their children—and only their children—to library resources. Parents or legal guardians who do not want their children to have access to certain library services, materials or facilities, should so advise their children. Librarians and governing bodies cannot assume the role of parents or the functions of parental authority in the private relationship between parent and child. Librarians and governing bodies have a public and professional obligation to provide equal access to all library resources for all library users.

Librarians have a professional commitment to ensure that all members of the community they serve have free and equal access to the entire range of library resources regardless of content, approach, format, or amount of detail. This principle of library service applies equally to all users, minors as well as adults. Librarians and governing bodies must uphold this principle in order to provide adequate and effective service to minors.

Adopted June 30, 1972; amended July 1, 1981; July 3, 1991, by the ALA Council.

Free Access to Libraries for
Minors: History

The question of whether or not intellectual freedom in libraries applies to children and young adults has been debated by librarians since the early years of the profession's involvement with intellectual freedom. The question was considered many times by the Intellectual Freedom Committee, and led to the preconference institute on Intellectual Freedom and the Teenager, held in San Francisco, June 23–25, 1967.

Sponsored jointly by the Intellectual Freedom Committee, the Young Adult Services Division, and the American Association of School Librarians, and attended by approximately 400 librarians, the preconference featured a variety of speakers of national reputation, including author Kenneth Rexroth, attorneys Stanley Fleishman and Alex P. Allain, book review editor Robert Kirsh, and library young adult consultant Esther Helfand. The most outspoken panelist was Edgar L. Freidenberg, author of *Coming of Age in America,* who told participants:

> The library is just one more place where the kids are taught they are second-class citizens. They learn this not only from the books pressed upon them by the helpful librarian but even more so from the very atmosphere of the place.[1]

In his summary of the three-day meeting, Ervin Gaines, chair of the IFC, dwelt at length on Freidenberg's comments, saying:

> He made the assumption that intellectual freedom was an inalienable right and that age is not a morally relevant factor and that adults have themselves no right to determine for youth access to

---

1. *San Francisco Examiner & Chronicle* June 25, 1967.

ideas. This assumption which came at the very beginning of this talk echoed and re-echoed throughout the conference. There was surprising unanimity of opinion on this particular point.[2]

As the preconference progressed, there was also surprising unanimity that not only teenagers were the focus of the discussions, but all young people. This was reflected in one of the major recommendations of the institute, "that free access to all books in a library collection be granted to young people."[3]

Later, during the 1967 Annual Conference, Gaines moved that the Council adopt a revised version of the Library Bill of Rights. He introduced his motion with the following remarks:

> At a meeting of the Intellectual Freedom Committee yesterday two minor amendments were suggested to this text [the revised Library Bill of Rights]. In section 5 we suggest that the word "age" be inserted. . . . This suggestion comes as a result of recommendations from the preconference on Intellectual Freedom and the Teenager, which was held last week.

The change was approved by the Council, and the Association, well in advance of society in general, took a significant stand, approving free access for minors to all the materials in a library collection.

After 1967, the word "age" in the Library Bill of Rights was a constant source of confusion. Did it mean children should be able to take home any materials in a library collection or were some restrictions permissible? What about double card systems or multiple card systems, restricting minors to use of only part of the collection? These and other questions accrued until the IFC's 1972 Midwinter Meeting. Twenty hours of meetings were dominated by discussions of minors and library access problems, all related to the word "age" in the Library Bill of Rights.

After the meeting, the committee announced plans to develop a position statement concerning access to libraries for minors. A draft was subsequently sent, in the spring of 1972, to the boards of the Public Library Association, the American Association of School Librarians, the Children's Services Division, the Young Adult Services Division, and the American Library Trustee Association. At its annual meeting in June 1972, the IFC approved the statement and recommended it to the ALA Council which adopted it on June 30, 1972,

---

2. *Newsletter on Intellectual Freedom* 16:54 (Sept. 1967).

3. Ibid., p.55.

as an ALA policy entitled Free Access to Libraries for Minors. The statement read:

> Some library procedures and practices effectively deny minors access to certain services and materials available to adults. Such procedures and practices are not in accord with the Library Bill of Rights and are opposed by the American Library Association.
>
> Restrictions take a variety of forms, including, among others, restricted reading rooms for adult use only, library cards limiting circulation of some materials to adults only, closed collections for adult use only, and interlibrary loan service for adult use only.
>
> All limitations in minors' access to library materials and services violate article 5 of the Library Bill of Rights, which states, "The rights of an individual to the use of a library should not be denied or abridged because of his age. . . ." Limiting access to some services and materials to only adults abridges the use of libraries for minors. "Use of the library" includes use of, and access to, all library materials and services.
>
> Restrictions are often initiated under the assumption that certain materials are "harmful" to minors, or in an effort to avoid controversy with parents who might think so. The librarian who would restrict the access of minors to materials and services because of actual or suspected parental objection should bear in mind that he is not *in loco parentis* in his position as librarian. Individual intellectual levels and family backgrounds are significant factors not accommodated by a uniform policy based upon age.
>
> In today's world, children are exposed to adult life much earlier than in the past. They read materials and view a variety of media on the adult level at home and elsewhere. Current emphasis upon early childhood education has also increased opportunities for young people to learn and to have access to materials, and has decreased the validity of using chronological age as an index to the use of libraries. The period of time during which children are interested in reading materials specifically designed for them grows steadily shorter, and librarians must recognize and adjust to this change if they wish to maintain the patronage of young people.
>
> The American Library Association holds that it is the parent—and only the parent—who may restrict his children—and only *his* children—from access to library materials and services. The parent who would rather his child did not have access to certain materials should so advise the child.
>
> The word "age" was incorporated into article 5 of the Library Bill of Rights as a direct result of a preconference entitled Intellectual Freedom and the Teenager, held in San Francisco in June 1967. One recommendation of the preconference participants was "that free access to all books in a library collection be granted to

young people." The preconference generally concluded that young people are entitled to the same access to libraries and to the materials in libraries as are adults and that materials selection should not be diluted on that account.

This does not mean, for instance, that issuing different types of borrowers' cards to minors and adults is, *per se*, contrary to the Library Bill of Rights. If such practices are used for purposes of gathering statistics, the various kinds of cards carry no implicit or explicit limitations on access to materials and services. Neither does it mean that maintaining separate children's collections is a violation of the Library Bill of Rights, provided that no patron is restricted to the use of only certain collections.

The Association's position does not preclude isolating certain materials for legitimate protection of irreplaceable or very costly works from careless use. Such "restricted-use" areas as rare book rooms are appropriate if the materials so classified are genuinely rare, and not merely controversial.

Unrestrictive selection policies, developed with care for principles of intellectual freedom and the Library Bill of Rights, should not be vitiated by administrative practices which restrict minors to the use of only part of a library's collections and services.

Following adoption of the 1980 revision of the Library Bill of Rights, the IFC reviewed the document anew. Working closely with the intellectual freedom committees of the Young Adult Services Division and the Association for Library Service to Children (previously the Children's Services Division), at the 1981 Midwinter Meeting and Annual Conference, the committee made several changes aimed not only at eliminating sex-linked language, but also at strengthening the impact of the interpretation. Reference to the 1967 preconference was deleted as a historical detail irrelevant to a broad public statement of policy, and several key paragraphs were rewritten to communicate the Association's stand with greater force and clarity.

The Intellectual Freedom Committee also decided to delete from the document all references to specific administrative practices such as dual card systems and restricted-use areas which, while not always in violation of the principles of the Library Bill of Rights, have been employed at times in ways which unfairly limit minors' access to library resources. Limiting discussion of the intellectual freedom implications of such administrative practices to their effects on minors' access in itself tended to legitimize their misuse, and, the committee concluded, the treatment in the document weakened its overall thrust by appearing to qualify the policy and limit its application. The committee therefore decided to discuss such practices separately and in a more all-sided way by developing a new interpretation, to be entitled Administrative

Policies and Procedures Affecting Access to Library Resources and Services.

On July 1, 1981, the revision of Free Access to Libraries for Minors was adopted by the Council. It read as follows:

> Some library procedures and practices effectively deny minors access to certain services and materials available to adults. Such procedures and practices are not in accord with the Library Bill of Rights and are opposed by the American Library Association.
>
> Restrictions take a variety of forms, including, among others, restricted reading rooms for adult use only, library cards limiting circulation of some materials to adults only, closed collections for adult use only, collections limited to teacher use, or restricted according to a student's grade level, and interlibrary loan service for adult use only.
>
> Article 5 of the Library Bill of Rights states that, "A person's right to use a library should not be denied or abridged because of origin, age, background, or views." All limitations on minors' access to library materials and services violate that article. The "right to use a library" includes use of, and access to, all library materials and services. Thus, practices which allow adults to use some services and materials which are denied to minors abridge the use of libraries based on age.
>
> Material selection decisions are often made and restrictions are often initiated under the assumption that certain materials may be "harmful" to minors, or in an effort to avoid controversy with parents. Libraries or library boards which would restrict the access of minors to materials and services because of actual or suspected parental objections should bear in mind that they do not serve in loco parentis. Varied levels of intellectual development among young people and differing family background and child-rearing philosophies are significant factors not accommodated by a uniform policy based upon age.
>
> In today's world, children are exposed to adult life much earlier than in the past. They read materials and view a variety of media on the adult level at home and elsewhere. Current emphasis upon early childhood education has also increased opportunities for young people to learn and to have access to materials, and has decreased the validity of using chronological age as an index to the use of libraries. The period of time during which children are interested in reading materials specifically designed for them grows steadily shorter, and librarians must recognize and adjust to this change if they wish to serve young people effectively. Librarians have a responsibility to ensure that young people have access to a wide range of informational and recreational materials and ser-

vices that reflects sufficient diversity to meet the young person's needs.

The American Library Association opposes libraries restricting access to library materials and services for minors and holds that it is the parents—and only parents—who may restrict their children—and only their children—from access to library materials and services. Parents who would rather their children did not have access to certain materials should so advise their children. The library and its staff are responsible for providing equal access to library materials and services for all library users.

The word "age" was incorporated into article 5 of the Library Bill of Rights because young people are entitled to the same access to libraries and to the materials in libraries as are adults. Materials selection should not be diluted on that account.

Ten years later, at the 1991 Midwinter Meeting, a further revised Free Access to Libraries for Minors was adopted by the IFC. The committee had extensively reworked the document to make the protections for minors access more explicit and to outline with greater precision librarians' responsibilities toward minors and all library users. The new policy emphasized the role of librarians as information providers and placed the burden of guiding minors squarely on the shoulders of parents.

The definition of library usage was expanded to include use of facilities as well as materials and services. Library trustees were implicated in the new policy as being coresponsible with librarians for providing equal access to all library resources for all library users.

The Midwinter version also included a list of practices which librarians have used to restrict indirectly minors' access to expensive, controversial, or otherwise objectionable materials, including issuing limited access cards; barring entry to stacks, reserve areas, or reading rooms; charging fees; and simply refusing to perform a service based solely on the age or educational level of the user. This list was intended to alert librarians to specific practices that inhibited minors' access to library materials, services, and facilities, and to discourage these all-too-common practices.

At the 1991 Annual Conference, the Council deleted the list of examples from the final interpretation before approving it as ALA policy. Many councilors believed that ALA's official position would be more effective and adaptable to changing societal circumstances if it were written in broad terms, rather than including a list of potential violations of the principle.

The list of examples which follows is not comprehensive, but suggestive of some of the most commonly used practices which violate the

Library Bill of Rights. Copies are available upon request from the Office for Intellectual Freedom.

Examples of Age-Based Access Limitations

Some specific examples of denial of equal access include, but are not limited to:

- restricting access to reading or reference rooms, or to otherwise open stack areas, based on the age or school grade level of the user;
- issuing limited access library cards, or otherwise restricting the circulation of materials, based on the age or school grade level of the user;
- assigning materials to special collections, such as parenting, teacher/professional, historical/genealogical collections, and restricting access to these collections, based on the age or school grade level of the user;
- using manual or computerized registration or circulation systems which restrict access to materials, based on the age or school grade level of the user;
- sequestering or otherwise restricting access to material because of its content, based on the age or school grade level of the user;
- requiring or soliciting written permission from parent or guardian to access or restrict materials because of their content, based on the age or school grade level of the user;
- restricting access to interlibrary loan, FAX, and electronic reference services, based on the age or school grade level of the user;
- restricting access to materials because of their format and/or their cost, such as computer software, compact discs, periodicals, microfilm/fiche, and videocassettes, based on the age or school grade level of the user;
- charging fees or requiring deposits to access services, materials, or facilities, based on the age or school grade level of the user;
- refusing to process interlibrary loans, reserves, or reference requests for materials classified as juvenile;
- assigning professional/non-professional staff to reference searches, based on the age or school grade level of the user;
- restricting access to library-sponsored programs or events otherwise designed for general audiences, based on the age or school grade level of the user;
- restricting access to public facilities, such as meeting rooms, display cases, and notice boards, based on the age or school grade level of the user.

2.2

REGULATIONS, POLICIES, AND PROCEDURES AFFECTING ACCESS TO LIBRARY RESOURCES AND SERVICES

An Interpretation of the Library Bill of Rights

American libraries exist and function within the context of a body of law derived from the United States Constitution, defined by statute, and implemented by regulations, policies, and procedures established by their governing bodies and administrations. These regulations, policies, and procedures reflect the function and character of the library, define its operations, and protect its mission and the rights of its users.

"The library is one of the great symbols of our democracy. It is a living embodiment of the First Amendment because it includes voices of dissent."[1] Libraries of all types adhere to this ideal. Publicly supported libraries serve as traditional public forums, open to the collection, use, and dissemination of all forms of recorded human expression that are expressly dedicated to the unfettered competition of the marketplace of ideas. It is essential to this purpose that the library function as neutral ground in that marketplace. Viewpoint-based discrimination has no place in publicly supported library collections or services; for the library to espouse partisan causes or favor particular viewpoints violates its mission.

"A public library is not only a designated public forum, but also a quintessential, traditional public forum whose accessibility affects the bedrock of our democratic system. A place where ideas are communicated freely through the written word"[2] and other means of recorded expression "is as integral to a democracy and to First Amendment rights as an available public space where citizens can communicate their ideas through the spoken word."[3] The fact of public sponsorship of a

---

1. *Richard R. Kreimer* v. *Bureau of Police for the Town of Morristown, et al.,* 765 F. Supp. 181 (D.N.J. 1991).
2. Ibid.
3. Ibid.

library in no way implies endorsement of any of the myriad viewpoints contained within a library's collection. Nor should a funding source dictate its contents. The United States Supreme Court has recognized that "the university is a traditional sphere of free expression so fundamental to the functioning of our society that the Government's ability to control speech within that sphere by means of conditions attached to the expenditures of Government funds, is restricted by the vagueness and overbreadth doctrines of the First Amendment. . . ."4 The same principles apply with equal force to publicly supported libraries. These principles restrict any attempt to control expression within a publicly supported library or to dictate or limit the contents of its collections, programs, displays, or publications through conditions attached to funding.

Libraries serve the function of making ideas and information available to all members of the society, without discrimination. Publicly supported libraries provide access to information for all without imposing barriers which limit or prevent library users, including the indigent or the economically disadvantaged, from exercising their full constitutional rights. Publicly supported libraries' traditional commitment to free public service is integral to their nature and function. Publicly supported libraries, like public schools and universities, are supported in part from a recognition that information and education are essential components of informed self-government.

The right of free access to information for all individuals is basic to all library service. The central thrust of the Library Bill of Rights is to protect and encourage the free flow of information and ideas. Article 5 protects the rights of an individual to use a library regardless of origin, age, background, or views. The American Library Association urges all libraries to set policies and procedures that reflect the basic tenets of the Library Bill of Rights, within the framework of constitutional imperatives and limitations.

Many libraries adopt administrative policies and procedures to govern their order and use, the comfort and safety of patrons and staff, and the protection of resources, services, and facilities. Such policies and procedures affect access, and must not become a convenient means for removing or restricting access to controversial materials, limiting access to facilities, programs, or exhibits, or for discriminating against specific individuals or groups of library patrons. Administrative policies and procedures which infringe on equitable access to library buildings, services, and resources, the privacy of the individual, or the right to read, violate the Library Bill of Rights. Further, if such policies have the effect of impermissible discrimination against individuals or particular groups of

---

4. *Rust, et al.* v. *Sullivan*, 59 U.S.L.W. 4451, 111 S.Ct. 1759 (1991).

library users, they are likely to violate First Amendment rights. The U.S. Supreme Court has recognized that " 'the right to receive ideas follows ineluctably from the *sender's* First Amendment right to send them. . . . More importantly, the right to receive ideas is a necessary predicate to the *recipient's* meaningful exercise of his own rights such as speech, press, and political freedom' (emphasis in original) *Board of Education, Island Trees Union Free School District No. 26* v. *Pico*, 457 U.S. 853, 866–67 (1982) (plurality opinion)."[5] Respect for these rights is central to the function of any government supported library for these rights define the library's purpose.

Because publicly supported libraries are institutions dedicated to the free flow of information, it is essential that the regulations, policies, and procedures which libraries develop and use embody the principles of free expression. Information about their operations must be made available in full compliance with confidentiality, privacy, freedom of information, and sunshine laws. The application of policies and procedures for the use of library services and resources should be consistently applied to both members of the public and library employees. Policies and procedures for responding to complaints about library materials— including individual items in a collection, library programs and services, or publications and other material produced or published by the library— should be uniformly applied regardless of the source of the complaint, whether coming from a member of the public, staff, or governing authority.

---

5. *Richard R. Kreimer* v. *Bureau of Police for the Town of Morristown, et al.,* 765 F. Supp. 181 (D.N.J. 1991).

Adopted January 1982, as Administrative Policies and Procedures Affecting Access to Library Resources and Services; amended with title change July 3, 1991, by the ALA Council.

Regulations, Policies, and Procedures Affecting Access to Library Resources and Services: History

During the process of revising Free Access to Libraries for Minors following the 1980 revision of the Library Bill of Rights, the Intellectual Freedom Committee received many comments concerning the misuse of certain necessary administrative policies and procedures to restrict library service to minors. Many libraries have formulated regulations governing reference services which discriminate against minors. Libraries with special or rare book collections, in the course of legitimate efforts to protect valuable resources, have restricted access to these materials solely according to age. While the problem is most acute with respect to restrictions on the rights of minors, in principle many administrative policies and procedures governing the order and protection of library materials and facilities may be misused—intentionally or unintentionally—to remove or restrict access in several ways which violate the tenets of the Library Bill of Rights.

As previously noted, the committee had addressed this problem to some extent in the original version of the policy Free Access to Libraries for Minors. At the 1980 Annual Conference in New York, however, the committee concluded that, judging from the extent of comments received, the matter needed to be addressed in its own right. Moreover, it was believed that separate treatment would strengthen the impact of the Free Access to Libraries for Minors document.

Therefore several draft documents were prepared and discussed at the 1981 national meeting. At the 1982 Midwinter Meeting in Denver, J. Dennis Day, IFC chair, presented a final draft to the Council, which approved the new policy on January 27, 1982. The policy read:

> The right of free access to information for all individuals is basic to all aspects of library service regardless of type of library. Article 5 of the Library Bill of Rights protects the rights of an

individual to use a library regardless of origin, age, background, or views. The central thrust of the Library Bill of Rights is to protect and encourage the free flow of information and ideas. The American Library Association urges that all libraries set policies and procedures that reflect the basic tenets of the Library Bill of Rights.

Many libraries have adopted administrative policies and procedures regulating access to resources, services, and facilities, i.e., specific collections, reference services, interlibrary loan, programming, meeting rooms, exhibit space. Such policies and procedures governing the order and protection of library materials and facilities, and the planning of library programs and exhibits, could become a convenient means for removing or restricting access to controversial materials, limiting access to programs or exhibits, or for discriminating against specific groups of library patrons. Such abuse of administrative procedures and policies is in opposition to the Library Bill of Rights.

The American Library Association recommends that all libraries with rare or special collections formulate policies and procedures for such collections so as not to restrict access and use due to age or the nature of the patron interest in the materials. Restricted access to such collections is solely for the protection of the materials and must in no way limit access to the information and ideas contained in the materials.

The Model Interlibrary Loan Code of the American Library Association recommends that all library patrons be eligible for interlibrary loan, in accordance with article 5 of the Library Bill of Rights and the policy statement Free Access to Libraries for Minors. The Model Interlibrary Loan Code states the importance of considering the needs and interests of all users, including children and young adults. Borrowing libraries should provide the resources to meet the ordinary needs of all of its primary clientele, and any members of its clientele should be eligible for interlibrary loan. When libraries adhere to the Model Interlibrary Loan Code, access to information is protected.

Library administrative policies should examine all restrictions to resources or services associated with age, as all are violations of article 5 of the Library Bill of Rights and the statement on restricted access to library materials. For example, privileges associated with library cards should be consistent for all library users, no matter what the age. Library policies in which certain patrons, usually minors, are denied library privileges available to other library patrons are not endorsed by the American Library Association, as they violate article 5 of the Library Bill of Rights, as well as the statement on Free Access to Libraries for Minors. It is parents and only parents who may restrict their children—and only their children—from access to library materials and services.

Reference service policies and procedures, such as library policies limiting the time spent on answering telephone refere..ce questions, should provide for equitable service to all library patrons, regardless of age or type of question. These policies must apply to both adult and child patrons.

Policies governing the use of meeting rooms and exhibits should be examined to ensure that minors are not excluded from a program of interest to them based on age. Meeting rooms and exhibit spaces should also be available on an "equitable basis, regardless of the beliefs or affiliations of individuals or groups requesting their use," and should not be denied to anyone based solely on age.

Policies should reflect that a person's right to attend a library-initiated program "should not be denied or abridged because of origin, age, background, or views," as stated in Library-Initiated Programs as a Resource, an interpretation of the Library Bill of Rights.

In 1990, the IFC began to revise Administrative Policies and Procedures Affecting Access to Library Resources and Services. The new interpretation, Regulations, Policies, and Procedures Affecting Access to Library Resources and Services, responds to issues raised in two 1991 court cases which have important implications for libraries. The policy also addresses intellectual freedom concerns raised by incidents of challenges to materials that were inappropriately handled, the challenges having been originated within libraries by librarians or library staff.

The two significant Court decisions affecting the process of revision were issued in May 1991. The first was *Rust* v. *Sullivan*,[1] a United States Supreme Court decision upholding Department of Health and Human Services (HHS) regulations which prohibited recipients of Title X funds (family planning clinics) from providing information about abortion or any abortion counseling whatsoever to their clients. The majority of the Court in this 5–4 decision held that this was a permissible government choice, to favor some "activities" over others. In a stinging dissent, Justice Blackmun pointed out that for the first time, the Court had sanctioned outright viewpoint-based discrimination in a federally funded program. In other words, the Supreme Court had said that it was permissible for the federal government to selectively fund speech, promoting one point of view while prohibiting mention of the opposing position.

Recognizing the dire implications of the HHS regulations for publicly funded libraries, the Freedom to Read Foundation (FTRF) and

---

1. *Rust* v. *Sullivan*, 59 U.S.L.W. 4451, 111 S.Ct. 1759 (1991).

ALA had submitted an *amicus curiae* brief outlining their concerns about the negative implications this case presented for First Amendment rights.

The brief stated that, while libraries take no position on the underlying issues, they do provide materials and information from all points of view on topics of current and historical interest, including abortion. It pointed out that the "gagging" of medical professionals could be expanded to libraries. Apparently, these fears were justified. Although the Court limited the application of its decision to the Title X program, an Office of Management and Budget (OMB) staff member almost immediately suggested, in a private conversation, expanding the rule to all programs administered by federal agencies. When the suggestion became public, several organizations, representing the legal, artistic, university, and library communities, wrote a letter of concern to OMB Director Frank Hodsoll.

Further evidence of government desires to expand the Court's ruling came shortly after the *Rust* decision when the Department of Justice filed a supplemental letter in a pending case called *Bullfrog Films* v. *Wick*,[2] a challenge to USIA regulations governing the certification of films as educational for export. The Justice Department attorney, representing USIA, contended that the *Rust* decision allowed it to discriminate among films and label some "propaganda."

The Court issued the *Rust* decision in an atmosphere of severe fiscal conservancy, when many public libraries already had experienced massive funding cuts. The potential for those cuts to be linked to ideological, viewpoint-based restrictions on library collections was clear.

The other significant court decision, *Kreimer* v. *Morristown*,[3] came from the United States District Court in New Jersey. In that case, Richard Kreimer, a homeless man, challenged rules and regulations of the Morristown (NJ) Public Library, on the grounds that they discriminated against homeless and economically disadvantaged patrons. The library admitted that it had designed certain of these rules specifically to bar Mr. Kreimer from the institution. Library officials contended that he annoyed other patrons, exuded a body odor so offensive as to interfere with other patrons' use of the library, stared at people, and followed children around in the stacks.

The court found that the library's regulations prohibiting patrons from staring or annoying other patrons were overbroad and vague, and

2. *Bullfrog Films* v. *Wick*, Nos. 89-55945 and 88-6310 (9th Circuit); reference letter dated May 31, 1991.

3. *Richard R. Kriemer* v. *Bureau of Police for the Town of Morristown, et al.*, 765 F. Supp. 181 (D.N.J. 1991)

therefore unconstitutional. While recognizing and firmly supporting the right and responsibility of public libraries to make rules governing their use and patron behavior, the court also firmly upheld the First Amendment right to receive information in publicly funded libraries. The court held that, in the interest of all patrons, library rules should be specific, necessary and neutral, and not susceptible to discriminatory application. In addition, they must not be so vague that their application is subject to the whims of individual library staff members.

The *Morristown* decision was regarded by the Freedom to Read Foundation and ALA's Intellectual Freedom Committee as a win-win situation for libraries. The judge's opinion eloquently and firmly upheld First Amendment rights to receive information in libraries, providing a powerful argument supporting libraries' resistance to censorship. At the same time, the judge recognized the necessity of specific, necessary and neutral rules, which govern patron behavior and ensure equal access for all.

A highly publicized and controversial library censorship case also had an influence on the interpretation's revision. At the Los Angeles Public Library, in celebration of Gay Pride Week, the library staff had developed bibliographies and banners featuring a quote from Langston Hughes. After receiving complaints about the use of a Langston Hughes' quote in connection with Gay Pride Week, the library director removed the banners and bibliographies and had them reissued without the quote. Staff at the library contended that this was an act of censorship every bit as objectionable as a citizen's attempt to remove materials.

The Los Angeles controversy and the issues raised by the *Rust* and *Morristown* decisions were an integral part of the discussions surrounding the revision of Administrative Policies and Procedures Affecting Access to Library Resources and Services. Whenever possible, the IFC seeks to clearly express the relationship between intellectual freedom policies and established legal principles and constitutional law, as expressed in case law. In so doing, ALA can easily refute the often-heard claim by would-be censors that ALA's intellectual freedom policies are merely opinion.

Concern for the issue of public sponsorship of speech, the rights of the indigent, and sensitivity to equity in handling censorship controversies, regardless of whether they are internally (within the library staff or administration) generated or externally (patron complaints) generated, resulted in the 1991 revision and retitling of the interpretation. Now called, Regulations, Policies, and Procedures Affecting Access to Library Resources and Services, the new interpretation quotes from both the *Rust* and *Morristown* decisions, and reaffirms ALA's position that publicly funded libraries are traditional, quintessential, open public forums which must not be subject to ideological restrictions linked to funding, nor to internally generated restrictions or rules which are not reasonable, necessary, neutral, and specific.

The Council adopted the new Interpretation at the Annual Conference on July 3, 1991.

2.3

STATEMENT ON LABELING

An Interpretation of the Library Bill of Rights

Labeling is the practice of describing or designating materials by affixing a prejudicial label and/or segregating them by a prejudicial system. The American Library Association opposes these means of predisposing people's attitudes toward library materials for the following reasons:

1. Labeling is an attempt to prejudice attitudes and as such, it is a censor's tool.

2. Some find it easy and even proper, according to their ethics, to establish criteria for judging publications as objectionable. However, injustice and ignorance rather than justice and enlightenment result from such practices, and the American Library Association opposes the establishment of such criteria.

3. Libraries do not advocate the ideas found in their collections. The presence of books and other resources in a library does not indicate endorsement of their contents by the library.

A variety of private organizations promulgate rating systems and/or review materials as a means of advising either their members or the general public concerning their opinions of the contents and suitability or appropriate age for use of certain books, films, recordings, or other materials. For the library to adopt or enforce any of these private systems, to attach such ratings to library materials, to include them in bibliographic records, library catalogs, or other finding aids, or otherwise to endorse them would violate the Library Bill of Rights.

While some attempts have been made to adopt these systems into law, the constitutionality of such measures is extremely questionable. If such legislation is passed which applies within a library's jurisdiction, the library should seek competent legal advice concerning its applicability to library operations.

Publishers, industry groups, and distributors sometimes add ratings to material or include them as part of their packaging. Librarians should not endorse such practices. However, removing or obliterating such ratings—if placed there by or with permission of the copyright holder—could constitute expurgation, which is also unacceptable.

The American Library Association opposes efforts which aim at closing any path to knowledge. This statement, however, does not exclude the adoption of organizational schemes designed as directional aids or to facilitate access to materials.

Adopted July 13, 1951. Amended June 25, 1971; July 1, 1981; June 26, 1990, by the ALA Council.

Statement on Labeling: History

In late 1950, the Intellectual Freedom Committee received a report that the Montclair, New Jersey, chapter of the Sons of the American Revolution (SAR) was exerting pressure on New Jersey libraries to put a prominent label or inscription on "publications which advocate or favor communism, or which are issued or distributed by any communist organization or any other organization formally designated by any authorized government official or agency as communistic or subversive." The SAR said further that such publications "should not be freely available in libraries to readers or in schools to pupils, but should be obtainable only by signing suitable applications."[1]

Rutherford D. Rogers, at the time chair of the IFC, reported the matter to the ALA Council on July 13, 1951, and said groups other than the SAR have tried to use such labeling as a means of limiting the freedom to read. He cited religious groups which sometimes asked libraries to label "objectionable" publications, and mentioned that other "patriotic" organizations were moving toward similar proposals. Rogers also reported that in April 1951, the Association received a letter from the Montclair chapter of the SAR requesting ALA to adopt a policy advocating that communistic and subversive materials not only be labeled, but also be segregated from other materials in the library collection and given out only upon written and signed application.

The Intellectual Freedom Committee believed such practices violated intellectual freedom principles and the labeling of books by points of view should not be undertaken by any library. The committee also noted that it was not clear who would do such labeling, who would decide what is communistic or subversive, or by what criteria such decisions would be made. In addition, the process was envisioned as

---

1. *ALA Bulletin* 45:241 (July/Aug. 1951).

expensive and time-consuming, involving examination of all materials in a library collection. The impracticality and financial problems of such a project, however, were not deemed relevant to the Association's policy concerning the practice. As Rogers pointed out, policy was to be based on the principle involved.

The IFC's study of the SAR proposal resulted in a six-point statement. Before presenting the statement to the Council for adoption as an ALA policy, the committee conducted an informal survey of twenty-four libraries around the country. Twenty responded, all agreeing that labeling violated basic principles of intellectual freedom and should not be practiced by libraries. The IFC's six-point Statement on Labeling was approved by the Council as an ALA policy on July 13, 1951:

> 1. Although totalitarian states find it easy and even proper, according to their ethics, to establish criteria for judging publications as "subversive," injustice and ignorance rather than justice and enlightenment result from such practices, and the American Library Association has a responsibility to take a stand against the establishment of such criteria in a democratic state.
>
> 2. Libraries do not advocate the ideas found in their collections. The presence of a magazine or book in a library does not indicate an endorsement of its contents by the library.
>
> 3. No one person should take the responsibility of labeling publications. No sizeable group of persons would be likely to agree wether on the types of materials which should be labeled or the sources of information which should be regarded with suspicion. As a practical consideration, a librarian who labeled a book or magazine pro-communist might be sued for libel.
>
> 4. Labeling is an attempt to prejudice the reader, and as such, it is a censor's tool.
>
> 5. Labeling violates the spirit of the Library Bill of Rights.
>
> 6. Although we are all agreed that communism is a threat to the free world, if materials are labeled to pacify one group, there is no excuse for refusing to label any item in the library's collection. Because communism, fascism, or other authoritarianisms tend to suppress ideas and attempt to coerce individuals to conform to a specific ideology, American librarians must be opposed to such "isms." We are, then, anticommunist, but we are also opposed to any other group which aims at closing any path to knowledge.

The 1951 Statement on Labeling was adopted as policy by many libraries, and over the years was a useful tool in combating this brand of censorship. One incident involving attempt to label library materials occurred at the St. Charles County Library, St. Charles, Missouri, in 1968 and concluded with a unique twist. The case began when Nina S. Ladof, the librarian, was presented with a petition requesting the removal of *Ramparts* magazine. The library dismissed the petition, explaining that *Ramparts* was purchased in accordance with the library's book selection policy, which included the Library Bill of Rights and The Freedom to Read.

After the initial attempt to remove *Ramparts* several months passed. Eventually, though, the original complainant presented the librarian with a sheaf of petitions from the Veterans of Foreign Wars, the American Legion, the Lions Club, and a church. With variations, the petitions read:

> We, the undersigned, do hereby petition the Library Board of the County of St. Charles, requesting that any book or publication on file in the St. Charles County Library System authored, published, or edited by any individual or group of individuals having been cited by any official Federal or State UnAmerican Activities Committee or Fact-Finding Committee as subversive or unAmerican in nature or belonging to any organization having been cited as subversive or unAmerican, be so explicitly labeled in a conspicuous manner for the information of the patrons of the St. Charles County Libraries.

Ladof pointed out that Dr. Benjamin Spock, author of *The Common Sense of Baby Care*, was sentenced on charges of aiding young men to avoid military service. Would this book require a label? Pursuing this example further, Ladof wrote to Spock's publishers to ask what action they would take if she did, in fact, affix a label to his works. Two replied that they would consider it possible grounds for legal action against the library. Dr. Spock's own attorney concurred.

Both the American Civil Liberties Union and the Freedom of Information Center at the University of Missouri provided Nina Ladof with the legal opinion that labeling a work, as requested in the petition, would be grounds for a libel action by the author whose works were involved because of the injury to the sale of his works that might result. Even if the label were factual, such as "so-and-so was a member of the Communist Party in 1941," he would have grounds to prove such injury. In fact, injury need not actually occur; it need only be a possibility for a court to award substantial damages to a plaintiff in such a case. And, since library boards of trustees cannot be sued as a body, each member would be liable for the damages awarded.

Armed with this information, and with the board's unanimous belief that labels are forms of censorship, and, as such, completely opposed to basic library policies, the library issued a firm statement rejecting the proposed labeling. The statement included information from legal sources and paraphrased and expanded the six points of the ALA Statement on Labeling. All persons interested in the matter were sent copies with an explanatory letter. *Ramparts* and other literature written by so-called subversives continued to circulate unlabeled.

The 1951 Statement on Labeling stood without revision until 1971. At that time, study of the policy confirmed that some sections were framed in language which reflected the Association's response to a specific threat—the labeling of "subversive" or "communist" materials. The Intellectual Freedom Community concluded that, while these sections once met a particular need, they limited the document's usefulness.

To make the Statement on Labeling application to a broader range of labeling problems, even encompassing "harmful matter," the Intellectual Freedom Committee recommended a revised version to the Council. The 1971 revision was designated an Interpretation of the Library Bill of Rights to emphasize the relationship between articles 1, 2, and 3 of that document and the Statement on Labeling. The revision was adopted by the Council on June 25, 1971:

> Because labeling violates the spirit of the Library Bill of Rights, the American Library Association opposes the technique of labeling as a means of predisposing readers against library materials for the following reasons:
>
> 1. Labeling* is an attempt to prejudice the reader, and as such it is a censor's tool.
>
> 2. Although some find it easy and even proper, according to their ethics, to establish criteria for judging publications as objectionable, injustice and ignorance rather than justice and enlightenment result from such practices, and the American Library Association must oppose the establishment of such criteria.
>
> 3. Libraries do not advocate the ideas found in their collections. The presence of a magazine or book in a library does not indicate an endorsement of its contents by the library.
>
> 4. No one person should take the responsibility of labeling publications. No sizeable group of persons would be likely to agree either on the types of material which should be labeled or the sources of information which should be regarded with suspicion. As a practical consideration, a librarian who labels a book or magazine might be sued for libel.
>
> 5. If materials are labeled to pacify one group, there is no excuse for refusing to label any item in the library's collection. Because authoritarians tend to suppress ideas and attempt to coerce individuals to conform to a specific ideology, the American

---

* "Labeling," as it is referred to in the Statement on Labeling, is the practice of describing or designating certain library materials, by affixing a prejudicial label to them or segregating them by a prejudicial system, so as to predispose readers against the materials.

Library Association opposes such efforts which aim at closing any path to knowledge.

Following the 1980 revision of the Library Bill of Rights, the IFC again reviewed the statement, recommending three major changes. First, the committee noted that relegating definition of the labeling practice to a footnote detracted from the policy's unity and effectiveness and suggested incorporating the definition in the opening paragraph. Second, the committee recommended that points 4 and 5 be dropped, since these were not considerations of principle but, rather, "practical" objections to labeling.

While librarians should certainly be aware that the labeling of library materials could provoke legal action, and, though it is certainly true that adoption of labels at the instigation of one group might open a veritable Pandora's box of labeling demands by others, neither of these considerations lies at the basis of the Association's opposition to labeling. The American Library Association opposes labeling of library materials not because this is impractical or legally dangerous, but because this practice flagrantly violates both the spirit and the letter of the Library Bill of Rights, and stands in fundamental opposition to the most basic principles of intellectual freedom.

In addition, the committee recommended adding a sentence to the statement indicating that the Association's objections to labeling should not be construed as opposition to legitimate organizational schemes designed to facilitate access. The second revision of the Statement on Labeling was adopted by the Council on July 1, 1981. It read:

> Labeling is the practice of describing or designating certain library materials by affixing a prejudicial label to them or segregating them by a prejudicial system. The American Library Association opposes this as a means of predisposing people's attitudes towards library materials for the following reasons:
>
> 1. Labeling is an attempt to prejudice attitudes and as such, it is a censor's tool.
>
> 2. Some find it easy and even proper, according to their ethics, to establish criteria for judging publications as objectionable. However, injustice and ignorance rather than justice and enlightenment result from such practices, and the American Library Association opposes the establishment of such criteria.
>
> 3. Libraries do not advocate the ideas found in their collections. The presence of books and other resources in a library does not indicate endorsement of their contents by the library.
>
> The American Library Association opposes efforts which aim at closing any path to knowledge. This statement does not, how-

ever, exclude the adoption of organizational schemes designed as
directional aids or to facilitate access to materials.

In keeping with the review of Library Bill of Rights interpretations, undertaken in response to the 1988 Minority Concerns Committee resolution, the Statement on Labeling was the first to be revised by
the Intellectual Freedom Committee at the June 1989 Annual Conference. The importance of this policy increased significantly in light of
attempts, in 1990, to pass legislation in Congress requiring warning
labels for musical recordings with allegedly obscene lyrics or lyrics
deemed offensive or unsuitable for minors.

Policy revisions made clear the ALA's opposition to labeling, and
emphasized librarians' responsibility to prevent the imposition of private or voluntary labeling schemes on library materials, while leaving
permanently affixed labels intact to avoid expurgation of copyrighted
material. The new interpretation also encourages librarians to become
familiar with local laws and regulations on the issue.

Following adoption by the IFC in June 1989, the revised Statement
on Labeling was circulated to other ALA units. At the 1990 Midwinter
Meeting, the revision was reconsidered in light of comments received
from the other units. The final version of this interpretation was accepted by the Committee and then adopted by the Council on June 26,
1990.

2.4

ACCESS FOR CHILDREN AND YOUNG PEOPLE TO VIDEOTAPES AND OTHER NONPRINT FORMATS

An Interpretation of the Library Bill of Rights

Library collections of videotapes, motion pictures, and other nonprint formats raise a number of intellectual freedom issues, especially regarding minors.

The interests of young people, like those of adults, are not limited by subject, theme, or level of sophistication. Librarians have a responsibility to ensure young people have access to materials and services that reflect diversity sufficient to meet their needs.

To guide librarians and others in resolving these issues, the American Library Association provides the following guidelines.

Article 5 of The Library Bill of Rights says, "A person's right to use a library should not be denied or abridged because of origin, age, background, or views."

ALA's Free Access to Libraries For Minors: An Interpretation of the Library Bill of Rights states:

> The "right to use a library" includes free access to, and unrestricted use of, all the services, materials, and facilities the library has to offer. Every restriction on access to, and use of, library resources, based solely on the chronological age, educational level, or legal emancipation of users violates Article 5.
>
> ... [P]arents—and only parents—have the right and responsibility to restrict the access of their children—and only their children—to library resources. Parents or legal guardians who do not want their children to have access to certain library services, materials or facilities, should so advise their children. Librarians and governing bodies cannot assume the role of parents or the functions of parental authority in the private relationship between parent and child. Librarians and governing bodies have a public and professional obli-

gation to provide equal access to all library resources for all library users.

Policies which set minimum age limits for access to videotapes and/ or other audiovisual materials and equipment, with or without parental permission, abridge library use for minors. Further, age limits based on the cost of the materials are unacceptable. Unless directly and specifically prohibited by law from circulating certain motion pictures and video productions to minors, librarians should apply the same standards to circulation of these materials as are applied to books and other materials.

Recognizing that libraries cannot act *in loco parentis*, ALA acknowledges and supports the exercise by parents of their responsibility to guide their own children's reading and viewing. Published reviews of films and videotapes and/or reference works which provide information about the content, subject matter, and recommended audiences can be made available in conjunction with nonprint collections to assist parents in guiding their children without implicating the library in censorship. This material may include information provided by video producers and distributors, promotional material on videotape packaging, and Motion Picture Association of America (MPAA) ratings *if they are included on the tape or in the packaging by the original publisher* and/or if they appear in review sources or reference works included in the library's collection. Marking out or removing ratings information from videotape packages constitutes expurgation or censorship.

MPAA and other rating services are private advisory codes and have no legal standings*. For the library to add such ratings to the materials if they are not already there, to post a list of such ratings with a collection, or to attempt to enforce such ratings through circulation policies or other procedures constitutes labeling, "an attempt to prejudice attitudes" about the material, and is unacceptable. The application of locally generated ratings schemes intended to provide content warnings to library users is also inconsistent with the Library Bill of Rights.

---

* For information on case law, please contact the ALA Office for Intellectual Freedom.

See also: Statement on Labeling and Expurgation of Library Materials, interpretations of the Library Bill of Rights.

Adopted June 28, 1989, by the ALA Council; the quotation from Free Access to Libraries for Minors was changed after the Council adopted the July 3, 1991, revision of that interpretation.

Access for Children and Young People to Videotapes and Other Nonprint Formats: History

In January 1989, the IFC examined the interpretation on Circulation of Motion Pictures and Video Productions in response to urgings from the ALA youth divisions and to the Minority Concerns Committee's request for a review of the Library Bill of Rights. The IFC concluded that a new interpretation was necessary to fully address the issue of minors access to videos and to provide similar guarantees for nonprint formats resulting from new technologies.

The committee also sought to provide clearer guidelines for librarians, emphasizing the importance of parental—not librarian—responsibility for guiding a child's viewing or choice of other library materials, opposing the use of cost-based restrictions to inhibit minors access to materials, and rejecting the imposition of private rating systems and the unapproved editing of films or other copyright materials for classroom use.

The new draft interpretation was presented to the committee at the June 1989 ALA Annual Conference. After discussion with representatives from the youth divisions and the Professional Ethics Committee, which resulted in minor editorial changes, the interpretation was adopted and recommended to the Council. On June 28, 1989, the Council adopted the new interpretation in place of the former Circulation of Motion Pictures and Video Productions. The latter was then rescinded by the Council.

2.5

EXPURGATION OF LIBRARY MATERIALS

An Interpretation of the Library Bill of Rights

Expurgating library materials is a violation of the Library Bill of Rights. Expurgation as defined by this interpretation includes any deletion, excision, alteration, editing, or obliteration of any part(s) of books or other library resources by the library, its agent, or its parent institution (if any). By such expurgation, the library is in effect denying access to the complete work and the entire spectrum of ideas that the work intended to express. Such action stands in violation of articles 1, 2, and 3 of the Library Bill of Rights, which state that "Materials should not be excluded because of the origin, background, or views of those contributing to their creation," that "Materials should not be proscribed or removed because of partisan or doctrinal disapproval," and that "Libraries should challenge censorship in the fulfillment of their responsibility to provide information and enlightenment."

The act of expurgation has serious implications. It involves a determination that it is necessary to restrict access to the complete work. This is censorship. When a work is expurgated, under the assumption that certain portions of that work would be harmful to minors, the situation is no less serious.

Expurgation of any books or other library resources imposes a restriction, without regard to the rights and desires of all library users, by limiting access to ideas and information.

Further, expurgation without written permission from the holder of the copyright on the material may violate the copyright provisions of the United States Code.

Adopted February 2, 1973; amended July 1, 1981; amended January 10, 1990, by the ALA Council.

45

Expurgation of Library
Materials: History

The December 1971 issue of *School Library Journal* (p.7) carried the following report submitted by one of its readers:

> Maurice Sendak might faint but a staff member of Caldwell Parish Library [Louisiana], knowing that the patrons of the community might object to the illustrations in *In the Night Kitchen*, solved the problem by diapering the little boys with white tempera paint. Other libraries might wish to do the same.

In response, Ursula Nordstrom, publisher of Harper Junior Books, sent a statement to over 380 librarians, professors, publishers, authors, and artists throughout the United States:

> [The news item sent to *School Library Journal*] is representative of several such reports about Maurice Sendak's *In the Night Kitchen*, a book for children, that have come out of public and school libraries throughout the country.
>
> At first, the thought of librarians painting diapers or pants on the naked hero of Sendak's book might seem amusing, merely a harmless eccentricity on the part of some prim few. On reconsideration, however, this behavior should be recognized for what it is: an act of censorship by mutilation rather than by obvious suppression.

Over 425 persons signed the statement of protest circulated by Miss Nordstrom.

The expurgation of *In the Night Kitchen* was brought to the attention of the Intellectual Freedom Committee by the Children's Book Council in June 1972. During its meeting at the 1972 ALA Annual Conference in Chicago, the committee decided, after considering whether expurgation was already covered by the Library Bill of Rights, that a statement should be issued specifically on expurgation. During the 1973 Midwinter Meeting in Washington, D.C., the committee approved a statement on expurgation of library materials and sent it to the ALA Council for approval. The statement which was adopted by the Council as an ALA policy on February 2, 1973, read:

> Library materials are chosen for their value and interest to the community the library serves. If library materials were acquired for these reasons and in accordance with a written statement on materials selection, then to expurgate must be interpreted as a violation of the Library Bill of Rights. For purposes of this statement, expurgation includes deletion, excision, alteration or obliteration. By such expurgation, the library is in effect denying access to the complete work and the full ideas that the work was intended to express; such action stands in violation of article 2 of the Library Bill of Rights, which states that "no library materials should be proscribed or removed from libraries because of partisan or doctrinal disapproval."
>
> The act of expurgation has serious implications. It involves a determination by an individual that it is necessary to restrict the availability of that material. It is, in fact, censorship.
>
> When a work is expurgated, under the assumption that certain sections of that work would be harmful to minors, the situation is no less serious. Expurgation of any library materials imposes a restriction, without regard to the rights and desires of all library users.

In 1981, during the review of all the interpretations of the Library Bill of Rights, the IFC reviewed the policy on expurgation and made several changes designed to add clarity to and strengthen the document. Most important, the IFC recommended basing the argument of the interpretation not only on article 2 of the Library Bill of Rights, but on articles 1 and 3 as well. The revision was adopted by the Council on July 1, 1981, and read:

> Books and other library resources are selected for their value, interest, and importance to the people of the community the library serves. Since books and other library resources are acquired for these reasons and in accordance with a written statement on materials selection, then expurgating them must be interpreted as a violation of the Library Bill of Rights. Expurgation as defined by this interpretation includes any deletion, excision, alteration, or obliteration of any part(s) of books or other library resources by the library. By such expurgation, the library is in effect denying access to the complete work and the entire spectrum of ideas that

the work intended to express; such action stands in violation of articles 1, 2, and 3 of the Library Bill of Rights, which state that "Materials should not be excluded because of the origin, background, or views of those contributing to their creation"; that "Materials should not be proscribed or removed because of partisan or doctrinal disapproval"; and that "Libraries should challenge censorship in the fulfillment of their responsibility to provide information and enlightenment."

The act of expurgation has serious implications. It involves a determination that it is necessary to restrict complete access to that material. This is censorship. When a work is expurgated, under the assumption that certain portions of that work would be harmful to minors, the situation is no less serious.

Expurgation of any books or other library resources imposes a restriction, without regard to the rights and desires of all library users, by limiting access to ideas and information.

At the June, 1989, Annual Conference in Dallas, the Interpretation on Expurgation of Library Materials was revised in accordance with the request of the Minority Concerns Committee for review of the Library Bill of Rights to ensure that discrimination on the basis of language and economic status would be addressed. The IFC adopted a revised version which was subsequently circulated for comments.

At the January, 1990, ALA Midwinter Meeting, minor editorial changes were made and the new draft was adopted and recommended to the Council. On January 10, 1990, the interpretation became ALA policy.

2.6

DIVERSITY IN COLLECTION DEVELOPMENT
An Interpretation of the Library Bill of Rights

Throughout history, censors' aims have varied from generation to generation. Books and other materials have not been selected or have been removed from library collections for prejudicial language and ideas, political content, economic theory, social philosophy, religious beliefs, sexual expression, and other topics of a potentially controversial nature.

Some examples of censorship may include removing or not selecting materials because they are considered by some as racist or sexist; not purchasing conservative religious materials; not selecting materials about or by minorities because it is thought these groups or interests are not represented in a community; or not providing information on or materials from nonmainstream political entities.

Librarians may seek to increase user awareness of materials on various social concerns by many means, including, but not limited to, issuing bibliographies and presenting exhibits and programs.

Librarians have a professional responsibility to be inclusive, not exclusive, in collection development and in the provision of interlibrary loan. Access to all materials legally obtainable should be assured to the user, and policies should not unjustly exclude materials even if they are offensive to the librarian or the user. Collection development should reflect the philosophy inherent in article 2 of the Library Bill of Rights: "Libraries should provide materials and information presenting all points of view on current and historical issues. Materials should not be proscribed or removed because of partisan or doctrinal disapproval." A balanced collection reflects a diversity of materials, not an equality of numbers. Collection development responsibilities include selecting materials in the languages in common use in the community which the library serves. Collection development and the selection of materials should be done according to professional standards and established selection and review procedures.

There are many complex facets to any issue, and variations of context in which issues may be expressed, discussed, or interpreted. Librarians have a professional responsibility to be fair, just, and equitable and to give all library users equal protection in guarding against violation of the library patron's right to read, view, or listen to materials and resources protected by the First Amendment, no matter what the viewpoint of the author, creator, or selector. Librarians have an obligation to protect library collections from removal of materials based on personal bias or prejudice, and to select and support the access to materials on all subjects that meet, as closely as possible, the needs and interests of all persons in the community which the library serves. This includes materials that reflect political, economic, religious, social, minority, and sexual issues.

Intellectual freedom, the essence of equitable library services, provides for free access to all expressions of ideas through which any and all sides of a question, cause, or movement may be explored. Toleration is meaningless without tolerance for what some may consider detestable. Librarians cannot justly permit their own preferences to limit their degree of tolerance in collection development, because freedom is indivisible.

Adopted July 14, 1982; amended January 10, 1990, by the ALA Council.

Diversity in Collection Development: History

During the 1971 Midwinter Meeting in Los Angeles, the ALA Intellectual Freedom Committee met with representatives of the International Conference of Police Associations' Executive Board. The meeting was to provide a forum for discussing police efforts to remove William Steig's *Sylvester and the Magic Pebble* from public and school libraries. During the meeting, the officers raised a provocative and embarrassing question for librarians. They asked why some librarians were quick to comply with requests to remove another children's book, *Little Black Sambo*, from their collections when blacks complained that its illustrations were degrading; yet now, when police officers found William Steig's pigs dressed as law enforcement officers to be degrading, librarians objected vociferously to taking the book out of their collections.

The evasive response from the IFC was generally to the effect that the committee had difficulties impressing upon members of the library profession the importance of the principles of intellectual freedom. The inability to answer the officers' charge adequately acknowledged the accusation implicit in the question: some librarians do employ a double standard when it comes to their practice of intellectual freedom and their commitment to it. Many librarians express a strong commitment to the principles of intellectual freedom, but fail to grasp that the concept of intellectual freedom, in its pure sense, promotes no causes, furthers no movements, and favors no viewpoints. *Little Black Sambo* and *Sylvester and the Magic Pebble* did not bring new issues before the library profession. These books only inherited the cloak of controversy that had already surrounded such diverse works as *Huckleberry Finn*, *Mother Goose Nursery Rhymes and Fairy Tales*, *Doctor Doolittle*, and *The Merchant of Venice*.

Article 2 of the Library Bill of Rights states that "no library materials should be proscribed or removed from libraries because of partisan or doctrinal disapproval." The phrase "no library materials" does not appear by accident. Before June 1967, the sentence concluded, "books or other reading matter of sound factual authority should not be proscribed or removed from library shelves because of partisan or doctrinal disapproval." Article 2 was revised in 1967 because some librarians used alleged lack of "sound factual authority" as a basis for removing library materials. To determine which materials lacked "sound factual authority," many deferred to their personal conceptions of "fact" and "authority." One of the most extreme examples, cited at the time of the revision, was of a Catholic librarian who excluded Protestant publications because they were not of "sound factual authority." Today, the simpler, broader phrase "no library materials" in the Library Bill of Rights leaves no room for interpretation. The revised statement reflects the philosophy that freedom is indivisible, and that tolerance, if it is to be meaningful, must be tolerance for all points of view.

At the 1972 Midwinter Meeting in Chicago, the Intellectual Freedom Committee reported its intention to prepare a statement making clear the meaning of the Library Bill of Rights as it pertains to attempts to censor library materials because of alleged racism, sexism, or any other "isms." The statement was approved by the IFC on June 25, 1972. It was subsequently submitted to the ALA Council at the 1973 Midwinter Meeting in Washington, D.C., and approved as an ALA policy on February 2, 1973. Entitled "Sexism, Racism, and Other -Isms in Library Materials," it read:

> Traditional aims of censorship efforts have been to suppress political, sexual, or religious expressions. The same three subjects have also been the source of most complaints about materials in library collections. Another basis for complaints, however, has become more and more frequent. Due, perhaps, to increased awareness of the rights of minorities and increased efforts to secure those rights, libraries are being asked to remove, restrict or reconsider some materials which are allegedly derogatory to specific minorities or which supposedly perpetuate stereotypes and false images of minorities. Among the several recurring "isms" used to describe the contents of the materials objected to are "racism" and "sexism."
>
> Complaints that library materials convey a derogatory or false image of a minority strike the personal social consciousness and sense of responsibility of some librarians who—accordingly—comply with the requests to remove such materials. While such efforts to counteract injustices are understandable, and perhaps even

commendable as reflections of deep personal commitments to the ideal of equality for all people, they are—nonetheless—in conflict with the professional responsibility of librarians to guard against encroachments upon intellectual freedom.

This responsibility has been espoused and reaffirmed by the American Library Association in many of its basic documents on intellectual freedom over the past thirty years. The most concise statement of the Association's position appears in article 2 of the Library Bill of Rights, which states that "Libraries should provide books and materials presenting all points of view concerning the problems and issues of our times; no library materials should be proscribed or removed because of partisan or doctrinal disapproval."

While the application of this philosophy may seem simple when dealing with political, religious, or even sexual expressions, its full implications become somewhat difficult when dealing with ideas, such as racism or sexism, which many find abhorrent, repugnant and inhumane. But, as stated in The Freedom to Read:

> It is inevitable in the give and take of the democratic process that the political, the moral, or the aesthetic concepts of an individual or group will occasionally collide with those of another individual or group. In a free society each individual is free to determine for himself what he wishes to read, and each group is free to determine what it will recommend to its freely associated members. But no group has the right to take the law into its own hands, and to impose its own concept of politics or morality upon other members of a democratic society. Freedom is no freedom if it is accorded only to the accepted and the inoffensive. . . . We realize that the application of these propositions may mean the dissemination of ideas and manners of expression that are repugnant to many persons. We do not state these propositions in the comfortable belief that what people read is unimportant. We believe rather that what people read is deeply important; that ideas can be dangerous; but that the suppression of ideas is fatal to a democratic society. Freedom itself is a dangerous way of life, but it is ours.

Some find this creed acceptable when dealing with materials for adults but cannot extend its application to materials for children. Such reluctance is generally based on the belief that children are more susceptible to being permanently influenced—even damaged—by objectionable materials than are adults. The Library Bill of Rights, however, makes no distinction between materials and services for children and adults. Its principles of free access to all materials available apply to every person; as stated in article 5, "The rights of an individual to the use of a library should not be denied or abridged because of his age, race, religion, national origins or social or political views."

Some librarians deal with the problem of objectionable materials by labeling them or listing them as "racist" or "sexist." This kind of action, too, has long been opposed by the American Library Association through its Statement on Labeling, which says,

> If materials are labeled to pacify one group, there is no excuse for refusing to label any item in the library's collection. Because authoritarians tend to suppress ideas and attempt to coerce individuals to conform to a specific ideology, the American Library Association opposes such efforts which aim at closing any path to knowledge.

Others deal with the problem of objectionable materials by instituting restrictive circulation or relegating materials to closed or restricted collections. This practice, too, is in violation of the Library Bill of Rights as explained in Restricted Access to Library Materials, which says,

> Too often only "controversial" materials are the subject of such segregation, leading to the conclusion that factors other than theft and mutilation were the true considerations. The distinction is extremely difficult to make, both for the librarian and the patron. Selection policies, carefully developed on the basis of principles of intellectual freedom and the Library Bill of Rights, should not be vitiated by administrative practices such as restricted access.

The American Library Association has made clear its position concerning the removal of library materials because of partisan or doctrinal disapproval, or because of pressures from interest groups, in another policy statement, the Resolution on Challenged Materials:

> The American Library Association declares as a matter of firm principle that no challenged material should be removed from any library under any legal or extra-legal pressure, save after an independent determination by a judicial officer in a court of competent jurisdiction and only after an adversary hearing, in accordance with well-established principles of law.

Intellectual freedom, in its purest sense, promotes no causes, furthers no movements, and favors no viewpoints. It only provides for free access to all ideas through which any and all sides of causes and movements may be expressed, discussed, and argued. The librarian cannot let his own preferences limit his degree of tolerance, for freedom is indivisible. Toleration is meaningless without toleration for the detestable.

It soon became apparent that this lengthy and somewhat unwieldy document had been formulated to address a specific situation arising in the late 1960s and early 1970s. During this time many people of a liberal or leftist political orientation, who, in the past, had stood in the forefront of the anticensorship battle, were falling, intentionally or not, into the very practice they had previously opposed when espoused by others. By the end of the 1970s, however, though the problem addressed by the policy continued, new instances of censorship had arisen in which other would-be censors also sought to justify their actions by support for broadly accepted social values. In reviewing the policy in the early 1980s, the IFC concluded that a broader statement covering the influence of conflicting values, philosophies and points of view on library collections, and reaffirming the library's commitment to the inclusion of all, would be more appropriate.

At first the committee tried to expand the number of "isms" covered by the policy to include such phenomena as anti-Semitism, communism and anti-communism, homosexuality, and the like. But it was quickly obvious that this approach would not only be extremely awkward, but, like the original policy, would tie the document to the temporal particularities of the period in which it was written. The committee therefore decided to formulate and present to the Council a new interpretation, expanding more broadly on the call in the Library Bill of Rights for libraries "to provide materials and information presenting all points of view on current and historical issues."

The new policy was entitled Diversity in Collection Development. These words were not lightly chosen. Indeed, the IFC initially had preferred the title Balanced Collections. In the early 1980s, however, several groups and individuals actively involved in increasing censorship pressures, largely from the right of center, also had raised the demand for "balance" in library holdings. Insofar as this was a call for libraries to be more inclusive in collection development, it was welcomed by ALA. Many, however, also saw in the demand for "balance" a dangerous, if hidden, threat of censorship.

The concept of balanced collections may be misunderstood to presuppose a bias toward moderation, and to place limitations on the acquisition of materials thought to be "extreme," because these might skew the "balance" of the collection. The requirement that a library collection be "balanced" could be construed to imply that, for instance, leftist materials cannot be acquired if there is no equivalent material from the right, or vice versa. If balance is sought in this formal sense, librarians are placed in a position where they must act as validators of opinion by assigning values, or "weights," to differing points of view across the spectrum of opinion. In other words, a misconceived, if well-intentioned requirement for balance may also make of the librarian a kind of censor.

Recognizing this possible misapplication of the notion of balance, the Committee opted to emphasize instead the concept of diversity. Not only is the library obliged to include many differing views in its collection, but materials representing the broadest diversity of human thought and creativity should, in general, be actively sought, irrespective of the opinions, prejudices, values, and tastes of the librarian, and whether or not a given numerical or other balance of views can be achieved at a given moment. The committee completed work on the document at the 1982 Annual Conference in Philadelphia and on July 14, 1982, the Council approved the new interpretation of the Library Bill of Rights, noting that it replaced the former policy on Racism, Sexism and Other -Isms in Library Materials, which was then rescinded. The new policy read:

> Throughout history, the focus of censorship has vacillated from generation to generation. Books and other materials have not been selected or have been removed from library collections for many reasons, among which are prejudicial language and ideas, political content, economic theory, social philosophies, religious beliefs, and/or sexual forms of expression.
>
> Some examples of this may include removing or not selecting materials because they are considered by some as racist or sexist; not purchasing conservative religious materials; not selecting materials about or by minorities because it is thought these groups or interests are not represented in a community; or not providing information on or materials from nonmainstream political entities.
>
> Librarians may seek to increase user awareness of materials on various social concerns by many means, including, but not limited to, issuing bibliographies and presenting exhibits and programs.
>
> Librarians have a professional responsibility to be inclusive, not exclusive, in collection development and in the provision of interlibrary loan. Access to all materials legally obtainable should be assured to the user and policies should not unjustly exclude materials even if offensive to the librarian or the user. Collection development should reflect the philosophy inherent in article 2 of the Library Bill of Rights: "Libraries should provide materials and information presenting all points of view on current and historical issues. Materials should not be proscribed or removed because of partisan or doctrinal disapproval." A balanced collection reflects a diversity of materials, not an equality of numbers. Collection development and the selection of materials should be done according

to professional standards and established selection and review procedures.

There are many complex facets to any issue, and variations of context in which issues may be expressed, discussed, or interpreted. Librarians have a professional responsibility to be fair, just, equitable, and to give all library users equal protection in guarding against violation of the library patrons' liberty to read, view, or listen to materials and resources protected by the First Amendment, no matter what the viewpoint of the author, creator, or selector. Librarians have an obligation to protect library collections from removal of materials based on personal bias or prejudice, and to select and support the access to materials on all subjects that meet, as closely as possible, the needs and interests of all persons in the community which the library serves. This includes materials that reflect political, economic, religious, social, minority, and sexual issues.

Intellectual freedom, the essence of equitable library services, promotes no causes, furthers no movements, and favors no viewpoints. It only provides for free access to all expressions of ideas through which any and all sides of a question, cause, or movement may be explored. Toleration is meaningless without tolerance for what some may consider detestable. Librarians cannot justly permit their own preferences to limit their degree of tolerance in collection development, because freedom is indivisible.

Note: This policy replaces the policy Racism, Sexism, and Other -Isms in Library Materials.

The interpretation on Diversity in Collection Development was revised in 1989 to acknowledge the responsibility of all librarians to be sensitive to the language(s) in common use in the community the library serves. Finally, the phrase claiming that intellectual freedom "promotes no causes, furthers no movements, and favors no viewpoints" was deleted from the text.

The newly revised interpretation was adopted by the Council on January 10, 1990.

2.7

EVALUATING LIBRARY COLLECTIONS
An Interpretation of the Library Bill of Rights

The continuous review of library materials is necessary as a means of maintaining an active library collection of current interest to users. In the process, materials may be added and physically deteriorated or obsolete materials may be replaced or removed in accordance with the collection maintenance policy of a given library and the needs of the community it serves. Continued evaluation is closely related to the goals and responsibilities of libraries and is a valuable tool of collection development. This procedure is not to be used as a convenient means to remove materials presumed to be controversial or disapproved of by segments of the community. Such abuse of the evaluation function violates the principles of intellectual freedom and is in opposition to the preamble and articles 1 and 2 of the Library Bill of Rights, which state:

> The American Library Association affirms that all libraries are forums for information and ideas, and that the following basic policies should guide their services.
>
> 1. Books and other library resources should be provided for the interest, information, and enlightenment of all people of the community the library serves. Materials should not be excluded because of the origin, background, or views of those contributing to their creation.
>
> 2. Libraries should provide materials and information presenting all points of view on current and historical issues. Materials should not be proscribed or removed because of partisan or doctrinal disapproval.

The American Library Association opposes such "silent censorship" and strongly urges that libraries adopt guidelines setting forth the positive purposes and principles of evaluation of materials in library collections.

Adopted February 2, 1973; amended July 1, 1981, by the ALA Council.

58

Evaluating Library Collections: History

In both theory and practice, library collections undergo continual re-evaluation to ensure that they fulfill and remain responsive to the goals of the institution and the needs of library patrons. The reevaluation process, however, can also be used to achieve the purposes of the censor, purposes manifestly inconsistent with articles 1 and 2 of the Library Bill of Rights.

At the 1972 Midwinter Meeting in Chicago, the Intellectual Freedom Committee realized the necessity of an interpretation of the Library Bill of Rights with regard to the more general issues involved in reevaluating library collections. Accordingly, the committee announced its intent to prepare a statement on reevaluation. The document was approved by the Intellectual Freedom Committee at the 1972 Annual Conference in Chicago. It was submitted to the ALA Council at the 1973 Midwinter Meeting in Washington, D.C., and was adopted on February 2, 1973, under the title Reevaluating Library Collections:

> The continuous review of library collections to remove physically deteriorated or obsolete materials is one means to maintain active library collections of current interest to users.* Continued reevaluation is closely related to the goals and responsibilities of libraries and is a valuable tool of collection building. This procedure, however, is sometimes used as a convenient means to remove materials thought to be too controversial or disapproved of by segments of the community. Such abuse of the reevaluation function violates the principles of intellectual freedom and is in

---

* The traditional term "weeding," implying "the removal of a noxious growth," is purposely avoided because of the imprecise nature of the term.

opposition to articles 1 and 2 of the Library Bill of Rights, which
state that:

> As a responsibility of library service, books and other li-
> brary materials selected should be chosen for values of interest,
> information and enlightenment of all the people of the commu-
> nity. In no case should library materials be excluded because of
> the race or nationality or the social, political, or religious views
> of the authors.
>
> Libraries should provide books and other materials present-
> ing all points of view concerning the problems and issues of our
> times; no library materials should be proscribed or removed
> from libraries because of partisan or doctrinal disapproval.
>
> The American Library Association opposes such "silent cen-
> sorship," and recommends that libraries adopt guidelines setting
> forth the positive purposes and principles for reevaluation of mate-
> rials in library collections.

In 1981 the policy was rewritten by the IFC to reflect the changes
which had been made in the 1980 version of the Library Bill of Rights.
In the process, a number of editorial changes were made in the text
with the aim of increasing its forcefulness. The most significant amendment recommended by the IFC was a change in the title of the document from Reevaluating Library Collections to Evaluating Library
Collections. The change was suggested because the process of evaluating library materials for acquisition or retention is a single ongoing
process and, in principle, is never completed and then *redone*. Moreover, the Intellectual Freedom Committee thought that it could be
falsely inferred from the word "reevaluating" that initial "evaluations"
of works had been incorrect. The revision was approved by the Council
on July 1, 1981.

2.8

CHALLENGED MATERIALS
An Interpretation of the Library Bill of Rights

The American Library Association declares as a matter of firm principle that it is the responsibility of every library to have a clearly defined materials selection policy in written form which reflects the Library Bill of Rights, and which is approved by the appropriate governing authority.

Challenged materials which meet the criteria for selection in the materials selection policy of the library should not be removed under any legal or extra-legal pressure. The Library Bill of Rights states in article 1 that "Materials should not be excluded because of the origin, background, or views of those contributing to their creation," and in Article 2, that "Materials should not be proscribed or removed because of partisan or doctrinal disapproval." Freedom of expression is protected by the Constitution of the United States, but constitutionally protected expression is often separated from unprotected expression only by a dim and uncertain line. The Constitution requires a procedure designed to focus searchingly on challenged expression before it can be suppressed. An adversary hearing is a part of this procedure.

Therefore, any attempt, be it legal or extra-legal, to regulate or suppress materials in libraries must be closely scrutinized to the end that protected expression is not abridged.

Adopted June 25, 1971; amended July 1, 1981; amended January 10, 1990, by the ALA Council.

Challenged Materials: History

The Library Bill of Rights states that library materials should not be "excluded because of the origin, background, or views" of their creators. The document states further that "materials should not be proscribed or removed because of partisan or doctrinal disapproval." Nevertheless, libraries are still pressured by many groups and individuals to remove certain materials because they find their sexual, political, or religious content objectionable.

Particularly when sexually explicit materials are the object of censorship efforts, librarians and boards of trustees are often unaware of the legal procedures required to effect the removal of such items. Many attorneys, even when employed by state or local governing bodies, are not aware of the procedures to determine whether or not a work is obscene under the law. According to U.S. Superme Court decisions, a work is not obscene until found to be so by a court of law, and only after an adversary hearing to determine the question of obscenity. Until a work is specifically found to be unprotected by the First Amendment, the title remains a legal library acquisition and need not be removed.

In 1971, several attempts to ban publications from libraries involved charges that the works were obscene, and therefore not legal or proper acquisitions for the library. In Groton, Connecticut, in a case involving *Evergreen Review*, the librarian and the board of trustees were threatened with prosecution under a state obscenity statute if they refused to remove the magazine from the library. The board, after several months of resisting efforts to remove the magazine, capitulated in the face of this threat to prosecute them as individuals.

The Groton, Connecticut, case prompted the Intellectual Freedom Committee, with the aid of legal counsel, to study U.S. Supreme Court and federal circuit court decisions concerning procedures whereby materials are determined to be obscene. Three cases in particular were reviewed: *Bantam Books, Inc.* v. *Sullivan* (372 U.S. 58, 83 S. Ct. 631 [1963]); *Marcus* v. *Search Warrants* (367 U.S. 717, 732; 81 S. Ct. 1708, 1716 [1961]); and *A Quantity of Copies of Books* v. *Kansas* (378 U.S. 205, 211; 84 S. Ct. 1723 [1964]).

Using the language of these three decisions as a basis, the Intellectual Freedom Committee developed the Resolution on Challenged Materials. The statement was submitted to the ALA Council during the 1971 Annual Conference in Dallas, and was adopted as an ALA policy on June 25, 1971. It read:

> WHEREAS, The Library Bill of Rights states that no library materials should be proscribed or removed because of partisan or doctrinal disapproval; and
>
> WHEREAS, Constitutionally protected expression is often separated from unprotected expression only by a dim and uncertain line; and
>
> WHEREAS, Any attempt, be it legal or extra-legal, to regulate or suppress material must be closely scrutinized to the end that protected expression is not abridged in the process; and
>
> WHEREAS, The Constitution requires a procedure designed to focus searchingly on the question before speech can be suppressed; and
>
> WHEREAS, The dissemination of a particular work which is alleged to be unprotected should be completely undisturbed until an independent determination has been made by a judicial officer, including an adversary hearing.
>
> THEREFORE, THE PREMISES CONSIDERED, BE IT RESOLVED, That the American Library Association declares as a matter of firm principle that no challenged library material should be removed from any library under any legal or extra-legal pressure, save after an independent determination by a judicial officer in a court of competent jurisdiction and only after an adversary hearing, in accordance with well-established principles of law.

A decade later, legal standards for determining obscenity had changed significantly. Nevertheless, the basic principle—that expression is protected by the First Amendment until it has been determined through an adversary procedure that such expression is obscene, libelous, or otherwise unprotected—remained firmly established in U.S. constitutional law. In reviewing the 1971 resolution in 1981, however, the IFC found that a major revision still was necessary. The principal difficulties were twofold. The first problem was the rather simple matter of format. Written as a formal resolution, with an implementary paragraph preceded by a series of "whereas clauses," the Resolution on Challenged Materials was inconsistent in form with other interpretations of the Library Bill of Rights, and lacked clarity and force as a document directed toward the general public as well as library professionals.

The second problem was more substantive. The materials selection policies of most libraries correctly provide opportunities for patron input and citizen requests for reconsideration of library materials. Yet the policy seemed to make a mockery of such procedures by declaring in advance that "no challenged library material should be removed" unless the library is ordered to do so by a court of law. Moreover, many librarians complained that such an inflexible declaration served to tie the library's own hands in its efforts to correct the inevitable mistakes which will occur in any selection process.

With these considerations in mind, the IFC presented the Council with a new version of the document, written in a format similar to the other interpretations of the Library Bill of Rights and more appropriate for a broader audience. The new version linked the decision to remove or retain challenged materials to the maintenance of clear guidelines consistent with the Library Bill of Rights and established by the library's materials selection policy. The revision designated the maintenance of a "clearly defined" selection policy a "responsibility" of all libraries. The new version offered libraries and patrons alike greater flexibility in the consideration of challenges while, at the same time, reaffirming the principles of the Library Bill of Rights and calling for the closest scrutiny of all efforts to remove materials and the maintenance of due process in the reconsideration procedure. On July 1, 1981, the Council adopted the revised statement on Challenged Materials as a policy of the American Library Association:

> The American Library Association declares as a matter of firm principle that it is the responsibility of every library to have a clearly defined materials selection policy in written form which reflects the Library Bill of Rights, and which is approved by the appropriate governing authority.
>
> Challenged materials which meet the materials selection policy of the library should not be removed under any legal or extralegal pressure. The Library Bill of Rights states in article 1 that "Materials should not be excluded because of the origin, background, or views of those contributing to their creation," and in article 2, that "Materials should not be proscribed or removed because of partisan or doctrinal disapproval." Freedom of expression is protected by the Constitution of the United States, but constitutionally protected expression is often separated from unprotected expression only by a dim and uncertain line. The Constitution re-

quires a procedure designed to focus searchingly on challenged expression before it can be suppressed. An adversary hearing is a part of this procedure.

Therefore, any attempt, be it legal or extralegal, to regulate or suppress materials in libraries must be closely scrutinized to the end that protected expression is not abridged.

As part of the interpretation review process initiated in 1989, one minor change was made in this policy to explicitly state that materials must meet criteria stated in materials selection policies rather than simply meeting the policy, *per se*. No substantive changes were recommended.

On January 10, at the 1990 Midwinter Meeting, the Council adopted the Challenged Materials interpretation, as amended.

In response to inquiries from librarians facing book or material challenges for the first time, the Intellectual Freedom Committee developed the following list of definitions to clarify terminology associated with such challenges:

Expression of Concern. An inquiry that has judgmental overtones.

Oral Complaint. An oral challenge to the presence and/or appropriateness of the material in question.

Written Complaint. A formal, written complaint filed with the institution (library, school, etc.), challenging the presence and/or appropriateness of specific material.

Public Attack. A publicly disseminated statement challenging the value of the material, presented to the media and/or others outside the institutional organization in order to gain public support for further action.

Censorship. A change in the access status of material, based on the content of the work and made by a governing authority or its representatives, including: exclusion, restriction, removal, or age/grade level changes.

2.9

RESTRICTED ACCESS TO
LIBRARY MATERIALS
An Interpretation of the Library Bill of Rights

Libraries are a traditional forum for the open exchange of information. Attempts to restrict access to library materials violate the basic tenets of the Library Bill of Rights.

Historically, attempts have been made to limit access by relegating materials into segregated collections. These attempts are in violation of established policy. Such collections are often referred to by a variety of names, including "closed shelf," "locked case," "adults only," "restricted shelf," or "high demand." Access to some materials also may require a monetary fee or financial deposit. In any situation which restricts access to certain materials, a barrier is places between the patron and those materials. That barrier may be age related, linguistic, economic, or psychological in nature.

Because materials placed in restricted collections often deal with controversial, unusual, or "sensitive" subjects, having to ask a librarian or circulation clerk for them may be embarrassing or inhibiting for patrons desiring the materials. Needing to ask for materials may pose a language barrier or a staff service barrier. Because restricted collections often are composed of materials which some library patrons consider "objectionable," the potential user may be predisposed to think of the materials as "objectionable" and, therefore, are reluctant to ask for them.

Barriers between the materials and the patron which are psychological, or are affected by language skills, are nonetheless limitations on access to information. Even when a title is listed in the catalog with a reference to its restricted status, a barrier is placed between the patron and the publication (see also Statement on Labeling).

There may be, however, countervailing factors to establish policies to protect library materials—specifically, for reasons of physical preservation including protection from theft or mutilation. Any such policies must be carefully formulated and administered with extreme attention to the principles of intellectual freedom. This caution is also in keeping with ALA policies, such as Evaluating Library Collections, Free Access to Libraries for Minors, and the Preservation Policy.

Finally, in keeping with the Joint Statement on Access of the American Library Association and Society of American Archivists, restrictions that result from donor agreements or contracts for special collections materials must be similarly circumscribed. Permanent exclusions are not acceptable. The overriding impetus must be to work for free and unfettered access to all documentary heritage.

Adopted February 2, 1973; amended July 1, 1981; July 3, 1991, by the ALA Council.

Restricted Access to Library Materials: History

On January 11, 1971, the City Council of San Jose, California, received a formal request from T.J. Owens, president of the San Jose branch of the National Association for the Advancement of Colored People (NAACP), that the book *Epaminondas and His Auntie* be removed from general circulation in the San Jose libraries. Owens charged that the book depicts a black child in a manner that makes him look "completely idiotic and stupid."[1]

Subsequent to a discussion of the book with Owens, Homer L. Fletcher, city librarian, recommended to the city council that *Epaminondas and His Auntie* be retained on open shelf in all the city's libraries and that the option remain for children's librarians to reorder the book should they choose to do so. Fletcher's recommendation was based on his view that any other action would be inconsistent with the Library Bill of Rights, which stated that "no library materials should be proscribed or removed from libraries because of partisan or doctrinal disapproval." Despite the recommendation of the city librarian, the San Jose City Council voted to remove the book from general circulation in city libraries, and to put the book on reserve, thereby necessitating that each individual who wished to use it make a special request to the librarian. On March 29, 1971, however, the City Council reconsidered its action and, upon recommendation of the Library Commission, adopted the Library Bill of Rights as city policy and removed the restrictions on the book.

An advisory statement concerning restricted circulation of library materials, drafted in response to the problem in San Jose, was approved by the Intellectual Freedom Committee during the 1971 ALA Annual Conference in Dallas. This statement, in slightly amended

---

1. *San Jose News*, March 2, 1971.

form, was submitted to the Council at the 1973 Midwinter Meeting in Washington, D.C., and approved as an ALA policy on February 2, 1973:

Restricting access of certain titles and certain classes of library materials is a practice common to many libraries in the United States. Collections of these materials are referred to by a variety of names such as "closed shelf," "locked case," "adults only," or "restricted shelf" collections.

Three reasons generally advanced to justify restricted access are:

1. It provides a refuge for materials that belong in the collection but which may be considered "objectionable" by some library patrons.

2. It provides a means for controlling distribution of materials which allegedly should not be read by those who are not "prepared" for such materials by experience, education, or age.

3. It provides a means to protect certain materials from theft and mutilation.

Though widely used—and often practical—restricted access to library materials is frequently in opposition to the principles of intellectual freedom. While the limitation differs from direct censorship activities, such as removal of library materials or refusal to purchase certain publications, it nonetheless constitutes censorship, albeit in a subtle form. As a form of censorship, restricted access violates the spirit of the Library Bill of Rights in the following ways:

1. It violates that portion of article 2 which states that "no library materials should be proscribed . . . because of partisan or doctrinal disapproval."

The word "proscribed," as used in article 2, means "suppressed." Restricted access achieves de facto suppression of certain materials.

Even when a title is listed in the card catalog with a reference to its restricted shelf status, a barrier is placed between the patron and the publication. Because a majority of materials placed in restricted collections deal with controversial, unusual, or "sensitive" subjects, asking a librarian or circulation clerk for them is an embarrassment for patrons desiring the materials. Because restricted collections are often composed of materials which some library patrons consider "objectionable," the potential user is predisposed to thinking of the materials as "objectionable," and is accordingly inhibited from asking for them. Although the barrier between the materials and the patron is psychological, it is nonetheless a tangible limitation on his access to information.

> 2. It violates article 5, which states that "the rights of an individual to the use of a library should not be denied or abridged because of his age. . . ."

> Limiting access of certain materials to adults only abridges the use of the library for minors. "Use of the library" includes use of, and access to, library materials. Such restrictions are generally instituted under the assumption that certain materials are "harmful" to minors, or in an effort to avoid controversy with parents who might think so.

> The librarian who would restrict the availability of materials to minors because of actual or suspected parental objection should bear in mind that he is not *in loco parentis* in his position as librarian. The American Library Association holds that it is the parent—and only the parent—who may restrict his children—and only his children—in reading matter. The parent who would rather his child did not read certain materials or certain kinds of materials should so advise the child.*

When restricted access is implemented to protect materials from theft or mutilation, the use of the practice may be legitimate. However, segregation of materials to protect them must be administered with extreme attention to the rationale for restricting access. Too often only "controversial" materials are the subject of such segregation, leading to the conclusion that factors other than theft and mutilation were the true considerations. The distinction is extremely difficult to make, both for the librarian and the patron.

Selection policies, carefully developed on the basis of principles of intellectual freedom and the Library Bill of Rights, should not be vitiated by administrative practices such as restricted access.

As part of the overall review of all interpretations of the Library Bill of Rights following that document's revision in 1980, the IFC recommended several relatively minor changes in the policy on restricted access, mainly aimed at removing sex-linked pronoun usage and strengthening the arguments against restricting access for minors. The recommendations were presented to the Council, which adopted the revised policy on July 1, 1981. It read:

> Restricting access of certain titles and classes of library materials is a practice common to many libraries in the United States. Collections of these materials are referred to by a variety of names such as "closed shelf," "locked case," "adults only," or "restricted shelf."

---

* *See also* Free Access to Libraries for Minors, adopted June 30, 1972, by the ALA Council.

Three reasons generally advanced to justify restricted access are:

1. It provides a refuge for materials that belong in the collection but which may be considered "objectionable" by some library patrons;

2. It provides a means for controlling distribution of materials to those who are allegedly not "prepared" for such materials, or who have been labeled less responsible, because of experience, education, or age;

3. It provides a means to protect certain materials from theft the mutilation.

Restricted access to library materials is frequently in opposition to the principles of intellectual freedom. While the limitation differs from direct censorship activities, such as removal of library materials or refusal to purchase certain publications, it nonetheless constitutes censorship, albeit in a subtle form. Restricted access often violates the spirit of the Library Bill of Rights in the following ways:

1. It violates that portion of article 2 which states that "no library materials should be proscribed . . . because of partisan or doctrinal disapproval."

"Materials . . . proscribed" as used in article 2 includes "suppressed" materials. Restricted access achieves de facto suppression of certain materials.

Even when a title is listed in the catalog with a reference to its restricted status, a barrier is placed between the patron and the publication. Because a majority of materials placed in restricted collections deal with controversial, unusual, or "sensitive" subjects, asking a librarian or circulation clerk for them may be embarrassing for patrons desiring the materials. Because restricted collections are often composed of materials which some library patrons consider "objectionable," the potential user is predisposed to thinking of the materials as "objectionable," and may be reluctant to ask for them. Although the barrier between the materials and the patron is psychological, it is nonetheless a limitation on access to information.

2. It violates article 5, which states that, "A person's right to use a library should not be denied or abridged because of . . . age."

Limiting access of certain materials only to adults abridges the use of the library for minors. Access to library materials is an integral part of the right to use a library. Such restrictions are generally instituted under the assumption that certain materials are "harmful" to minors, or in an effort to avoid controversy with adults who might think so.

Libraries and library boards who would restrict the availability of materials to minors because of actual or anticipated parental objection should bear in mind that they do not serve *in loco parentis*. The American Library Association holds that it is parents—and only parents—who may restrict their children—and only their children—from access to library materials and services. Parents who would rather their children not have access to certain materials should so advise their children.

When restricted access is implemented solely to protect materials from theft or mutilation, the practice may be legitimate. However, segregation of materials to protect them must be administered with extreme attention to the reason for restricting access. Too often only "controversial" materials are the subject of such segregation, indicating that factors other than theft and mutilation—including content—were the true considerations. When loss rates of items popular with young people are high, this cannot justify the labeling of all minors as irresponsible and the adoption of prejudiced restrictions on the right of minors to use library services and materials.

Selection policies, carefully developed to include principles of intellectual freedom and the Library Bill of Rights, should not be vitiated by administrative practices such as restricted access.

Note: *See also* Free Access to Libraries for Minors, adopted June 30, 1972; amended July 1, 1981, by ALA Council.

In 1990, Restricted Access to Library Materials was substantially revised. Barriers between materials and patrons which were deemed psychological, linguistic, or related to other patron characteristics were addressed. New language relating to preservation of library materials, referencing related interpretations of the Library Bill of Rights, including Evaluating Library Collections and Free Access to Libraries for Minors, as well as ALA's Preservation Policy was added. Also added was an explanation of how the Library Bill of Rights applies to restrictions resulting from agreements made with donors of materials or contracts for special collections materials. The new version of Restricted Access to Library Materials was adopted by the Council on July 3, 1991.

2.10a

MEETING ROOMS
An Interpretation of the Library Bill of Rights

Many libraries provide meeting rooms for individuals and groups as part of a program of service. Article 6 of the Library Bill of Rights states that such facilities should be made available to the public served by the given library "on an equitable basis, regardless of the beliefs or affiliations of individuals or groups requesting their use."

Libraries maintaining meeting room facilities should develop and publish policy statements governing use. These statements can properly define time, place, or manner of use; such qualifications should not pertain to the content of a meeting or to the beliefs or affiliations of the sponsors. These statements should be made available to any commonly used language within the community served.

If meeting rooms in libraries supported by public funds are made available to the general public for nonlibrary sponsored events, the library may not exclude any group based on the subject matter to be discussed or based on the ideas that the group advocates. For example, if a library allows charities and sports clubs to discuss their activities in library meeting rooms, then the library should not exclude partisan political or religious groups from discussing their activities in the same facilities. If a library opens its meeting rooms to a wide variety of civic organizations, then the library may not deny access to a religious organization. Libraries may wish to post a permanent notice near the meeting room stating that the library does not advocate or endorse the viewpoints of meetings or meeting room users.

Written policies for meeting room use should be stated in inclusive rather than exclusive terms. For example, a policy that the library's facilities are open "to organizations engaged in educational, cultural, intellectual, or charitable activities" is an inclusive statement of the limited uses to which the facilities may be put. This defined limitation would permit religious groups to use the facilities because they engage in intellectual activities, but would exclude most commercial uses of the facility.

A publicly supported library may limit use of its meeting rooms to strictly "library-related" activities, provided that the limitation is clearly circumscribed and is viewpoint neutral.

Written policies may include limitations on frequency of use and whether or not meetings held in library meeting rooms must be open to the public. If state and local laws permit private as well as public sessions of meetings in libraries, libraries may choose to offer both options. The same standard should be applicable to all.

If meetings are open to the public, libraries should include in their meeting room policy statement a section which addresses admission fees. If admission fees are permitted, libraries shall seek to make it possible that these fees do not limit access to individuals who may be unable to pay, but who wish to attend the meeting. Article 5 of the Library Bill of Rights states that "a person's right to use a library should not be denied or abridged because of origin, age, background, or views." It is inconsistent with Article 5 to restrict indirectly access to library meeting rooms based on an individual's or group's ability to pay for that access.

Adopted July 2, 1991, by the ALA Council.

2.10b

EXHIBIT SPACES AND
BULLETIN BOARDS
An Interpretation of the Library Bill of Rights

Libraries often provide exhibit space and bulletin boards. The uses made of these spaces should conform to the Library Bill of Rights: Article 1 states, "Materials should not be excluded because of the origin, background, or views of those contributing to their creation." Article 2 states, "Materials should not be proscribed or removed because of partisan or doctrinal disapproval." Article 6 maintains that exhibit space should be made available "on an equitable basis, regardless of the beliefs or affiliations of individuals or groups requesting their use."

In developing library exhibits, staff members should endeavor to present a broad spectrum of opinion and a variety of viewpoints. Libraries should not shrink from developing exhibits because of controversial content or because of the beliefs or affiliations of those whose work is represented. Just as libraries do not endorse the viewpoints of those whose works are represented in their collections, libraries also do not endorse the beliefs or viewpoints of topics which may be the subject of library exhibits.

Exhibit areas often are made available for use by community groups. Libraries should formulate a written policy for the use of these exhibit areas to assure that space is provided on an equitable basis to all groups which request it.

Written policies for exhibit space use should be stated in inclusive rather than exclusive terms. For example, a policy that the library's exhibit space is open "to organizations engaged in educational, cultural, intellectual, or charitable activities" is an inclusive statement of the limited uses of the exhibit space. This defined limitation would permit religious groups to use the exhibit space because they engage in intellectual activities, but would exclude most commercial uses of the exhibit space.

A publicly supported library may limit use of its exhibit space to strictly "library-related" activities, provided that the limitation is clearly circumscribed and is viewpoint neutral.

Libraries may include in this policy rules regarding the time, place, and manner of use of the exhibit space, so long as the rules are content-neutral and are applied in the same manner to all groups wishing to use the space. A library may wish to limit access to exhibit space to groups within the community served by the library. This practice is acceptable provided that the same rules and regulations apply to everyone, and that exclusion is not made on the basis of the doctrinal, religious, or political beliefs of the potential users.

The library should not censor or remove an exhibit because some members of the community may disagree with its content. Those who object to the content of any exhibit held at the library should be able to submit their complaint and/or their own exhibit proposal to be judged according to the policies established by the library.

Libraries may wish to post a permanent notice near the exhibit area stating that the library does not advocate or endorse the viewpoints of exhibits or exhibitors.

Libraries which make bulletin boards available to public groups for posting notices of public interest should develop criteria for the use of these spaces based on the same considerations as those outlined above. Libraries may wish to develop criteria regarding the size of material to be displayed, the length of time materials may remain on the bulletin board, the frequency with which material may be posted for the same group, and the geographic area from which notices will be accepted.

Adopted July 2, 1991 by the ALA Council.

Meeting Rooms, Exhibit Spaces, and Bulletin Boards: History

Use of library exhibit spaces and meeting rooms became a subject of developing controversy in the 1970s. These years saw several publicized efforts to deny access to such facilities to controversial groups or exhibitors. In North Carolina, for example, an exhibit sponsored by the Ku Klux Klan at a public library sparked a violent confrontation with protestors. At the University of California library at Berkeley, Turkish students protested the "one-sidedness" of an exhibit on the early twentieth-century massacre of Armenians by the Turks, which had been placed in the library by students of Armenian ancestry. In several places, attempts were made to deny use of such facilities to certain groups on the grounds either that the groups themselves were advocates of violence, or that the threat of violence associated with their meetings—including threats made against these meetings by the groups' opponents—posed a danger to library employees and patrons or to library property. At the same time, exhibits mounted by libraries themselves sometimes came under fire. In Virginia, for instance, an exhibit of books about homosexuality in a public library collection was accused of promoting this practice and of obscenity. All these efforts were in violation of article 6 of the Library Bill of Rights.

Yet the 1970s were also marked by some confusion within ALA about the applicability of article 6, as it was formulated in the 1967 version of the Library Bill of Rights. In particular, academic and school libraries pointed out that the provision was written to apply in reality only to public libraries. And public librarians noted that not enough flexibility existed even to accommodate the varying situations of public libraries.

The 1980 revision of the Library Bill of Rights took account of these objections, and the revision of article 6 in that year successfully remedied its major defects (*see* p.3). At the 1980 Annual Conference in

New York, however, the IFC, with Frances C. Dean as chair, decided that, given both the increasing number of incidents and the admitted complexity of applying even the revised article in practice, a written policy interpreting the article would be desirable.

The Intellectual Freedom Committee agreed that the key to applying the article was the need to maintain flexibility, while upholding a standard of fairness. On this basis a policy was prepared and, at the 1981 Midwinter Meeting in Washington, D.C., presented to the Council, which adopted it as an ALA policy on February 4, 1981. It read:

> As part of their program of service, many libraries provide meeting rooms and exhibit spaces for individuals and groups. Article 6 of the Library Bill of Rights states that such facilities should be made available to the public served by the given library "on an equitable basis, regardless of the beliefs or affiliations of individuals or groups requesting their use."
>
> In formulating this position, the American Library Association sought to accommodate the broad range of practices among public, academic, school and other libraries, while upholding a standard of fairness. Libraries maintaining exhibit and meeting room facilities for outside groups and individuals should develop and publish policy statements governing their use. These statements can properly define and restrict eligibility for use as long as the qualifications do not pertain to the content of a meeting or exhibit or to the beliefs or affiliations of the sponsors.
>
> It is appropriate for a library to limit access to meeting rooms or exhibit space to members of the specific community served by the library or to groups of a specific category. It is not proper to apply such limitations in ways which favor points of view or organizations advocating certain viewpoints. For example, some libraries permit religious groups to use meeting facilities, while others do not. According to article 6, both policies are acceptable as long as all religious groups are treated in the same way, irrespective of their doctrines.
>
> Exhibits and meetings sponsored by the library itself should be organized in a manner consistent with the Library Bill of Rights, especially article 2 which states that "libraries should provide materials and information presenting all points of view." However, in granting meeting or exhibit space to outside individuals and groups, the library should make no effort to censor or amend the content of the exhibit or meeting. Those who object to or disagree with the content of any exhibit or meeting held at the library should be entitled to submit their own exhibit or meeting proposals which should be judged according to the policies established by the library.
>
> The library may properly limit the use of its meeting rooms to meetings which are open to the public, or it may make space avail-

able for both public and private sessions. Again, however, the same standard should be applicable to all.

In 1989, revisions were undertaken to reflect nondiscrimination on the basis of language or economic status. Discussion on appropriate changes in the interpretation continued through June 26, 1990, at which time the committee voted to rescind two sentences of the interpretation as an interim measure. Those two sentences were:

"For example, some libraries permit religious groups to use meeting facilities, while others do not. According to article 6, both policies are acceptable as long as all religious groups are treated in the same way, irrespective of their doctrines." The policy then read:

> As part of their program of service, many libraries provide meeting rooms and exhibit spaces for individuals and groups. Article 6 of the Library Bill of Rights states that such facilities should be made available to the public served by the given library "on an equitable basis, regardless of the beliefs or affiliations of individuals or groups requesting their use."
>
> In formulating this position, the American Library Association sought to accommodate the broad range of practices among public, academic, school and other libraries, while upholding a standard of fairness. Libraries maintaining exhibit and meeting room facilities for outside groups and individuals should develop and publish policy statements governing their use. These statements can properly define and restrict eligibility for use as long as the qualifications do not pertain to the content of a meeting or exhibit or to the beliefs or affiliations of the sponsors.
>
> It is appropriate for a library to limit access to meeting rooms or exhibit space to members of the specific community served by the library or to groups of a specific category. The library may properly limit the use of its meeting rooms to meetings which are open to the public, or it may make space available for both public and private sessions. It is not proper to apply such limitations in ways which favor points of view or organizations advocating certain viewpoints.
>
> Exhibits and meetings sponsored by the library itself should be organized in a manner consistent with the Library Bill of Rights, especially article 2 which states that "libraries should provide materials and information presenting all points of view." However, in granting meeting or exhibit space to outside individuals and groups, the library should make no effort to censor or amend the content of the exhibit or meeting. Those who object to or disagree with the content of any exhibit or meeting held at the library should be entitled to submit their own exhibit or meeting proposals which should be judged according to the policies established by the library.

Continuing concerns about the meaning of "viewpoint neutral restrictions" and "designated public forums" and about commercial uses of library meeting rooms, however, led to a consensus decision to totally rewrite the policy.

In January, 1991, two separate interpretations—one on Meeting Rooms and the other on Exhibit Spaces and Bulletin Boards—were introduced. Recent court decisions supporting the right of religious groups to have access to public forums for their meetings raised questions which were best dealt with in a discrete meeting room policy, rather than trying to include meeting rooms, exhibit spaces, and bulletin boards under the same policy rubric. After additional discussion about fees, commercial uses, and disclaimers to clarify the library's position as a neutral host and not an advocate of particular meetings or exhibits, the committee voted to adopt the two interpretations for circulation to all ALA units, the Council, and the executive Board for comment.

The two separate policies were adopted as revised on July 2, 1991, at the Annual Conference.

2.11

LIBRARY-INITIATED PROGRAMS AS A RESOURCE

An Interpretation of the Library Bill of Rights

Library-initiated programs support the mission of the library by providing users with additional opportunities for information, education, and recreation. Article 1 of the Library Bill of Rights states: "Books and other library resources should be provided for the interest, information, and enlightenment of all people of the community the library serves."

Library-initiated programs take advantage of library staff expertise, collections, services, and facilities to increase access to information and information resources. Library-initiated programs introduce users and potential users to the resources of the library and to the library's primary function as a facilitator of information access. The library may participate in cooperative or joint programs with other agencies, organizations, institutions, or individuals as part of its own effort to address information needs and to facilitate information access in the community the library serves.

Library-initiated programs on site and in other locations include, but are not limited to, speeches, community forums, discussion groups, demonstrations, displays, and live or media presentations.

Libraries serving multilingual or multicultural communities make efforts to accommodate the information needs of those for whom English is a second language. Library-initiated programs across language and cultural barriers introduce otherwise unserved populations to the resources of the library and provide access to information.

Library-initiated programs "should not be proscribed or removed (or canceled) because of partisan or doctrinal disapproval" of the contents of the program or the views expressed by the participants, as stated in article 2 of the Library Bill of Rights. Library sponsorship of a program does not constitute an endorsement of the content of the program or the views expressed by the participants, any more than the purchase of material for the library collection constitutes an endorsement of the contents of the material or the views of its creator.

Library-initiated programs are a library resource, and as such, are developed in accordance with written guidelines, as approved and adopted by the library's policy-making body. These guidelines include an endorsement of the Library Bill of Rights and set forth the library's commitment to free and open access to information and ideas for all users.

Library staff select topics, speakers, and resource materials for library-initiated programs based on the interests and information needs of the community. Topics, speakers, and resource materials are not excluded from library-initiated programs because of possible controversy. Concerns, questions, or complaints about library-initiated program are handled according to the same written policy and procedures which govern reconsiderations of other library resources.

Library-initiated programs are offered free of charge and are open to all. Article 5 of the Library Bill of Rights states: "A person's right to use a library should not be denied or abridged because of origin, age, background, or views."

The "right to use a library" encompasses all of the resources the library offers, including the right to attend library-initiated programs. Libraries to not deny or abridge access to library resources, including library-initiated programs, based on an individual's economic background and ability to pay.

Adopted January 27, 1982. Amended June 26, 1990, by the ALA Council.

Library-Initiated Programs
as a Resource: History

As libraries have sought in recent years to broaden their appeal and to strengthen their ties with the communities they serve, library-initiated programs such as invited public speakers, film showings, reading clubs, and children's game groups, have become an increasingly important and visible part of library service. Such programming, however, also has increasingly become a target for would-be censors. In the 1970s, many communities witnessed efforts to ban controversial speakers from appearing in libraries. Elsewhere, showings of R-rated or allegedly "explicit" films were attacked. In New Rochelle, New York, an Italian-American group objected to a library showing of *The Godfather*, and in North Carolina a French comedy about a homosexual couple, *La Cage aux Folles*, was successfully banned from a public library.

In the early 1980s, some parents' groups objected to several library-sponsored "theme" programs for children, especially those emphasizing magic or the occult. In a few communities, citizens concerned about the alleged spread of occultism and witchcraft sought to terminate use of library facilities for organized playing of the popular game "Dungeons and Dragons."

In response to incidents of this sort and a growing number of inquiries from librarians and library users about the applicability of the Library Bill of Rights to such programs, in 1981, at the urging of the intellectual freedom committees of the Young Adult Services Division and the Association for Library Service to Children, the IFC, with J. Dennis Day as chair, decided to develop a policy statement. At the 1982 Midwinter Meeting in Denver, the committee approved the statement and recommended it to the Council, which adopted it on January 27, 1982, as an interpretation of the Library Bill of Rights, entitled Library-Initiated Programs as a Resource. It read:

Library-initiated programming is a library resource that provides information, education, and recreation to library users. Library-initiated programming utilizes library staff, books, library and community resources, resource people, displays, and media presentations. The library often incorporates cooperative programming with other agencies, organizations, and educational institutions, as well as other resources, to communicate with library users. Library-initiated programs should provide "for the interest, information, and enlightenment of all the people of the community the library serves," as stated in article 1 of the Library Bill of Rights.

The American Library Association believes that library-sponsored programs, as well as library resources, "should not be proscribed or removed (or canceled) because of partisan or doctrinal disapproval" (article 2 of the Library Bill of Rights).

A person's right to attend a library-initiated program "should not be denied or abridged because of origin, age, background, or views" (article 5 of the Library Bill of Rights).

A written policy on library-initiated programming, approved by the library's policy-making body, should reflect the library's philosophy regarding free access to information and ideas. Similarly, concerns expressed regarding library-initiated programs should be handled as they are for library resources.

Selection of library program topics, speakers, courses, classes, and resource materials should be made by library staff on the basis of the interests and needs of library users and the community. Library programming should not exclude topics, books, speakers, media, and other resources because they might be controversial.

Review of the interpretation on Library-Initiated Programs as a Resource began in January, 1989. A draft of a revised document was circulated in the spring of 1990. Comments received on the proposed draft raised questions of fees, access for handicapped and deaf patrons, and the practical problems of abolishing age-based restrictions on program attendance.

As a result of these comments, the interpretation was expanded to include library programs held on- and off-site, and those produced in cooperation with other groups. Provisions were included to encourage librarians to formulate written policies on programming that conform to the intellectual freedom standards set by the Library Bill of Rights.

In addition, librarians were exhorted to consider the multicultural or multilingual composition of their communities in planning library events and not to shrink from addressing controversial topics. A special provision was added to emphasize the librarian's duty to assure equal access to all patrons, explicitly stating that economic background and ability to pay cannot be used to restrict access to library-sponsored events.

The new interpretation was adopted by the Council on June 26, 1990.

2.12

ACCESS TO RESOURCES AND SERVICES IN THE SCHOOL LIBRARY MEDIA PROGRAM
An Interpretation of the Library Bill of Rights

The school library media program plays a unique role in promoting intellectual freedom. It serves as a point of voluntary access to information and ideas and as a learning laboratory for students as they acquire critical thinking and problem solving skills needed in a pluralistic society. Although the educational level and program of the school necessarily shapes the resources and services of a school library media program, the principles of the Library Bill of Rights apply equally to all libraries, including school library media programs.

School library media professionals assume a leadership role in promoting the principles of intellectual freedom within the school by providing resources and services that create and sustain an atmosphere of free inquiry. School library media professionals work closely with teachers to integrate instructional activities in classroom units designed to equip students to locate, evaluate, and use a broad range of ideas effectively. Through resources, programming, and educational processes, students and teachers experience the free and robust debate characteristic of a democratic society.

School library media professionals cooperate with other individuals in building collections of resources appropriate to the developmental and maturity levels of students. These collections provide resources which support the curriculum and are consistent with the philosophy, goals, and objectives of the school district. Resources in school library media collections represent diverse points of view and current as well as historical issues.

While English is, by history and tradition, the customary language of the United States, the languages in use in any given community may vary. Schools serving communities in which other languages are used make efforts to accommodate the needs of students for whom English is a second language. To support these efforts, and to ensure equal access to resources and services, the school library media program provides resources which reflect the linguistic pluralism of the community.

Members of the school community involved in the collection development process employ educational criteria to select resources unfettered by their personal, political, social, or religious views. Students and educators served by the school library media program have access to resources and services free of constraints resulting from personal, partisan, or doctrinal disapproval. School library media professionals resist efforts by individuals to define what is appropriate for all students or teachers to read, view, or hear.

Major barriers between students and resources include: imposing age or grade level restrictions on the use of resources, limiting the use of interlibrary loan and access to electronic information, charging fees for information in specific formats, requiring permissions from parents or teachers, establishing restricted shelves or closed collections, and labeling. Policies, procedures, and rules related to the use of resources and services support free and open access to information.

The school board adopts policies that guarantee students access to a broad range of ideas. These include policies on collection development and procedures for the review of resources about which concerns have been raised. Such policies, developed by persons in the school community, provide for a timely and fair hearing and assure that procedures are applied equitably to all expressions of concern. School library media professionals implement district policies and procedures in the school.

Adopted July 2, 1986; amended January 10, 1990, by the ALA Council.

Access to Resources and Services in the School Library Media Program: History

During the early 1950s, as the anticommunist reaction of McCarthyism swept across the United States, school librarians and school curriculum planners were affected no less than persons in journalism, entertainment, and government. Schools were coerced to ban works that were alleged to contain "un-American" thinking.

The issue of selecting school library materials was raised during the meeting of the board of directors of the American Association of School Librarians (AASL), during the 1953 ALA Annual Conference in Los Angeles. Sue Hefley, chair of the school libraries discussion group at the second Conference on Intellectual Freedom (held at Whittier College, June 20–21), reported on her group's consensus concerning the need for a policy statement on the matter of selection.

In response to Hefley's report, the board voted "that a committee be appointed to consider the advisability of preparing a statement on book selection in defense of liberty in schools of a democracy, and in considering this problem to make use of the excellent statement prepared at the Conference on Intellectual Freedom. Furthermore, that this committee make recommendations as to what further action AASL should take in this matter."[1]

In preparation for the AASL meeting at the 1954 Annual Conference in Minneapolis, the Committee on Book Selection in Defense of Liberty in Schools of a Democracy submitted a draft for a School Library Bill of Rights. At the 1955 Midwinter Meeting, the AASL officially accepted the School Library Bill of Rights, and, on July 8, 1955, it was adopted by the ALA Council.

In the years following the adoption of the School Library Bill of Rights, the Library Bill of Rights underwent several basic changes.

---

1. *School Libraries 3*, no. 1:8 (Oct. 1953).

(For full discussion, *see* Library Bill of Rights, pp.4–13.) Because of changes in the Library Bill of Rights, affirmed by the School Library Bill of Rights of 1955, as well as changes in the conception of the range of materials to be provided by libraries, the AASL Board of Directors appointed a committee in 1968 to consider revising the 1955 School Library Bill of Rights.

At the 1969 ALA Annual Conference in Atlantic City, the revised School Library Bill of Rights was brought before the AASL Board of Directors. Making only minor corrections, the board voted to accept the revised version:

> The American Association of School Librarians reaffirms its belief in the Library Bill of Rights of the American Library Association. Media personnel are concerned with generating understanding of American freedoms through the development of informed and responsible citizens. To this end the American Association of School Librarians asserts that the responsibility of the school library media center is:
>
> To provide a comprehensive collection of instructional materials selected in compliance with basic written selection principles, and to provide maximum accessibility to these materials;
>
> To provide materials that will support the curriculum, taking into consideration the individual's needs, and the varied interests, abilities, socioeconomic backgrounds, and maturity levels of the students served;
>
> To provide materials for teachers and students that will encourage growth in knowledge, and that will develop literary, cultural and aesthetic appreciation, and ethical standards;
>
> To provide materials which reflect the ideas and beliefs of religious, social, political, historical, and ethnic groups and their contribution to the American and world heritage and culture, thereby enabling students to develop an intellectual integrity in forming judgments;
>
> To provide a written statement, approved by the local boards of education, of the procedures for meeting the challenge of censorship of materials in school library media centers; and
>
> To provide qualified professional personnel to serve teachers and students.

It soon became clear, however, that the existence of two different documents with very similar titles could be a source of confusion. Moreover, with the 1967 amendment of the Library Bill of Rights to oppose discrimination against library users by age, the School Library Bill of

Rights became largely redundant. As increasing numbers of librarians pointed out, the school document simply repeated in different language the principles enunciated more forcefully in the Library Bill of Rights. This served only to detract attention from and, hence, to weaken the impact of the Association's most basic document on intellectual freedom.

The problem was discussed extensively in both the Intellectual Freedom Committee and AASL. At the 1976 Annual Conference in Chicago, the Board of Directors of the American Association of School Librarians withdrew the School Library Bill of Rights and endorsed the Library Bill of Rights.

Since 1976 and particularly in the 1980s, the challenge to materials in school libraries and media centers have increased in volume and intensity. The need became apparent for an interpretation of the Library Bill of Rights that spoke directly to the unique role of school libraries and media centers in the educational process. A clear statement of the responsibility of school library media professionals for the selection process and of the centrality of intellectual freedom principles in this process was perceived as the central focus for this interpretation.

In 1985–86, an interpretation was drafted by the AASL with the cooperation of the IFC. At the 1986 Annual Conference in New York, Access to Resources and Services in the School Library Media Program was adopted by the ALA Council. It read:

> The school library media program plays a unique role in promoting intellectual freedom. It serves as a point of voluntary access to information and ideas and as a learning laboratory for students as they acquire critical thinking and problem solving skills needed in a pluralistic society. Although the educational level and program of the school necessarily shape the resources and services of a school library media program, the principles of the Library Bill of Rights apply equally to all libraries, including school library media programs.
>
> School library media professionals assume a leadership role in promoting the principles of intellectual freedom within the school by providing resources and services that create and sustain an atmosphere of free inquiry. School library media professionals work closely with teachers to integrate instructional activities in classroom units designed to equip students to locate, evaluate, and use a broad range of ideas effectively. Through resources, programming, and educational processes, students and teachers experience the free and robust debate characteristic of a democratic society.

School library media professionals cooperate with other individuals in building collections of resources appropriate to the developmental and maturity levels of students. These collections provide resources which support the curriculum and are consistent with the philosophy, goals, and objectives of the school district. Resources in school library media collections represent diverse points of view and current as well as historic issues.

Members of the school community involved in the collection development process employ educational criteria to select resources unfettered by their personal, political, social, or religious views. Students and educators served by the school library media program have access to resources and services free of constraints resulting from personal, partisan, or doctrinal disapproval. School library media professionals resist efforts by individuals to define what is appropriate for all students or teachers to read, view or hear.

Major barriers between students and resources include: imposing age or grade level restrictions on the use of resources, limiting the use of interlibrary loan and access to electronic information, charging fees for information in specific formats, requiring permissions from parents or teachers, establishing restricted shelves or closed collections, and labeling. Policies, procedures, and rules related to the use of resources and services support free and open access to information.

The school board adopts policies that guarantee student access to a broad range of ideas. These include policies on collection development and procedures for the review of resources about which concerns have been raised. Such policies, developed by persons in the school community, provide for a timely and fair hearing and assure that procedures are applied equitably to all expressions of concern. School library media professionals implement district policies and procedures in the school.

A revised interpretation was circulated for comment in the fall of 1989. The sole substantive change was the addition of a paragraph stating that the school library media program should attempt to accommodate needs of students for whom English is a second language. To ensure equality of access, librarians must provide resources reflecting the linguistic pluralism of the community which they serve.

At the 1990 Midwinter Meeting, comments received from AASL, OLPR, SCOLE, and the Professional Ethics Committee resulted in minor editorial changes. The policy was recommended to the Council and adopted on January 10, 1990.

2.13

THE UNIVERSAL RIGHT TO FREE EXPRESSION

An Interpretation of the Library Bill of Rights

Freedom of expression is an inalienable human right and the foundation for self-government. Freedom of expression encompasses the freedoms of speech, press, religion, assembly, and association, and the corollary right to receive information.

The American Library Association endorses this principle, which is also set forth in the Universal Declaration of Human Rights, adopted by the United Nations General Assembly. The Preamble of this document states that "... recognition of the inherent dignity and of the equal and inalienable rights of all members of the human family is the foundation of freedom, justice, and peace in the world..." and "... the advent of a world in which human beings shall enjoy freedom of speech and belief and freedom from fear and want has been proclaimed as the highest aspiration of the common people...."

Article 18 of this document states:

> Everyone has the right to freedom of thought, conscience and religion; this right includes freedom to change his religion or belief, and freedom, either alone or in community with others and in public or private, to manifest his religion or belief in teaching, practice, worship, and observance.

Article 19 states:

> Everyone has the right to freedom of opinion and expression; this right includes freedom to hold opinions without interference and to seek, receive and impart information and ideas through any media regardless of frontiers.

Article 20 states:

> 1. Everyone has the right to freedom of peaceful assembly and association.
> 2. No one may be compelled to belong to an association.

We affirm our belief that these are inalienable rights of every person, regardless of origin, age, background, or views. We embody our professional commitment to these principles in the Library Bill of Rights and Code of Professional Ethics, as adopted by the American Library Association.

We maintain that these are universal principles and should be applied by libraries and librarians throughout the world. The American Library Association's policy on International Relations reflects these objectives: ". . . to encourage the exchange, dissemination, and access to information and the unrestricted flow of library materials in all formats throughout the world."

We know that censorship, ignorance, and limitations on the free flow of information are the tools of tyranny and oppression. We believe that ideas and information topple the walls of hate and fear and build bridges of cooperation and understanding far more effectively than weapons and armies.

The American Library Association is unswerving in its commitment to human rights and intellectual freedom; the two are inseparably linked and inextricably entwined. Freedom of opinion and expression is not derived from or dependent on any form of government or political power. This right is inherent in every individual. It cannot be surrendered, nor can it be denied. True justice comes from the exercise of this right.

We recognize the power of information and ideas to inspire justice, to restore freedom and dignity to the oppressed, and to change the hearts and minds of the oppressors.

Courageous men and women, in difficult and dangerous circumstances throughout human history, have demonstrated that freedom lives in the human heart and cries out for justice even in the face of threats, enslavement, imprisonment, torture, exile, and death. We draw inspiration from their example. They challenge us to remain steadfast in our most basic professional responsibility to promote and defend the right of free expression.

There is no good censorship. Any effort to restrict free expression and the free flow of information aids the oppressor. Fighting oppression with censorship is self-defeating.

Threats to the freedom of expression of any person anywhere are threats to the freedom of all people everywhere. Violations of human rights and the right of free expression have been recorded in virtually every country and society across the globe.

In response to these violations, we affirm these principles:

> The American Library Association opposes any use of governmental prerogative that leads to the intimidation of individuals which prevents them from exercising their rights to

hold opinions without interference, and to seek, receive, and impart information and ideas. We urge libraries and librarians everywhere to resist such abuse of governmental power, and to support those against whom such governmental power has been employed.

The American Library Association condemns any governmental effort to involve libraries and librarians in restrictions on the right of any individual to hold opinions without interference, and to seek, receive, and impart information and ideas. Such restrictions pervert the function of the library and violate the professional responsibilities of librarians.

The American Library Association rejects censorship in any form. Any action which denies the inalienable human rights of individuals only damages the will to resist oppression, strengthens the hand of the oppressor, and undermines the cause of justice.

The American Library Association will not abrogate these principles. We believe that censorship corrupts the cause of justice, and contributes to the demise of freedom.

Adopted by the ALA Council, January 16, 1991.

The Universal Right to Free Expression: History

Out of a long and emotional debate about support for sanctions—including books and informational materials—against South Africa, a new interpretation of the Library Bill of Rights was created. Modeled after article 19 of the United Nations Universal Declaration of Human Rights, the Universal Right to Free Expression advocates the free flow of information within all countries across national boundaries.

In 1989, the ALA was asked to support the Association of American Publishers in its efforts to end the book boycott against South Africa. The Council asked the IFC for its recommendation. Concurrently, the Social Responsibilities Round Table (SRRT) had proposed a set of guidelines for librarians interacting with South Africa which were opposed by the IFC. The debate within the ALA over South African policy was emotional, vigorous, and sometimes vituperative. It became clear that no extant ALA policy provided an adequate framework from which to respond fully to the complicated international intellectual freedom and human rights questions raised during the course of the debate.

In 1990, the IFC began work on an international free flow of information policy to address this glaring need. The new policy was to provide a secure foundation from which to respond to the AAP's request and from which to address other international intellectual freedom issues. The drafters used articles 18, 19, and 20 of the Universal Declaration of Human Rights as models for the new policy.

In January 1991, the IFC considered comments on the Free Flow of Information draft. The title of the interpretation was changed to The Universal Right to Free Expression, and the IFC voted to seek endorsements of other units of the ALA and to present the interpretation to the Council.

On January 16, 1991, the Council voted to adopt the policy as the most recent addition to the Library Bill of Rights and its interpretations.

2.14

DEALING WITH CONCERNS ABOUT LIBRARY RESOURCES

Procedural Statement

As with any public service, libraries receive complaints and expressions of concern. One of the librarian's responsibilities is to handle these complaints in a respectful and fair manner. The complaints that librarians often worry about the most are those dealing with library resources or free access policies. The key to successfully handling these complaints is to be sure the library staff and the governing authorities are all knowledgeable about the complaint procedures and their implementation. As normal operating procedure each library should:

1. *Maintain a materials selection policy.* It should be in written form and approved by the appropriate governing authority. It should apply to all library materials equally.

2. *Maintain a library service policy.* This should cover registration policies, programming, and services in the library that involve access issues.

3. *Maintain a clearly defined method for handling complaints.* The complaint must be filed in writing and the complainant must be properly identified before action is taken. A decision should be deferred until fully considered by appropriate administrative authority. (A sample form may be found in part V, figure 2, with Procedures for Handling Complaints.) The process should be followed, whether the complaint originates internally or externally.

4. *Maintain in-service training.* Conduct periodic in-service training to acquaint staff, administration, and the governing authority with the materials selection policy and library service policy and procedures for handling complaints.

5. *Maintain lines of communication with civic, religious, educational, and political bodies of the community.* Library board and staff participation in local civic organizations and presentations to these orga-

nizations should emphasize the library's selection process and intellectual freedom principles.

6. *Maintain a vigorous public information program on behalf of intellectual freedom.* Newspapers, radio, and television should be informed of policies governing resource selection and use, and of any special activities pertaining to intellectual freedom.

7. *Maintain familiarity with any local municipal and state legislation pertaining to intellectual freedom and First Amendment rights.*

Adoption of these practices will not preclude receiving complaints from pressure groups or individuals but should provide a base from which to operate when these concerns are expressed. When a complaint is made, follow one or more of the steps listed below:

a. Listen calmly and courteously to the complaint. Remember the person has a right to express concern. Use of good communication skills helps many people understand the need for diversity in library collections and the use of library resources. In the event the person is not satisfied, advise the complainant of the library policy and procedures for handling library resource statements of concern. If a person does fill out a form about their concern, make sure a prompt written reply related to the concern is sent.

b. It is essential to notify the administration and/or the governing authority (library board, etc.) of the complaint and assure them that the library's procedures are being followed. Present full, written information giving the nature of the complaint and identifying the source.

c. When appropriate, seek the support of the local media. Freedom to read and freedom of the press go hand in hand.

d. When appropriate, inform local civic organizations of the facts and enlist their support. Meet negative pressure with positive pressure.

e. Assert the principles of the Library Bill of Rights as a professional responsibility. Laws governing obscenity, subversive material, and other questionable matter are subject to interpretation by courts. Library materials found to meet the standards set in the materials selection policy should not be removed from public access until after an adversary hearing resulting in a final judicial determination.

f. Contact the ALA Office for Intellectual Freedom and your state intellectual freedom committee to inform them of the complaint and to enlist their support and the assistance of other agencies.

The principles and procedures discussed above apply to all kinds of resource-related complaints or attempts to censor and are supported by groups such as the National Education Association, the American Civil Liberties Union and the National Council of Teachers of English, as well as the American Library Association. While the practices provide positive means for preparing for and meeting pressure-group complaints, they serve the more general purpose of supporting the Library Bill of Rights, particularly article 3, which states that: "Libraries should challenge censorship in the fulfillment of their responsibility to provide information and enlightenment."

Dealing with Concerns about Library Resources: History

The Library Bill of Rights and its interpretations are all broad statements of policy. Their purpose is to clarify application of the basic principles of intellectual freedom to libraries. As statements of policy, they offer general guidance for the resolution of practical problems, but they are not in and of themselves practical or procedural documents. Yet in the course of applying the principles of the Library Bill of Rights, librarians frequently encounter pressures and concerns from those who, consciously or not, may seek to distort the library into an instrument of their own beliefs. Dealing with Concerns about Library Resources outlines basic procedural and practical measures for responding to such pressure.

Dealing with Concerns about Library Resources is a procedural document. Its goal being to assist librarians in implementing ALA's intellectual freedom policies, it is not itself a policy statement. Its roots, however, lie in a previous interpretation of the Library Bill of Rights, entitled How Libraries Can Resist Censorship, first adopted in 1962 but rescinded by the ALA Council at the request of the IFC in 1981.

The early 1960s saw increased censorship attacks on libraries and strenuous assaults on the freedom to read; "witch hunts" in Georgia, censorship of some best sellers, and heated controversy over Henry Miller's *Tropic of Cancer* were prominent during the period. In response to this situation, a group of librarians and publishers met in Washington, D.C., on January 5, 1962, to draft a statement on censorship. The committee was composed of David H. Clift, executive director of the American Library Association; Dan Lacy, managing director of the American Book Publishers Council; Margaret Dudley, executive secretary of the National Book Committee; Emerson Greenaway, chair of the ALA Legislative Committee; and Archie McNeal, chair of the

ALA Intellectual Freedom Committee. The statement this group wrote, entitled How Libraries and Schools Can Resist Censorship, gave support and step-by-step guidelines to ways a library can thwart the censor.

In introducing the statement to the ALA Council, McNeal urged its support, especially in light of the countrywide attempts at censorship. How Libraries and Schools Can Resist Censorship was approved unanimously by the ALA Council on February 1, 1962. The statement was endorsed by the Adult Education Association Executive Committee, the Amerian Book Publishers Council, the American Civil Liberties Union, the National Book Committee, the National Council of Teachers of English, the National Education Association Commission on Professional Rights and Responsibilities, and the National Education Association Department of Class Room Teachers.

At the 1972 Midwinter Meeting of the Intellectual Freedom Committee, the original statement on resisting censorship was altered to include all types of libraries, not just school and public libraries, and "library materials" was substituted for "books." The new document, How Libraries Can Resist Censorship, was adopted by the ALA Council on January 28, 1972:

> Libraries of all sizes and types continue to be targets of pressure from groups and individuals who wish to use the library as an instrument of their own tastes and views. The problem differs somewhat between the public library, with a responsibility to present as wide a spectrum of materials as its budget can afford, and the school or academic library, whose collection is designed to support the educational objectives of the institution. Both, however, involve the freedom of the library to meet its professional responsibilities to the whole community.
>
> To combat censorship efforts from groups and individuals, every library should take certain measures to clarify policies and establish community relations. While these steps should be taken regardless of any attack or prospect of attack, they will provide a firm and clearly defined position if selection policies are challenged. As normal operating procedure, each library should:
>
> 1. Maintain a definite materials selection policy. It should be in written form and approved by the appropriate regents or other governing authority. It should apply to all library materials equally.
>
> 2. Maintain a clearly defined method for handling complaints. Basic requirements should be that the complaint be filed in writing and the complainant be properly identified before his request is considered. Action should be deferred until full consideration by appropriate administrative authority.

3. Maintain lines of communication with civic, religious, educational, and political bodies of the community. Participation in local civic organizations and in community affairs is desirable. Because the library and the school are key centers of the community, the librarian should be known publicly as a community leader.

4. Maintain a virorous public relations program on behalf of intellectual freedom. Newspapers, radio, and television should be informed of policies governing materials selection and use, and of any special activities pertaining to intellectual freedom.

Adherence to the practices listed above will not preclude confrontations with pressure groups or individuals but may provide a base from which to counter efforts to place restraints on the library. If a confrontation does occur, librarians should remember the following:

1. Remain calm. Don't confuse noise with substance. Require the deliberate handling of the complaint under previously established rules. Treat the group or individual who complains with dignity, courtesy, and good humor. Given the facts, most citizens will support the responsible exercise of professional freedom by teachers and librarians, and will insist on protecting their own freedom to read.

2. Take immediate steps to assure that the full facts surrounding a complaint are known to the administration and the governing authority. The school librarian-media specialist should go through the principal to the superintendent and the school board; the public librarian, to the board of trustees or to the appropriate governing authority of the community; the college or university librarian, to the president and through him to the board of trustees. Present full, written information giving the nature of the complaint and identifying the source.

3. Seek the support of the local press when appropriate. The freedom to read and freedom of the press go hand in hand.

4. Inform local civic organizations of the facts and enlist their support when appropriate. Meet negative pressure with positive pressure.

5. In most cases, defend the principle of the freedom to read and the professional responsibility of teachers and librarians. Only rarely is it necessary to defend the individual item. Laws governing obscenity, subversive material, and other questionable matter are subject to interpretation by courts. Responsibility for removal of any library materials from public access rests with this established process.

6. Inform the ALA Office for Intellectual Freedom and other appropriate national and state organizations concerned with intellectual freedom of the nature of the problem. Even though censorship must be fought at the local level, there is value in the support and assistance of agencies outside the area which have no personal

involvement. They can often cite parallel cases and suggest methods of meeting an attack.

The principles and procedures discussed above apply to all kinds of censorship attacks and are supported by groups such as the National Education Association, the American Civil Liberties Union, and the National Council of Teachers of English, as well as the American Library Association. While the practices provide positive means for preparing for and meeting pressure group complaints, they serve the more general purpose of supporting the Library Bill of Rights, particularly article 3, which states that "censorship should be challenged by libraries in the maintenance of their responsibility to provide public information and enlightenment." Adherence to this principle is especially necessary when under pressure.

During 1980–81, following the 1980 revision of the Library Bill of Rights, the Intellectual Freedom Committee reviewed How Libraries Can Resist Censorship and found that the bulk of the document was simply a procedural elaboration and repetitive of other policies. Stripped to its essentials, its main utility was as a concise statement of practical measures libraries can and should take in preparing for and responding to potentially censorious complaints and pressures. At the 1981 Annual Conference, the IFC voted to request ALA Council to rescind the former interpretation, which the Council did. Later that year, Dealing with Complaints about Resources, based in part on the former interpretation and on discussions by the IFC, was published as a procedural statement. At the 1983 Midwinter Meeting in San Antonio, the statement was again revised by the committee and retitled Dealing with Concerns about Library Resources. This document is the basis for part V of this manual, Before the Censor Comes: Essential Preparations.

PART II

Protecting the
Freedom to Read

1

THE FREEDOM TO READ

The freedom to read is essential to our democracy. It is continuously under attack. Private groups and public authorities in various parts of the country are working to remove books from sale, to censor textbooks, to label "controversial" books, to distribute lists of "objectionable" books or authors, and to purge libraries. These actions apparently rise from a view that our national tradition of free expression is no longer valid; that censorship and suppression are needed to avoid the subversion of politics and the corruption of morals. We, as citizens devoted to the use of books and as librarians and publishers responsible for disseminating them, wish to assert the public interest in the preservation of the freedom to read.

We are deeply concerned about these attempts at suppression. Most such attempts rest on a denial of the fundamental premise of democracy: that the ordinary citizen, by exercising critical judgment, will accept the good and reject the bad. The censors, public and private, assume that they should determine what is good and what is bad for their fellow-citizens.

We trust Americans to recognize propaganda, and to reject it. We do not believe they need the help of censors to assist them in this task. We do not believe they are prepared to sacrifice their heritage of a free press in order to be "protected" against what others think may be bad for them. We believe they still favor free enterprise in ideas and expression.

We are aware, of course, that books are not alone in being subjected to efforts at suppression. We are aware that these efforts are related to a larger pattern of pressures being brought against education, the press, films, radio, and television. The problem is not only one of actual censorship. The shadow of fear cast by these pressures leads, we suspect, to an even larger voluntary curtailment of expression by those who seek to avoid controversy.

Such pressure toward conformity is perhaps natural to a time of uneasy change and pervading fear. Especially when so many of our apprehensions are directed against an ideology, the expression of a dissident idea becomes a thing feared in itself, and we tend to move against it as against a hostile deed, with suppression.

And yet suppression is never more dangerous than in such a time of social tension. Freedom has given the United States the elasticity to endure strain. Freedom keeps open the path of novel and creative solutions, and enables change to come by choice. Every silencing of a heresy, every enforcement of an orthodoxy, diminishes the toughness and resilience of our society and leaves it the less able to deal with stress.

Now as always in our history, books are among our greatest instruments of freedom. They are almost the only means for making generally available ideas or manners of expression that can initially command only a small audience. They are the natural medium for the new idea and the untried voice from which come the original contributions to social growth. They are essential to the extended discussion which serious thought requires, and to the accumulation of knowledge and ideas into organized collections.

We believe that free communication is essential to the preservation of a free society and a creative culture. We believe that these pressures towards conformity present the danger of limiting the range and variety of inquiry and expression on which our democracy and our culture depend. We believe that every American community must jealously guard the freedom to publish and to circulate, in order to preserve its own freedom to read. We believe that publishers and librarians have a profound responsibility to give validity to that freedom to read by making it possible for the readers to choose freely from a variety of offerings.

The freedom to read is guaranteed by the Constitution. Those with faith in free people will stand firm on these constitutional guarantees of essential rights and will exercise the responsibilities that accompany these rights.

We therefore affirm these propositions:

1. *It is in the public interest for publishers and librarians to make available the widest diversity of views and expressions, including those which are unorthodox or unpopular with the majority.*

   Creative thought is by definition new, and what is new is different. The bearer of every new thought is a rebel until that idea is refined and tested. Totalitarian systems attempt to maintain themselves in power by the ruthless suppression of any concept which challenges the established orthodoxy. The power of a democratic system to adapt to change is vastly strengthened by the freedom of its citizens to choose widely from among conflicting opinions offered freely to them. To stifle every nonconformist idea at birth would mark the end of the democratic process. Furthermore, only through the constant activity of weighing and selecting can the democratic mind attain the strength demanded by times like these. We need to know not only what we believe but why we believe it.

2. *Publishers, librarians, and booksellers do not need to endorse every idea or presentation contained in the books they make available. It would conflict with the public interest for them to establish their own political, moral, or aesthetic views as a standard for determining what books should be published or circulated.*

   Publishers and librarians serve the educational process by helping to make available knowledge and ideas required for the growth of the mind and the increase of learning. They do not foster education by imposing as mentors the patterns of their own thought. The people should have the freedom to read and consider a broader range of ideas than those that may be held by any single librarian or publisher or government or church. It is wrong that what one can read should be confined to what another thinks proper.

3. *It is contrary to the public interest for publishers or librarians to determine the acceptability of a book on the basis of the personal history or political affiliations of the author.*

   A book should be judged as a book. No art or literature can flourish if it is to be measured by the political views or private lives of its creators. No society of free people can flourish which draws up lists of writers to whom it will not listen, whatever they may have to say.

4. *There is no place in our society for efforts to coerce the taste of others, to confine adults to the reading matter deemed suitable for adolescents, or to inhibit the efforts of writers to achieve artistic expression.*

   To some, much of modern literature is shocking. But is not much of life itself shocking? We cut off literature at the source if we prevent writers from dealing with the stuff of life. Parents and teachers have a responsibility to prepare the young to meet the diversity of experiences in life to which they will be exposed, as they have a responsibility to help them learn to think critically for themselves. These are affirmative responsibilities, not to be discharged simply by preventing them from reading works for which they are not yet prepared. In these matters taste differs, and taste cannot be legislated; nor can machinery be devised which will suit the demands of one group without limiting the freedom of others.

5. *It is not in the public interest to force a reader to accept with any book the prejudgment of a label characterizing the book or author as subversive or dangerous.*

   The idea of labeling presupposes the existence of individuals or groups with wisdom to determine by authority what is good or bad for the citizen. It presupposes that individuals must be directed in making up their minds about the ideas they examine. But Americans do not need others to do their thinking for them.

6. *It is the responsibility of publishers and librarians, as guardians of the people's freedom to read, to contest encroachments upon that freedom by individuals or groups seeking to impose their own standards or tastes upon the community at large.*

   It is inevitable in the give and take of the democratic process that the political, the moral, or the aesthetic concepts of an individual or group will occasionally collide with those of another individual or group. In a free society individuals are free to determine for themselves what they wish to read, and each group is free to determine what it will recommend to its freely associated members. But no group has the right to take the law into its own hands, and to impose its own concept of politics or morality upon other members of a democratic society. Freedom is no freedom if it is accorded only to the accepted and the inoffensive.

7. *It is the responsibility of publishers and librarians to give full meaning to the freedom to read by providing books that enrich the quality and diversity of thought and expression. By the exercise of this affirmative responsibility, they can demonstrate that the answer to a bad book is a good one, the answer to a bad idea is a good one.*

   The freedom to read is of little consequence when expended on the trivial; it is frustrated when the reader cannot obtain matter fit for that reader's purpose. What is needed is not only the absence of restraint, but the positive provision of opportunity for the people to read the best that has been thought and said. Books are the major channel by which the intellectual inheritance is handed down, and the principal means of its testing and growth. The defense of their freedom and integrity, and the enlargement of their service to society, requires of all publishers and librarians the utmost of their faculties, and deserves of all citizens the fullest of their support.

We state these propositions neither lightly nor as easy generalizations. We here stake out a lofty claim for the value of books. We do so because we believe that they are good, possessed of enormous variety and usefulness, worthy of cherishing and keeping free. We realize that the application of these propositions may mean the dissemination of ideas and manners of expression that are repugnant to many persons. We do not state these propositions in the comfortable belief that what people read is unimportant. We believe rather that what people read is deeply important; that ideas can be dangerous; but that the suppression of ideas is fatal to a democratic society. Freedom itself is a dangerous way of life, but it is ours.

This statement was originally issued in May of 1953 by the Westchester Conference of the American Library Association and the American Book Publishers Council, which in 1970 consolidated with the American Educational Publishers Institute to become the Association of American Publishers

Adopted June 25, 1953; revised January 28, 1972, January 16, 1991, by the ALA Council and the AAP Freedom to Read Committee.
A Joint Statement by:

American Library Association
Association of American Publishers

Subsequently Endorsed by:

American Booksellers Association
American Booksellers Foundation for Free Expression
American Civil Liberties Union
American Federation of Teachers AFL-CIO
Anti-Defamation League of B'nai B'rith
Association of American University Presses
Children's Book Council
Freedom to Read Foundation
International Reading Association
Thomas Jefferson Center for the Protection of Free Expression
National Association of College Stores
National Council of Teachers of English
P.E.N. - American Center
People for the American Way
Periodical and Book Association of America
Sex Information and Education Council of the U.S.
Society of Professional Journalists
Women's National Book Association
YWCA of the U.S.A.

The Freedom to Read: History

The Freedom to Read, best known of the American Library Association's documents supporting the principles of intellectual freedom as embodied in the Library Bill of Rights, had it beginnings during the Intellectual Freedom Committee's 1953 Midwinter Meeting in Chicago.[1] At that meeting, Chair William S. Dix suggested the committee "discuss the current wave of censorship and attacks on books and libraries"; "help clarify the stand which libraries might take and point to ways in which our own position might be strengthened in the minds of the public." The committee directed Dix to consider a small, off-the-record conference with in-depth discussion of the matter.

Dix's efforts resulted in a conference on the freedom to read, sponsored jointly by the American Library Association and the American Book Publishers Council, held at the Westchester Country Club, Rye, New York, May 2–3, 1953. The object of the meeting was to bring together nationally known figures representing librarians, publishers, and the public interest. Spokesmen for the public interest, viewed as vitally important to the success of the conference, included representatives of business, foundations, law, and education. Luther Evans, former Librarian of Congress and head of the United Nations Educational, Scientific and Cultural Organization, served as chair of the conference.

In their invitation to potential participants, the joint sponsors said:

> Recent months have seen the emergence in our country of a
> pattern of pressures whose effect must be to limit the range and
> variety of expression. This pattern has affected in one way or an-

---

1. For full details of national and international events surrounding the development of The Freedom to Read, see Everett T. Moore, "Intellectual Freedom," in *Research Librarianship: Essays in Honor of Robert B. Downs*, ed. Jerrold Orne (New York: Bowker, 1971).

other all the media of communications and indeed the entire area of free inquiry. Books are the last of the communications media to be affected by these pressures toward conformity. They remain preeminently the medium for the free expression of facts, ideas, and human experience in all its varieties. Librarians and publishers feel a deep responsibility for doing their part to see that this continues to be so, and they share with thoughtful men in every profession a conviction that freedom of communication is indispensable to a creative culture and a free society.

The objectives of the conference were the following:

1. To define the rights and responsibilities of publishers and librarians in maintaining the freedom of Americans to read what they choose;
2. To assay recent developments tending to restrict this freedom;
3. To consider where lines should be drawn between permissible expression and impermissible expression, and who is to draw the lines; and
4. To ascertain the public interest in this area and, if the group agrees, consider ways of asserting it.

Debate at the conference focused on the specific problem areas of obscenity and pornography and disloyalty and subversive materials. The participants considered a number of questions: What is the function of publishers and librarians in circulating ideas? Should they be responsible guides, or simply caterers to public taste? Do they have a special responsibility to make available nonconforming expression and unpopular views? Do citizens have a right to read everything not expressly prohibited by law? Should a book be judged only by its content, and the political and personal background of the author ignored? Is the role of the public library entirely neutral? Can books be subversive?

The conference resulted in substantial agreement on principles. A Continuations Committee was appointed to draft a statement based on the proceedings and to consider action and research projects designed to publicize and explore further the matters discussed. The Continuations Committee consisted of Arthur A. Houghton, Jr., president of Steuben Glass; Harold D. Lasswell, professor of law and political science at Yale Law School; Bernard Berelson, director of the Behavioral Sciences Division at the Ford Foundation; William S. Dix, librarian at Princeton University; and Dan Lacy, managing director of the American Book Publishers Council.

By the end of May, the Continuations Committee, with the assistance of other individuals, produced a final version of The Freedom to

Read for the approval of the Westchester Conference participants. On June 18, 1953, the following statement was endorsed by the Board of Directors of the American Book Publishers Council and on June 25, 1953, by the Council of the American Library Association:

The freedom to read is essential to our democracy. It is under attack. Private groups and public authorities in various parts of the country are working to remove books from sale, to censor textbooks, to label "controversial" books, to distribute lists of "objectionable" books or authors, and to purge libraries. These actions apparently rise from a view that our national tradition of free expression is no longer valid; that censorship and suppression are needed to avoid the subversion of politics and the corruption of morals. We, as citizens devoted to the use of books and as librarians and publishers responsible for disseminating them, wish to assert the public interest in the preservation of the freedom to read.

We are deeply concerned about these attempts at suppression. Most such attempts rest on a denial of the fundamental premise of democracy: that the ordinary citizen, by exercising his critical judgment, will accept the good and reject the bad. The censors, public and private, assume that they should determine what is good and what is bad for their fellow-citizens.

We trust Americans to recognize propaganda, and to reject obscenity. We do not believe they need the help of censors to assist them in this task. We do not believe they are prepared to sacrifice their heritage of a free press in order to be "protected" against what others think may be bad for them. We believe they still favor free enterprise in ideas and expression.

We are aware, of course, that books are not alone in being subjected to efforts at suppression. We are aware that these efforts are related to a larger pattern of pressures being brought against education, the press, films, radio, and television. The problem is not only one of actual censorship. The shadow of fear cast by these pressures leads, we suspect, to an even larger voluntary curtailment of expression by those who seek to avoid controversy.

Such pressure toward conformity is perhaps natural to a time of uneasy change and pervading fear. Especially when so many of our apprehensions are directed against an ideology, the expression of a dissident idea becomes a thing feared in itself, and we tend to move against it as against a hostile deed, with suppression.

And yet suppression is never more dangerous than in such a time of social tension. Freedom has given the United States the elasticity to endure strain. Freedom keeps open the path of novel and creative solutions, and enables change to come by choice. Every silencing of a heresy, every enforcement of an orthodoxy, diminishes the toughness and resilience of our society and leaves it the less able to deal with stress.

Now as always in our history, books are among our greatest instruments of freedom. They are almost the only means for making generally available ideas or manners of expression that can initially command only a small audience. They are the natural medium for the new idea and the untried voice from which come the original contributions to social growth. They are essential to the extended discussion which serious thought requires, and to the accumulation of knowledge and ideas into organized collections.

We believe that free communication is essential to the preservation of a free society and a creative culture. We believe that these pressures towards conformity present the danger of limiting the range and variety of inquiry and expression on which our democracy and our culture depend. We believe that every American community must jealously guard the freedom to publish and to circulate, in order to preserve its own freedom to read. We believe that publishers and librarians have a profound responsibility to give validity to that freedom to read by making it possible for the reader to choose freely from a variety of offerings.

The freedom to read is guaranteed by the Constitution. Those with faith in free men will stand firm on these constitutional guarantees of essential rights and will exercise the responsibilities that accompany these rights.

We therefore affirm these propositions:

1. It is in the public interest for publishers and librarians to make available the widest diversity of views and expressions, including those which are unorthodox or unpopular with the majority.

    Creative thought is by definition new, and what is new is different. The bearer of every new thought is a rebel until that idea is refined and tested. Totalitarian systems attempt to maintain themselves in power by the ruthless suppression of any concept which challenges the established orthodoxy. The power of a democratic system to adapt to change is vastly strengthened by the freedom of its citizens to choose widely from among conflicting opinions offered freely to them. To stifle every nonconformist idea at birth would mark the end of the democratic process. Furthermore, only through the constant activity of weighing and selecting can the democratic mind attain the strength demanded by times like these. We need to know not only what we believe but why we believe it.

2. Publishers and librarians do not need to endorse every idea or presentation contained in the books they make available.

It would conflict with the public interest for them to establish their own political, moral, or aesthetic views as the sole standard for determining what books should be published or circulated.

Publishers and librarians serve the educational process by helping to make available knowledge and ideas required for the growth of the mind and the increase of learning. They do not foster education by imposing as mentors the patterns of their own thought. The people should have the freedom to read and consider a broader range of ideas than those that may be held by any single librarian or publisher or government or church. It is wrong that what one man can read should be confined to what another thinks proper.

3. It is contrary to the public interest for publishers or librarians to determine the acceptability of a book solely on the basis of the personal history or political affiliations of the author.

A book should be judged as a book. No art or literature can flourish if it is to be measured by the political views or private lives of its creators. No society of free men can flourish which draws up lists of writers to whom it will not listen, whatever they may have to say.

4. The present laws dealing with obscenity should be vigorously enforced. Beyond that, there is no place in our society for extralegal efforts to coerce the taste of others, to confine adults to the reading matter deemed suitable for adolescents, or to inhibit the efforts of writers to achieve artistic expression.

To some, much of modern literature is shocking. But is not much of life itself shocking? We cut off literature at the source if we prevent serious artists from dealing with the stuff of life. Parents and teachers have a responsibility to prepare the young to meet the diversity of experiences in life to which they will be exposed, as they have a responsibility to help them learn to think critically for themselves. These are affirmative responsibilities, not to be discharged simply by preventing them from reading works for which they are not yet prepared. In these matters taste differs, and taste cannot be legislated; nor can machinery be devised which will suit the demands of one group without limiting the freedom of others. We deplore the catering to the immature, the retarded, or the maladjusted taste. But those concerned with freedom have the responsibility of seeing to it that each individual book or publication, whatever its contents, price or method of distribution, is dealt with in accordance with due process of law.

5.   It is not in the public interest to force a reader to accept with any book the prejudgment of a label characterizing the book or author as subversive or dangerous.

The idea of labeling presupposes the existence of individuals or groups with wisdom to determine by authority what is good or bad for the citizen. It presupposes that each individual must be directed in making up his mind about the ideas he examines. But Americans do not need others to do their thinking for them.

6.   It is the responsibility of publishers and librarians, as guardians of the people's freedom to read, to contest encroachments upon that freedom by individuals or groups seeking to impose their own standards or tastes upon the community at large.

It is inevitable in the give and take of the democratic process that the political, the moral, or the aesthetic concepts of an individual or group will occasionally collide with those of another individual or group. In a free society each individual is free to determine for himself what he wishes to read, and each group is free to determine what it will recommend to its freely associated members. But no group has the right to take the law into its own hands, and to impose its own concept of politics or morality upon other members of a democratic society. Freedom is no freedom if it is accorded only to the accepted and the inoffensive.

7.   It is the responsibility of publishers and librarians to give full meaning to the freedom to read by providing books that enrich the quality of thought and expression. By the exercise of this affirmative responsibility, bookmen can demonstrate that the answer to a bad book is a good one, the answer to a bad idea is a good one.

The freedom to read is of little consequence when expended on the trivial; it is frustrated when the reader cannot obtain matter fit for his purpose. What is needed is not only the absence of restraint, but the positive provision of opportunity for the people to read the best that has been thought and said. Books are the major channel by which the intellectual inheritance is handed down, and the principal means of its testing and growth. The defense of their freedom and integrity, and the enlargement of their service to society, requires of all bookmen the utmost of their faculties, and deserves of all citizens the fullest of their support.

We state these propositions neither lightly nor as easy generalizations. We here stake out a lofty claim for the value of books. We do so because we believe that they are good, possessed of enormous variety and usefulness, worthy of cherising and keeping free. We realize that the application of these propositions may mean the dissemination of ideas and manners of expression that are repugnant to many persons. We do not state these propositions in the comfortable belief that what people read is unimportant. We believe rather that what people read is deeply important; that ideas can be dangerous; but that the suppression of ideas is fatal to a democratic society. Freedom itself is a dangerous way of life, but it is ours.

Subsequently, The Freedom to Read was endorsed by many other organizations, including the American Booksellers Association, the Book Manufacturers' Institute, and the National Education Association.

For nearly twenty years, The Freedom to Read stood as the chief support of the principles enunciated in the Library Bill of Rights. In the late 1960s, however, several events led to consideration of either a revision of The Freedom to Read or a new position paper.

From a deceptively comfortable position in the middle of the 1960s, most librarians looked forward to the 1970s with optimism, hoping for a favorable climate for intellectual freedom. The U.S. Supreme Court extended constitutional support and protection in many areas of human and civil rights. Very encouraging to librarians was the expansion of freedom of expression and other First Amendment rights to allow publications that could not have been found fifteen years earlier. An unfettered climate in which all ideas could be freely exchanged seemed imminent.

But the sense of optimism was soon undercut as increased American involvement in the Vietnam war prompted rancorous divisions among citizens and members of the government. And then came 1968: On April 4, Dr. Martin Luther King was assassinated in Memphis, and the riots provoked in Washington, D.C., led President Johnson to call out troops. By April 14, violence had erupted in twenty-nine states. On June 6, Robert F. Kennedy died in Los Angeles, also victim of an assassin's bullet. From August 25 to 29, the Democratic National Convention in Chicago became the scene for violent clashes between the police and National Guard troops on one side and over ten thousand antiwar demonstrators on the other. This period of violent dissent, countered by equally violent reactions, continued into 1970 with the Kent State and Jackson, Mississippi incidents and battles between the Black Panther Party and police, and between the radical Weatherman group and police.

It became increasingly clear that such incidents of violent dissent and violent reactions, were gradually eroding prospects for the open society many had envisioned. The "permissive" atmosphere collided with demands for law and order. One effect of the collision was that, little by little, the supports in the society at large for intellectual freedom were weakened.

In the form of subpoenas, pressure was brought against news reporters, photographers, and television broadcasting corporations to divulge sources of information and to produce unpublished materials deleted from final reports. Vice President Spiro Agnew gave a series of speeches condemning the news media for biased reporting and calling on citizens to protest such reporting. President Richard Nixon promised to appoint conservatives to the Supreme Court.

Recognizing the increasing conservatism of the nation, and mindful that The Freedom to Read might be tied too closely to the McCarthy era, the IFC began, in the fall of 1968, to consider the need for and desirability of a new statement to serve the 1970s. A careful view of the document resulted in the following points:

> 1. Article 4, urging the vigorous enforcement of "the present laws dealing with obscenity," should be revised or deleted entirely.
> 2. The basic sentiments expressed in The Freedom to Read remain valid and should not be distorted.
> 3. The document has historical significance.
> 4. A new statement is needed dealing specifically with the pressures on today's society and those foreseen arising during the next decade.

Believing a new statement should at least be attempted, the IFC contacted the National Book Committee (NBC) and the American Book Publishers Council (ABPC), cosponsor of The Freedom to Read, to ask if they were interested in joining the undertaking. Both replied affirmatively. Theodore Waller and Peter Jennison met with the IFC during the 1969 Midwinter Meeting in Washington, D.C., and formed a subcommittee composed of representatives from ABPC, ALA, and NBC, charged with determining content and preparing a draft document.

Meeting during the Atlantic City Conference, June 1969, the subcommittee, composed of Edwin Castagna, Peter Jennison, Judith F. Krug, Dan Lacy, and Theodore Waller, discussed the two major items: (1) Should The Freedom to Read be revised, or should a new document be produced? (As did the IFC, they decided to design a new statement meeting the challenge of the '70s); and (2) What kind of ammunition is needed to meet the challenge of the '70s? The subcommittee also considered such questions as: Can freedom to read be separated from intellectual freedom? Is a broader concept of intellectual freedom, embracing the First Amendment together with other aspects of the Bill of Rights, such as the invasion of privacy, needed? Should all media—not just books—be considered? Should complete intellectual freedom be called for, or, in the end, must one retreat to the principle of the freedom to read?

The subcommittee next met in August of that year, with a membership augmented by the presence of William DeJohn, Freeman Lewis, Harriet Pilpel, and Richard Sullivan. They drafted several statements, and asked Jennison to assemble them into one cohesive document. Five drafts were subsequently produced, and the IFC, in a mail vote, approved the fifth draft by a ten-to-one vote. At the time of the 1970 Midwinter Meeting, however, a sixth draft had been prepared.

The ABPC Board of Directors received the draft and approved it by acclamation January 28. The sixth draft was resubmitted to the IFC, which approved it by a ten-to-one vote.

Following the 1970 Midwinter Meeting, the staff of the Office for Intellectual Freedom carefully reviewed the sixth draft of the document, tentatively entitled The Promise of the First Freedom: A Statement of Free Men. The staff could not agree with the IFC's endorsement of this document, and recommended to the IFC that The Freedom to Read be revised, as opposed to rewritten, to meet comtemporary needs. This decision was based on several factors:

1. The major part of The Freedom to Read remained valid.

2. Among those parts that needed change were the specific references to books, for libraries were concerned with all types of materials.

3. Although The Freedom to Read had historical significance, subsequent policy statements, as well as actions, of the Association, were in opposition to a few parts, primarily article 4.

4. The few parts in opposition were believed to be serious matters and should not be permitted to stand.

The revision was undertaken by the Office for Intellectual Freedom and W. Lester Smith of the Association of American Publishers (AAP), successor to the combined ABPC and the American Educational Publishers Institute. The new document differed from the 1953 version on only a few significant points: the earlier call for "vigorous enforcement of present obscenity laws" was omitted, as was the reference to "immature, the retarded, and the maladjusted taste."

The revised The Freedom to Read was approved by the ALA Council at the 1972 Midwinter Meeting and by the AAP as follows:

> The freedom to read is essential to our democracy. It is continuously under attack. Private groups and public authorities in vari-

ous parts of the country are working to remove books from sale, to censor textbooks, to label "controversial" books, to distribute lists of "objectionable" books or authors, and to purge libraries. These actions apparently rise from a view that our national tradition of free expression is no longer valid; that censorship and suppression are needed to avoid the subversion of politics and the corruption of morals. We, as citizens devoted to the use of books and as librarians and publishers responsible for disseminating them, wish to assert the public interest in the preservation of the freedom to read.

We are deeply concerned about these attempts at suppression. Most such attempts rest on a denial of the fundamental premise of democracy: that the ordinary citizen, by exercising his critical judgment, will accept the good and reject the bad. The censors, public and private, assume that they should determine what is good and what is bad for their fellow-citizens.

We trust Americans to recognize propaganda, and to reject it. We do not believe they need the help of censors to assist them in this task. We do not believe they are prepared to sacrifice their heritage of a free press in order to be "protected" against what others think may be bad for them. We believe they still favor free enterprise in ideas and expression.

We are aware, of course, that books are not alone in being subjected to efforts at suppression. We are aware that these efforts are related to a larger pattern of pressures being brought against education, the press, films, radio, and television. The problem is not only one of actual censorship. The shadow of fear cast by these pressures leads, we suspect, to an even larger voluntary curtailment of expression by those who seek to avoid controversy.

Such pressure toward conformity is perhaps natural to a time of uneasy change and pervading fear. Especially when so many of our apprehensions are directed against an ideology, the expression of a dissident idea becomes a thing feared in itself, and we tend to move against it as against a hostile deed, with suppression.

And yet suppression is never more dangerous than in such a time of social tension. Freedom has given the United States the elasticity to endure strain. Freedom keeps open the path of novel and creative solutions, and enables change to come by choice. Every silencing of a heresy, every enforcement of an orthodoxy, diminishes the toughness and resilience of our society and leaves it the less able to deal with stress.

Now as always in our history, books are among our greatest instruments of freedom. They are almost the only means for making generally available ideas or manners of expression that can initially command only a small audience. They are the natural medium for the new idea and the untried voice from which come the original contributions to social growth. They are essential to the extended discussion which serious thought requires, and to the accumulation of knowledge and ideas into organized collections.

We believe that free communication is essential to the preservation of a free society and a creative culture. We belive that these pressures towards conformity present the danger of limiting the range and variety of inquiry and expression on which our democracy and our culture depend. We believe that every American community must jealously guard the freedom to publish and to circulate, in order to preserve its own freedom to read. We believe that publishers and librarians have a profound responsibility to give validity to that freedom to read by making it possible for the readers to choose freely from a variety of offerings.

The freedom to read is guaranteed by the Constitution. Those with faith in free people will stand firm on these constitutional guarantees of essential rights and will exercise the responsibilities that accompany these rights.

We therefore affirm these propositions:

1. It is in the public interest for publishers and librarians to make available the widest diversity of views and expressions, including those which are unorthodox or unpopular with the majority.

    Creative thought is by definition new, and what is new is different. The bearer of every new thought is a rebel until that idea is refined and tested. Totalitarian systems attempt to maintain themselves in power by the ruthless suppression of any concept which challenges the established orthodoxy. The power of a democratic system to adapt to change is vastly strengthened by the freedom of its citizens to choose widely from among conflicting opinions offered freely to them. To stifle every nonconformist idea at birth would mark the end of the democratic process. Furthermore, only through the constant activity of weighing and selecting can the democratic mind attain the strength demanded by times like these. We need to know not only what we believe but why we believe it.

2. Publishers, librarians, and booksellers do not need to endorse every idea or presentation contained in the books they make available. It would conflict with the public interest for them to establish their own political, moral, or aesthetic views as a standard for determining what books should be published or circulated.

    Publishers and librarians serve the educational process by helping to make available knowledge and ideas required for the growth of the mind and the increase of learning. They do not foster education by imposing as mentors the patterns of their own thought. The people should have the freedom to read and consider a broader range of ideas than those that may be held by any single librarian or publisher or government or church. It is wrong that what one can read should be confined to what another thinks proper.

3. It is contrary to the public interest for publishers or librarians to determine the acceptability of a book on the basis of the personal history or political affiliations of the author.

A book should be judged as a book. No art or literature can flourish if it is to be measured by the political views or private lives of its creators. No society of free men can flourish which draws up lists of writers to whom it will not listen, whatever they may have to say.

4. There is no place in our society for efforts to coerce the taste of others, to confine adults to the reading matter deemed suitable for adolescents, or to inhibit the efforts of writers to achieve artistic expression.

To some, much of modern literature is shocking. But is not much of life itself shocking? We cut off literature at the source if we prevent writers from dealing with the stuff of life. Parents and teachers have a responsibility to prepare the young to meet the diversity of experiences in life to which they will be exposed, as they have a responsibility to help them learn to think critically for themselves. These are affirmative responsibilities, not to be discharged simply by preventing them from reading works for which they are not yet prepared. In these matters taste differs, and taste cannot be legislated; nor can machinery be devised which will suit the demands of one group without limiting the freedom of others.

5. It is not in the public interest to force a reader to accept with any book the prejudgment of a label characterizing the book or author as subversive or dangerous.

The ideal of labeling presupposes the existence of individuals or groups with wisdom to determine by authority what is good or bad for the citizen. It presupposes that each individual must be directed in making up his mind about the ideas he examines. But Americans do not need others to do their thinking for them.

6. It is the responsibility of publishers and librarians, as guardians of the people's freedom to read, to contest encroachments upon that freedom by individuals or groups seeking to impose their own standards or tastes upon the community at large.

It is inevitable in the give and take of the democratic process that the political, the moral, or the aesthetic concepts of an individual or group will occasionally collide with those of another individual or group. In a free society each individual is free to determine for himself what he wishes to read, and each group is free to determine what it will recommend to its freely associated members. But no group has the right to take the law into its own hands, and to impose its own concept of politics or morality upon other members of a democratic society. Freedom is no freedom if it is accorded only to the accepted and the inoffensive.

7. It is the responsibility of publishers and librarians to give full meaning to the freedom to read by providing books that enrich the quality and diversity of thought and expression. By the exercise of this affirmative responsibility, bookmen can demonstrate that the answer to a bad book is a good one, the answer to a bad idea is a good one.

The freedom to read is of little consequence when expended on the trivial; it is frustrated when the reader cannot obtain matter fit for his purpose. What is needed is not only the absence of restraint, but the positive provision of opportunity for the people to read the best that has been thought and said. Books are the major channel by which the intellectual inheritance is handed down, and the principal means of its testing and growth. The defense of their freedom and integrity, and the enlargement of their service to society, requires of all bookmen the utmost of their faculties, and deserves of all citizens the fullest of their support.

We state these propositions neither lightly nor as easy generalizations. We here stake out a lofty claim for the value of books. We do so because we believe that they are good, possessed of enormous variety and usefulness, worthy of cherishing and keeping free. We realize that the application of these propositions may mean the dissemination of ideas and manners of expression that are repugnant to many persons. We do not state these propositions in the comfortable belief that what people read is unimportant. We believe rather that what people read is deeply important; that ideas can be dangerous; but that the suppression of ideas is fatal to a democratic society. Freedom itself is a dangerous way of life, but it is ours.

The document was subsequently endorsed by many other organizations: American Booksellers Association; American Civil Liberties Union; American Federation of Teachers, AFL-CIO; Anti-Defamation

League of B'nai B'rith; Association of American University Presses; Bureau of Independent Publishers and Distributors; Children's Book Council; Freedom of Information Center; Freedom to Read Foundation; Magazine Publishers Association; Motion Picture Association of America; National Association of College Stores; National Board of the Young Women's Christian Association of the U.S.A.; National Book Committee; National Council of Negro Women; National Council of Teachers of English; National Library Week Program; P.E.N.— American Center; Periodical and Book Association of America; Sex Information and Education Council of the U.S.; and Women's National Book Association.

By 1990, both the IFC and the AAP Freedom to Read Committee were in agreement that the Freedom to Read statement needed minor revisions. In addition, it had recently had gone out of print. At the Annual Conference in June, Richard Kleeman of the Association of American Publishers recommended minor changes, including removal of gender-specific language. It was also suggested that the new draft incorporate international freedom to read concerns.

A major question in regard to a revised statement was whether it should be more explicitly inclusive of the arts and music—targets of many then-recent censorship battles. Again, the view was strongly expressed that the statement has stood the test of time and would only be diminished by major revisions. The IFC agreed to proceed with a review and report back at the 1991 Midwinter Meeting. Richard Kleeman said the AAP Freedom to Read Committee would follow the same timetable.

In January, 1991, the Committee considered two new drafts: one without gender-specific language and the other with a new international focus. Ultimately, the committee decided to adopt only the first version and to address international and other concerns in separate documents. On January 16, 1991, the committee adopted the revised Freedom to Read Statement and so informed the Council. Given the editorial nature of the changes, no action by the Council was required. On the same date, at its regular monthly meeting, the AAP Freedom to Read Committee adopted the same revision.

2

POLICY ON CONFIDENTIALITY
OF LIBRARY RECORDS

The Council of the American Library Association strongly recommends that the responsible officers of each library in the United States:

1. Formally adopt a policy which specifically recognizes its circulation records and other records identifying the name of library users to be confidential in nature.*

2. Advise all librarians and library employees that such records shall not be made available to any agency of state, federal, or local government except pursuant to such process, order, or subpoena as may be authorized under the authority of, and pursuant to, federal, state, or local law relating to civil, criminal, or administrative discovery procedures or legislative investigative power.

3. Resist the issuance or enforcement of any such process, order, or subpoena until such time as a proper showing of good cause has been made in a court of competent jurisdiction.**

*Note: See also ALA Policy Manual 54.15, Code of Ethics, point 3: "Librarians must protect each user's right to privacy with respect to information sought or received, and materials consulted, borrowed, or acquired."

**Note: Point 3, above, means that upon receipt of such process, order, or subpoena, the library's officers will consult with their legal counsel to determine if such process, order, or subpoena is in proper form and if there is a showing of good cause for its issuance; if the process, order, or subpoena is not in proper form or if good cause has not been shown, they will insist that such defects be cured.

Adopted January 20, 1971; revised July 4, 1975, by the ALA Council.

2

Suggested Procedures for Implementing Policy on Confidentiality of Library Records

When drafting local policies, libraries should consult with their legal counsel to insure these policies are based upon and consistent with applicable federal, state, and local law concerning the confidentiality of library records, the disclosure of public records, and the protection of individual privacy.

Suggested procedures include the following:

1. The library staff member receiving the request to examine or obtain information relating to circulation or other records identifying the names of library users, will immediately refer the person making the request to the responsible officer of the institution, who shall explain the confidentiality policy.
2. The director, upon receipt of such process, order, or subpoena, shall consult with the appropriate legal officer assigned to the institution to determine if such process, order, or subpoena is in good form if there is a showing of good cause for its issuance.
3. If the process, order, or subpoena is not in proper form or if good cause has not been shown, insistence shall be made that such defects be cured before any records are released. (The legal process requiring the production of circulation or other library records shall ordinarily be in the form of subpoena *duces tecum* [bring your records] requiring the responsible officer to attend court or the taking of his/her disposition and may require him/her to bring along certain designated circulation or other specified records.)
4. Any threat or unauthorized demands (i.e., those not supported by a process, order, or subpoena) concerning circulation and other records identfying the names of library users shall be reported to the appropriate legal officer of the institution.

5. Any problems relating to the privacy of circulation and other records identifying the names of library users which are not provided for above shall be referred to the responsible officer.

Adopted by the ALA Intellectual Freedom Committee, January 9, 1983; revised January 11, 1988

Policy on Confidentiality of Library Records: History

During the spring of 1970, the Milwaukee Public Library was visited by agents of the U.S. Treasury Department requesting permission to examine the circulation records of books and materials on explosives. Initially rebuffed by the assistant librarian, the agents later returned with an opinion from the city attorney's office that circulation records were public records, and that the agents should be allowed access to the files. The library complied. At about the same time, the ALA Office for Intellectual Freedom received reports of similar visits from treasury agents at public libraries in Cleveland, Ohio, and Richmond, California. On July 1 of that year, a report was received from Atlanta, Georgia, stating that in the Atlanta area, twenty-seven libraries and branches were visited.

On July 21, the ALA Executive Board issued an emergency advisory statement urging all libraries to make circulation records confidential as a matter of policy. The advisory statement read:

> The American Library Association has been advised that the Internal Revenue Service of the Treasury Department has requested access to the circulation records of public libraries in Atlanta, Georgia, and Milwaukee, Wisconsin, for the purpose of determining the identity of persons reading matter pertaining to the construction of explosive devices. The Association is further advised that such requests were not based on any process, order, or subpoena authorized by federal, civil, criminal, or administrative discovery procedures.
>
> The Executive Board of the ALA believes that the efforts of the federal government to convert library circulation records into "suspect lists" constitute an unconscionable and unconstitutional invasion of the right of privacy of library patrons and, if permitted

to continue, will do irreparable damage to the educational and social value of the libraries of this country.

Accordingly, the Executive Board of the American Library Association strongly recommends that the responsible officers in each U.S. library:

1. Formally adopt a policy which specifically recognizes its circulation records to be confidential in nature.

2. Advise all librarians and library employees that such records shall not be made available to any agency of state, federal, or local government except pursuant to such process, order, or subpoena as may be authorized under the authority of, and pursuant to, federal, state, or local law relating to civil, criminal, or administrative discovery procedures or legislative investigatory power.

3. Resist the issuance or enforcement of any such process, order, or subpoena until such time as a proper showing of good cause has been made in a court of competent jurisdiction.

David H. Clift, ALA executive director, and staff members met with Randolph W. Thrower, commissioner of the Internal Revenue Service (IRS), on August 5, 1970, to discuss their mutual concern over the inquiries. Little was agreed upon at the meeting except that "efforts would begin, in a spirit of cooperation, to develop guidelines acceptable to the American Library Association and the Internal Revenue Service." That afternoon, Mr. Clift received a copy of a letter sent to Senator Sam J. Ervin, Jr., chair of the Senate Subcommittee on Constitutional Rights, by Secretary of the Treasury David M. Kennedy in response to Senator Ervin's earlier expressed concern about the IRS inquiries. Secretary Kennedy's letter stated that the visits had been conducted to "determine the advisability of the use of library records as an investigative technique to assist in quelling bombings. That survey . . . has terminated and will not be repeated." But the door was not being closed on future surveys. The secretary added that "it is our judgment that checking such records in certain limited circumstances is an appropriate investigative technique," and that the Alcohol, Tobacco, and Firearms Division of the Treasury Department has the authority, under federal statute, to conduct limited investigations in specific cases.[1]

ALA indicated its awareness of the Internal Revenue Service's responsibility to enforce the statutes, but noted that the Association's primary concern was not the enforcement itself, but rather, the means by which this enforcement was undertaken regarding libraries. While

---

1. David M. Kennedy, letter to Sen. Sam J. Ervin, Jr., July 29, 1970 (copy in ALA files).

not intending to hinder effective enforcement of federal statutes, the Association made it clear that circulation records were "not to be made available to any agency of state, federal, or local government except pursuant to such process, order, or subpoena as may be authorized under the authority of, and pursuant to, federal, state, or local law relating to civil, criminal, or administrative discovery procedures or legislative investigatory power."

In anticipation of presenting the matter to the ALA Council at the 1971 Midwinter Meeting in Los Angeles, Intellectual Freedom Committee members were polled by telegram in October 1970, concerning a proposed draft of a policy statement. Suggestions for modification of the July statement were made by the IFC and the Executive Board at the latter's 1970 fall meeting. The board suggested that the original introductory paragraph be shortened, that the phrase "and other records identifying the names of library users with specific materials" be added to article 1, and that article 3 be clarified.

The Policy on Confidentiality of Library Records was formally adopted by the IFC at a special meeting in December 1970. It was submitted to the ALA Council at the 1971 Midwinter Meeting in Los Angeles, and was approved on January 20, 1971. On that date, in his progress report to the Council, IFC Chair David K. Berninghausen stated:

> When the time comes in any society that government officials seek information as to what people are reading, it must be presumed that they expect to use these records as evidence of dangerous *thinking*. And when a government takes action to control what its citizens are *thinking*, it is a tell-tale sign that all is not well in that society.
>
> We recognize that the U.S. Treasury agents probably did not realize that their investigations would be viewed as an invasion of privacy of readers or as an infringement on the freedom of thought guaranteed by the U.S. Constitution and Bill of Rights. But it is such small, beginning steps that lead a nation down the road to tyranny. We are pleased to note that these programs of inquiry have been stopped. We are proud of ALA's prompt action which helped to bring the investigations to an end.[2]

At the 1975 Annual Conference in San Francisco, a new problem of confidentiality was considered by the IFC. Earlier, the Intellectual Freedom Committee of the Washington Library Association had called ALA's attention to the fact that the policy on the confidentiality of

---

2. American Library Association, "Minutes of Council Meetings," vol. 14, 1971–1972, p. 76.

library records "identifying the names of library users with specific materials" had been used to justify the release of other kinds of library records on patrons to police officers.

After reviewing this issue, the IFC voted to recommend to Council that the phrase "with specific materials" be deleted from the policy, thus making it applicable to all patron records. The IFC's recommendation was accepted by Council at its meeting on July 4, 1975.

During the 1980–82 revision of ALA's intellectual freedom policies, the IFC considered several suggested revisions of the Policy on Confidentiality of Library Records. After considerable discussion and consultation with ALA counsel, however, the committee decided not to recommend any changes in the policy. At the 1983 Midwinter Meeting in San Antonio, however, it was voted to append to the document a note referring to point 3 of the ALA Code of Ethics protecting the library user's right to privacy. At San Antonio, the IFC also adopted a series of "suggested procedures" for implementing the confidentiality policy.

At the 1988 Midwinter Meeting in San Antonio, the IFC amended the suggested procedures. The emendations were made to bring the language in this document into conformance with the language in the policy, to stress the need for a court order before any records are released, and to emphasize the need for libraries to consult applicable federal, state and local law when drafting such a policy for local use.

Later in 1988, responding to concerns about whether the language in the Policy on Confidentiality was able to cover all records, rather than just registration or circulation records, the IFC reviewed both the policy and the procedures for implementing it. The committee decided the language of the policy was sufficient, but the language in the procedures was not uniformly inclusive and should be revised. The committee chair noted that the procedures should include a direction to librarians to ascertain the status of their state law on confidentiality of library records. In addition, the chair suggested that all state IFCs be encouraged to review their state statutes to determine the inclusivity of the records covered.

A new draft incorporating the above-mentioned concerns was adopted by the Committee on January 11, 1988. Procedures for implementing policy are institutional in nature and not official ALA policy; action by the Council, therefore, was not needed.

3

POLICY CONCERNING CONFIDENTIALITY OF PERSONALLY IDENTIFIABLE INFORMATION ABOUT LIBRARY USERS

The ethical responsibilities of librarians, as well as statutes in most states and the District of Columbia, protect the privacy of library users. Confidentiality extends to "information sought or received, and materials consulted, borrowed, or acquired," and includes database search records, reference interviews, circulation records, interlibrary loan records, and other personally identifiable uses of library materials, facilities, or services.

The First Amendment's guarantee of freedom of speech and of the press requires that the corresponding rights to hear what is spoken and read what is written be preserved, free from fear of government intrusion, intimidation, or reprisal. The American Library Association reaffirms its opposition to "any use of government prerogatives which lead to the intimidation of the individual or the citizenry from the exercise of free expression . . . [and] encourages resistance to such abuse of government power. . . ." (ALA Policy 53.4). In seeking access or in the pursuit of information, confidentiality is the primary means of providing the privacy that will free the individual from fear of intimidation or retaliation.

Libraries are one of the great bulwarks of democracy. They are living embodiments of the First Amendment because their collections include voices of dissent as well assent. Libraries are impartial resources providing information on all points of view, available to all persons regardless of age, race, religion, national origin, social or political views, economic status, or any other characteristic. The role of libraries as such a resource must not be compromised by an erosion of the privacy rights of library users.

The American Library Association regularly receives reports of visits by agents of federal, state, and local law enforcement agencies to libraries, where it is alleged they have asked for personally identifiable information about library users. These visits, whether under the rubric of simply informing libraries of agency concerns or for some other reason, reflect an insensitivity to the legal and ethical bases for confidentiality, and the role it plays in the preservation of First Amendment rights, rights also extended to foreign nationals while in the United States. The government's interest in library use reflects a dangerous and fallacious equation of what a person reads with what that person believes or how that person is likely to behave. Such a presumption can and does threaten the freedom of access to information. It also is a threat to a crucial aspect of First Amendment rights: that freedom of speech and of the press include the freedom to hold, disseminate and receive unpopular, minority, "extreme," or even "dangerous" ideas.

The American Library Association recognizes that, under limited circumstances, access to certain information might be restricted due to a legitimate "national security" concern. However, there has been no showing of a plausible probability that national security will be compromised by any use made of *unclassified* information available in libraries. Thus, the right of access to this information by individuals, including foreign nationals, must be recognized as part of the librarian's legal and ethical responsibility to protect the confidentiality of the library user.

The American Library Association also recognizes that law enforcement agencies and officers may occasionally believe that library records contain information which would be helpful to the investigation of criminal activity. If there is a reasonable basis to believe such records are *necessary* to the progress of an investigation or prosecution, the American judicial system provides the mechanism for seeking release of such confidential records: the issuance of a court order, following a showing of *good cause* based on *specific facts*, by a court of competent jurisdiction.

Adopted July 2, 1991, by the ALA Council

Policy Concerning Confidentiality of Personally Identifiable Information about Library Users: History

---

In 1989, the Intellectual Freedom Committee prepared a statement sent to then-FBI director William Sessions, outlining ALA's concerns about the FBI Library Awareness Program. Though the FBI had indicated it would exchange a similar statement of its own about the program, none was ever received by ALA. Inquiries to the OIF from librarians seeking assistance in handling law enforcement requests for confidential information about library users continued.

In response to the increasing number of inquiries, the lack of cooperation from the FBI, and concern about law enforcement requests for personally identifiable information about patrons whether found in library records *per se* or not, the ALA Council requested that a policy addressing the FBI and law enforcement issues be drafted.

The IFC revised and reformatted the statement prepared for the FBI in 1989 to explain library concerns about confidentiality to produce the Policy Concerning Confidentiality of Personally Identifiable Information about Library Users.

In 1991, the first draft was further revised to broaden the language concerning what constitutes personally identifiable information about library users. This was done in response to a case in Oregon, where law enforcement officials took fingerprints from library materials as part of a criminal investigation. Members questioned whether fingerprints could be considered personally identifiable information according to the policy.

The new draft also included a statement, expressing the ALA's contention that the use of unclassified materials in libraries cannot reasonably be deemed a national security threat, as alleged by the FBI in an attempt to justify the Library Awareness Program. The final version of the new policy was adopted by the Council on July 2, 1991.

4

POLICY ON GOVERNMENTAL INTIMIDATION

The American Library Association opposes any use of governmental prerogatives which leads to the intimidation of the individual or the citizenry from the exercise of free expression. ALA encourages resistance to such abuse of governmental power and supports those against whom such governmental power has been employed.

Adopted February 2, 1973; amended July 1, 1981, by the ALA Council.

Resolution on Governmental
Intimidation: History

The issue of the federal government's abuse of authority was brought
before the ALA membership at the Association's 1971 Annual Conference in Dallas. At the general membership meeting on June 23, Zoia
Horn and Patricia Rom (then librarians at Bucknell University, in
Lewisburg, Pennsylvania) introduced a resolution on governmental intimidation. Approved by the membership and two days later amended
and approved by the ALA Council, the original ALA statement on
governmental intimidation read as follows:

> WHEREAS, ALA is concerned with the preservation of intellectual
> freedom; and
>
> WHEREAS, The freedom to think, to communicate, and discuss
> alternatives are essential elements of intellectual freedom; and
>
> WHEREAS, These freedoms have been threatened by actions of the
> federal government through the use of informers, electronic sur-
> veillance, grand juries, and indictments under the Conspiracy Act
> of 1968 as demonstrated in the case of the Harrisburg 6, now
>
> THEREFORE BE IT RESOLVED,
>
> 1. That the ALA Membership Meeting at Dallas recognizes
>   the danger to intellectual freedom presented by the use of
>   spying in libraries by government agencies;
>
> 2. That ALA go on record against the use of the grand jury
>   procedure to intimidate anti-Vietnam War activists and
>   people seeking justice for minority communities;
>
> 3. That ALA deplore and go on record against the use of the
>   Conspiracy Act of 1968 as a weapon against the citizens of
>   this country who are being indicted for such overt acts as

meeting, telephoning, discussing alternative methods of bringing about change, and writing letters;

4. That the ALA Membership at Dallas assert the confidentiality of the professional relationships of librarians to the people they serve, that these relationships be respected in the same manner as medical doctors to their patients, lawyers to their clients, priests to the people they serve; and

5. That ALA assert that no librarian would lend himself to a role as informant, whether of voluntarily revealing circulation records or identifying patrons and their reading habits.

In March 1972, the Social Responsibilities Round Table asked the Executive Board to give the Association's moral support and financial aid to a librarian who had been called to testify in a federal court and, after refusing, had been jailed for civil contempt. The Social Responsibilities Round Table held that the Dallas Resolution on Governmental Intimidation committed the ALA to supporting this librarian. The Executive Board directed the IFC to review the resolution and "develop a statement which would interpret the resolution in terms of guidance for possible action."

At the 1972 Annual Conference in Chicago, the IFC spent a great portion of its scheduled meetings trying to fulfill this charge. The committee felt that it was unable to develop an interpretive statement because, in the committee's words, the 1971 statement was "good in intent, but inoperable . . . due to its narrowness of focus." Because the 1971 statement was tied to a specific piece of legislation and a specific incident, the Intellectual Freedom Committee felt the document was difficult to apply. Rather than developing an interpretive statement, the committee promised to develop a new resolution, expressing similar concerns, for presentation to the ALA Council at the Association's 1973 Midwinter Meeting. The IFC turned its full attention to preparing a new statement at the 1973 Midwinter Meeting. The new document was presented to the Council on February 2, 1973.

The committee originally moved that the resolution be adopted and substituted in its entirety for the 1971 Dallas statement. However, the Council felt that the new resolution omitted one important concern: an affirmation of the confidential nature of the librarian-patron relationship, covered by articles 4 and 5 of the Dallas resolution. To ensure that this point was retained as a part of official ALA policy, the Council rescinded all of the Dallas resolution except for articles 4 and 5. In addition, the Council amended the IFC's resolution, confirming the ALA's support of all those against whom governmental power has been employed. The Resolution on Governmental Intimidation, approved by the ALA Council on February 2, 1973, read as follows:

> WHEREAS, The principle of intellectual freedom protects the rights of free expression of ideas, even those which are in opposition to the policies and actions of government itself; and
>
> WHEREAS, The support of that principle is guaranteed by the First Amendment, thus insuring constitutional protection of individual or collective dissent; and
>
> WHEREAS, Government, at whatever level, national, state, or local, must remain ever vigilant to the protection of that principle; and
>
> WHEREAS, Government, although properly empowered to promulgate, administer, or adjudicate law, has no right to use illicitly its legally constituted powers to coerce, intimidate, or harass the individual or the citizenry from enunciating dissent; and
>
> WHEREAS, The illegitimate uses of legitimate governmental powers have become increasingly a matter of public record, among them being the misuse of the Grand Jury and other investigative procedures, the threat to deny licenses to telecommunications media, the indictment of citizens on charges not relevant to their presumed offenses, and the repressive classification, and hence denial, of documentary material to the very public taxed for its accumulation; and
>
> WHEREAS, These illicit uses not only constitute an abrogation of the right to exercise the principle of freedom of expression but also, and perhaps more dangerously, prefigure a society no longer hospitable to dissent;
>
> NOW THEREFORE BE IT RESOLVED, That the American Library Association, cognizant that in the scales of justice the strength of individual liberty may outweigh the force of power, expresses its unswerving opposition to any use of governmental prerogative which leads to the intimidation of the individual or the citizenry from the exercise of the constitutionally protected right of free expression; and
>
> BE IT FURTHER RESOLVED, That the American Library Association encourages its members to resist such improper uses of govermental power; and
>
> FURTHER, That the American Library Association supports those against whom such governmental power has been employed.

During the review of the ALA intellectual freedom policies and statements which followed Council's adoption in 1980 of the revision of the Library Bill of Rights, the Intellectual Freedom Committee determined that two problems existed with the Resolution on Govermental Intimidation. The first was the matter of format. It was a resolution and included a series of "whereas clauses," which were helpful in explaining the "policy" section but were not theoretically a part of the policy. The second problem related to the policy section itself, which the committee believed should stand alone without the necessity of explanatory phrases. As in all cases when examples are used, these tend to date the policy to the period of time in which it was originally created. They also tend to dilute the clarity and force of the policy statement.

The committee agreed that any policy on governmental intimidation should strongly oppose this activity and that, in addition, the policy should indicate ALA support of those who resist governmental intimidation. In presenting the amended policy to the ALA Council, the Intellectual Freedom Committee decided that the 1973 version would be maintained in full in the historical file and that it would be made available as necessary. The amended policy on governmental intimidation was adopted by the ALA Council on July 1, 1981.

5

POLICY ON ACCESS TO THE USE OF LIBRARIES AND INFORMATION BY INDIVIDUALS WITH PHYSICAL OR MENTAL IMPAIRMENT

WHEREAS, The Intellectual Freedom Committee is concerned with freedom of access; and

WHEREAS, The "Library Bill of Rights" states that "books and other library resources should be provided for the interests, information and enlightenment of all people of the community the library serves" and "a person's right to use a library should not be denied or abridged . . ."; and

WHEREAS, Federal and state constitutional and statutory laws forbid public institutions from discriminating against handicapped individuals, i.e., persons who have a physical or mental impairment; and

WHEREAS, Court opinions have clearly interpreted said laws as proscribing discrimination against persons who have acquired immune deficiency syndrome ("AIDS"), AIDS-related complex ("ARC"), or who test positive for the human immunodeficiency virus ("HIV"); and

WHEREAS, The American Medical Association and the United States Department of Health and Human Services have opined that while the human immunodeficiency virus that causes AIDS is a contagious disease, it cannot be transmitted by casual contact; now, therefore be it

RESOLVED, That the "Library Bill of Rights" of the American Library Association which insures access to library facilities, materials and services by all people of the community includes individuals with physical or mental impairments; and be it further

RESOLVED, That the American Library Association deplores discrimination against and denial or abridgment of library and information access to persons of all ages who have acquired immune deficiency syndrome ("AIDS"), AIDS-related complex ("ARC"), or who test positive for the human immunodeficiency virus ("HIV").

Adopted January 13, 1988, by the ALA Council.

Resolution on Access to the Use of Libraries and Information by Individuals with Physical or Mental Impairment: History

Immediately before the 1988 Midwinter Meeting in San Antonio, the Intellectual Freedom Committee received a request for a statement of ALA's position concerning access to libraries and information by those with physical and mental impairments, particularly persons with the AIDS virus.

The occasion for this request was the barring of a child in Lake City, Tennessee, from attendance at the public school because the child had AIDS. Public librarians in the area perceived a need for their boards to adopt a clear policy about the access rights of persons with AIDS. In the search for existing policy statements, the Intellectual Freedom Committee was contacted, but no such statements were found.

Recognizing the need for definitive language affirming the access rights of all physically and mentally impaired persons and in light of a rising hysteria over AIDS, the IFC took to the ALA Council the following resolution On Access to the Use of Libraries and Information by Individuals with Physical or Mental Impairment. It was adopted by the Council on January 13, 1988.

PART III

Intellectual Freedom: An All-Embracing Concept

1

Intellectual Freedom:
An All-Embracing Concept

When an institution is supported by public funds, taxpayers naturally believe they have the right, if not the obligation, to influence the operations of that institution. Where intellectual freedom is concerned, this belief is especially prevalent, regardless of the kind of library or library activity involved. Too often, however, librarians and others engaged in one particular kind of library or library activity believe their situation is so unique as not to have any relationship to intellectual freedom at all.

The following five articles written by experienced authorities on the philosophy and operation of the most common types of publicly supported libraries—public, school, academic, federal, and state—illustrate that intellectual freedom does indeed affect all types of libraries and library activities. These articles also outline librarians' professional responsibilities with regard to the modifications a particular library environment may impose on the nature and functioning of the all-embracing concept, intellectual freedom.

2

Public Libraries and Intellectual Freedom

Gordon M. Conable

> *If this nation is to be wise as well as strong, if we are to achieve our destiny, then we need more new ideas for more wise men reading more good books in more public libraries. These libraries should be open to all—except the censor. We must know all the facts and hear all the alternatives and listen to all the criticisms. Let us welcome controversial books and controversial authors. For the Bill of Rights is the guardian of our security as well as our Library.*
> —JOHN F. KENNEDY

American democracy is dependent upon a belief that the people are capable of self-government. To secure our basic rights, we believe that "governments are instituted among men deriving their just powers from the consent of the governed." In this country, we have taken this to mean "informed consent."

The concept of informed consent only has meaning if the full range of human ideas is accessible to the people. The proponents of the various points of view must be able to make their cases fully and openly, however popular or unpopular they may be, before the individual and collective judgment of their fellow citizens.

This principle is embodied in the First Amendment to the Constitution, which protects the free expression of ideas:

> Congress shall make no law respecting an establishment of religion, or prohibiting the free exercise thereof; or abridging the freedom of speech, or of the press; or the right of the people peaceably

Gordon M. Conable is the Director of the Monroe County Library System in Monroe, Michigan. He served on the ALA Intellectual Freedom Committee 1987–91, and was Chair 1989–91.

to assemble, and to petition the government for a redress of grievances.

American public libraries provide access to those ideas. By providing the information and resources necessary for strong, open, free, and unrestricted dialogue on all issues of concern, the public library preserves these freedoms.

It is the genius of the American system that we base our liberty on the broadest protection of each individual's rights to free expression and on the corollary right to access the expression of others. It is the genius of the American public library to be an institution dedicated to promoting the exercise of these rights.

American public libraries flourished out of a commitment to the principle that knowledge and access to information empower the individual. Libraries embody a firm belief that it is in the public interest that information not be the exclusive province of a privileged few, but that it be widely and freely available to all.

At the time that public library movement began, books and education were scarcer commodities. Today, with the quantity of information that is generated and distributed increasing exponentially, the issue of scarcity is superseded by new problems of access. But the function of the public library is much the same: to offer knowledge and information to the average citizen who cannot afford, with individual resources alone, to secure all the information necessary to meet his or her self-defined needs in a complex and challenging world. In this way, public libraries provide tangible commitment to free speech, self-government, and self-education by collecting, organizing, preserving, disseminating, and protecting everyone's rights of access to the rich diversity of human expression in all its recorded forms. This responsibility goes further to justify the existence and support of public libraries than any of the many other roles and functions that public libraries fulfill within their communities.

Libraries are repositories of, and as access, distribution, and retrieval centers for, an exploding body of human knowledge and opinion. They serve as neutral ground for opposing positions. Human beings, after all, are very different from each other. Fear and anger over those differences sometimes motivate individuals to attack the messages that elucidate, represent, or advocate ideas that seem to threaten their own beliefs, way of life, sense of security, understanding of the world, or desires and aspirations. Thus the contents of libraries sometimes become targets for censors who seek to have particular items removed from the library collection, restricted as to access, expurgated, labeled, or otherwise censored. A public librarian cannot remain unconcerned, but must understand the nature of censorship, the motives of censors, and what yielding to them means.

Such attacks are generally emotionally charged. They may represent the personal distress of an individual coming in contact with material that he or she is unprepared to deal with or finds frightening. Fear—often expressed as fear of harm that could be caused to children through exposure to certain books, films, videotapes, recordings, or ideas—motivates many complaints. Such a response is quite natural and human; parents are expected to protect their offspring. The fear may be real, but the requested response—the censorship of library materials—is an inappropriate means of dealing with real or perceived danger to children. Calm discussion will frequently provide the opportunity to reassure concerned parents, support the parents' role in guiding their own children's—and only their own children's—reading, and assist them in finding library materials that meet their own family needs.

The librarian must be able to respond sensitively to such complaints without comprising the rights of others or the integrity of the library collection and its policies. Supreme Court Justice Louis D. Brandeis spoke directly to the stakes involved: "Fear of serious injury cannot alone justify suppression of free speech and assembly. Men feared witches and burned women. It is the function of speech to free men from the bondage of irrational fears." Others have feared ideas and burned books. It is the function of libraries and librarians to protect ideas and books and access to them.

Other attacks on libraries or their collections represent the calculated political agenda of sophisticated, well-organized individuals or groups that see the issue of material in the library as a means of advancing other social or political interests within a broader framework. There are rarer than the spontaneous outrage of the individual reader, but they can be more difficult to handle.

Regardless of the motive or the specific target of the censor, the function of the library and the task of the librarian are the same. It is our duty to stand firm against such pressure. This is our trust and this is our purpose. With common sense, directness, honesty, and an open approach upon accountability and not defensiveness, directness and not ideology, many complaints about books can be handled without either escalating them into major public controversies or giving in to pressure.

When the occasional controversy does erupt, the process can provide a healthy demonstration of democracy and free speech in action. It should be approached in this manner and the library should utilize the experience as a means of making its point about the importance of the underlying issues of free expression. This can provide a wellspring of community support and good will that can last long after the shouting has died.

Reviewing the astonishing range of materials that have come under attack in public libraries in recent years, it is impossible to predict or anticipate which items may arouse anyone's wrath. Shakespeare, the Bible, and generally acknowledged classics have come under the censor's fire, but so have innumerable works of less literary merit, less recognized authority, and less successful authorship. The librarian must be willing and able to defend them all, for to sacrifice the trivial, the controversial, or the distasteful means sacrificing the ability to defend anything.

Supreme Court Justice Hugo Black put it like this: "It is my belief that there are 'absolutes' in our Bill of Rights, and that they were put there on purpose by men who knew what words meant and meant their prohibitions to to be 'absolutes.' " The First Amendment must apply to everyone or it will protect no one.

Living up to the public trust embodied in professional standards relating to intellectual freedom requires courage, creativity, humor, determination, wit, patience, and commitment. Those who would shirk these standards should seek other employment.

Joanne Goldsmith has said: "The librarian who quietly removes a book from the shelf because of a noisy complaint is more guilty of restricting intellectual freedom than the complainant. The librarian has responsibility to a tradition, a body of law, and to the procedures established and approved for dealing with complaints. Worse, once the librarian has surrendered on a single occasion, he or she is the first target in future assaults. Extremism feeds on success. It is made bolder and more demanding by victory."

The issues with which public libraries must deal relating to intellectual freedom are varied and complex. In addition to the defense of challenged materials, the range of related issues includes among others:

Fees: The imposition of service charges may provide a significant ecomonic barrier to information access.

Formats: Many libraries and librarians are committed to and effective in defending nonillustrated, printed material. Philosophical assumptions, cost, or ambivalence based upon other factors may lead to practices in the handling of video, sound recordings, film, or other nonprint formats that violate basic intellectual freedom standards.

Facilities: Libraries that provide public meeting rooms and display or exhibit facilities may be subject to pressure if the subject matter of meetings, exhibits, or displays is deemed controversial or offensive.

Political agendas: Supporters of particular causes may seek to have opposing points of view excluded from the library or may charge the library with bias or censorship if their viewpoint is underrepresented. Similarly, attempts to oppose racism and apartheid have led some jurisdictions to adopt legislation boycotting vendors who do business with South Africa. These and similar measures, if applied to libraries, may have the inadvertent effect of governmentally limiting the free flow of information.

User confidentiality and privacy: Failure to protect the rights of library users to utilize library materials and services privately can limit the practical exercise of First Amendment rights. Incursions of this sort—which are illegal in many jurisdictions— have been attempted by the FBI, police agencies, marketing firms, religious missonaries, the press, and others.

Public libraries operate in a public arena, and the legal structures that establish and finance library service, the reasonable requirements for public accountability, and the realities of political process provide the context in which libraries must carry out their mission. This context may appear to add to the pressures that librarians face in opposing censorship, but if properly understood, these factors provide significant tools for librarians in defending their collections and services from the censor's attacks. Law, the rights and protections of public employees (which in many ways surpass those offered to private employees), and the protection that comes from open process and public debate can all work to the librarian's advantage in exercising his or her ethical responsibilities.

Censorship can come from both sources external to the library and sources within the library itself. The external sources include:

Parents. Either singularly or in groups, parents may seek the removal of materials from a library's collection. Their concerns often center around materials that deal with sex in an explicit or realistic way, but they may also attack books dealing with witchcraft and the occult, and books that differ from their vision of the traditional family structure. In recent years there has been an increase in challenges to pictures books.

Religious groups. Either individual members of a religious group or the group as a whole may attack material. Moral issues, sexual issues, the role of women, "demonic" or "satanic" material, or the presentation of religion in a manner perceived to be negative are all common reasons for challenges.

Political groups. These people may charge a library with political bias on the basis of perceived imbalance within the collection or they may charge that material representing their political viewpoint is being systematically excluded by librarians with differing political views. Material describing communist societies still comes under fire.

Protected minority groups. Material that is considered racist or which presents specific ethnic groups in stereotyped ways or inaccurately treats their culture or history frequently comes under fire. Similar attacks on sexist or other stereotyped materials are also common.

Patriotic groups. These groups may protest materials criticizing the government or national traditions, or which outline alternative interpretations of American life and history.

Emotionally unstable individuals. Some individuals who are emotionally unstable may focus on any of the above causes as outlets for their frustration. It is important, however, to determine whether the underlying cause is a real intellectual confrontation of differing ideas and philosophies or an emotionally upset person who is striking out against the public library as a convenient target.

Sources of censorship from inside the institution may include the following:

Trustees or governing bodies. Since such groups are the policy-making bodies, they may build censoring devices into policy. If the board demands the removal of a book because of local pressure, it has established a precedent severely limiting the materials that may be included in a collection. On the other hand, with the support of the board, the librarian can stand up to any would-be censor.

Library staff. One of the most difficult kinds of censorship to combat is that imposed by the library's own staff. Besides being catalogers, children's librarians, circulation clerks, and the like, staff members are also parents, church-goers, and members of political, patriotic, and a great variety of other groups holding particular viewpoints. These may appear threatened, maligned, or ridiculed by material the library owns and such materials may remain unordered, uncatalogued, uncirculated, or stolen simply because certain staff members object to them.

Managment. If top administrators shy away from controversial issues, they set the tone for the rest of the staff and this may have a chilling effect on library acquisitions. They may also establish procedures or recommend policies for board adoption

that limit access to materials on the basis of age, sequester controversial materials in locked cases or rooms, or take other steps
that negate accessibility.

Selection policies. A library's selection policy can be misused to
restrict intellectual freedom. Policies that are inclusive, that are
based upon the First Amendment, and that successfully balance
the issue of collection diversity and demand buying are much
stronger than those that narrowly limit collection scope on the
basis of purely subjective factors such as "quality" or "popular-
ity," which requires outside endorsement in the form of reviews
or recommended lists to justify every acquisition, or which are
written in a way to justify the exclusion of controversial material
from the collection.

Circulation and interlibrary loan policies. Some libraries still
limit children's borrowing of materials from the adult collection
or limit their access to certain informational formats such as
videotapes or other audiovisual materials. Along the same lines,
ILL services are sometimes denied to children or children's materials may be excluded from bibliographic databases that are
searched to obtain materials from other libraries. Such barriers
are a form of censorship and violate professional standards.

Public libraries need to remember that with proper groundwork,
preparation, and training, censorship attacks from without can be
withstood and that individuals and groups exist in the community who
will defend the library. Thoughtful determination and self-awareness
are required to confront censorship issues from within.

The active advocacy of intellectual freedom is a challenge that all
librarians accept when they join the profession. It is the essence of our
responsibility, the core of our public trust, our highest duty.

3

School Library Media Centers and Intellectual Freedom

Diane McAfee Hopkins

As the first library that many children and young adults are introduced to and use on a continuing basis, school library media centers play a vital role in promoting intellectual freedom. This brief article will examine intellectual freedom from the broad perspective of access, exploring the following issues: physical and intellectual access, collection development policy and procedures, sources of potential complaints, effectively dealing with challenges to materials, and promotion of intellectual freedom.

Access

It is important to view intellectual freedom in school library media centers as a major access issue. Basic access to resources for K–12 students may be affected by the organizational and hierarchial structure of the public school district, the age and grade level of the student, and the interest of people inside and outside the school community in the materials that are available for student use.

Intellectual and physical access are both important in assuring intellectual freedom for children and young adults. Physical access includes the basic access that results from the presence of the library media center, particularly one that is professionally staffed and accessible for use by students before, during and after regular school hours. A library media center also should offer a broad range of resources from which to choose and should be supported by a budget which provides for the ongoing and growing needs of students and faculty in the school.

Diane McAfee Hopkins is an assistant professor at the School of Library and Information Studies, University of Wisconsin–Madison. She is serving on the ALA intellectual Freedom Committee 1991–93.

The aim of intellectual freedom for students is unmet if access is limited to a single school library media center and its holdings. The basic principle of access for students extends to interlibrary loan of materials from other library media centers in the district as well as libraries located outside the district. Students should be encouraged and aided in gaining information from wherever it is available, without barriers such as fees and age-level restrictions. Access also includes computerized information networks or databases.

Professional practice, in terms of rules and regulations which govern student access to school library media centers, should be scrutinized to ascertain the promotion of intellectual freedom. Among questions to be asked are the following: Do the rules encourage or inhibit intellectual freedom for students? Is time in the library media center (LMC) restricted to rigidly scheduled classes? Are rules governing access to the LMC by students in study halls appropriate? Are students permitted and encouraged to use the LMC before school, during lunch, after school, and at other times during the school day? Are students discouraged from using nonprint materials?

In addition to rules and regulations, professional practice in the selection and evaluation of materials requires examination from the standpoint of intellectual freedom. Library media specialists must assure that access to information is promoted, not only in the English language but, where appropriate, in the languages which accomodate students for whom English is a second language.

The criteria for the selection of library media center materials, as set forth in the board-approved collection development policy, should be followed in the selection of materials. Decisions about selection or reevaluation should not be based on perceived notions about the controversial nature of materials. The school library medial specialist should assume the role of an advocate for youth, rather than a protector of youth.

Intellectual access to information includes the right of students to develop the skills necessary to permit them to acquire materials and critically examine and interpret the information they find. Libary media specialists should examine the nature of information skills instruction. Are library media skills taught in isolation from the instructional curriculum? Are there curriculum constraints such as a heavy reliance on textbook instruction?

In summary, access to information for children and young adults must include an examination of their opportunities for physical and intellectual access. The presence of an LMC alone is not sufficient to guarantee intellectual freedom for students.

Collection Development Policy and Procedures

Public school districts are governed by school boards which are legally responsible for the materials available to students. They delegate leadership and selection coordination of materials to certified library media specialists and administrators under whom the library media specialist works. The collection development policy, which is approved by the school board, establishes the climate in which and the criteria by which libary media collections are developed. The policy may encompass all instructional materials used in the district. The collection development policy should be formulated through the efforts of many who provide leadership and active participation including school library media specialists, teachers, administrators, students, and community members. The policy should promote intellectual freedom through a recognition of the value of information in a variety of formats. Materials should reflect the cultural diversity and pluralistic nature of contemporary American society. The policy should include the American Library Association's Library Bill of Rights and other appropriate intellectual freedom statements from professional associations such as the Association for Educational Communications and Technology, International Reading Association, National Council of Teachers of English, and the National Council for the Social Studies.

The procedures for the evaluation an selection of materials are central to the development of the library media center collection. Among procedures employed by library media specialists are the following: wide use of professional, reputable, selection resources in combination, where possible, with first-hand examination of materials; consultation with school faculty to ascertain their instructional needs and involve them in the selection and review of materials. The strengths and weaknesses of the existing collection, access to other collections, and educational goals at the district and school level also are important considerations in the evaluation and selection of library media center collections.

Library media specialists should give careful attention to the section of the collection development policy dealing with the procedures for reconsideration of materials. Such procedures must be clearly written and thoughtfully considered with a view toward promoting intellectual freedom on behalf of students and teachers. It is critical that the established procedures be systematically followed in dealing with each question, whether the question originates within the district itself or within the community. School library media center collections focus on a direct relationship to the school's instructional curriculum. However, the collection should also be reflective of student needs and interests. These include recreational interests of students, and may particularly include the fiction collection of the libary media center. The collection development policy, therefore, should reflect a recognition of personal and recreational reading, listening, and viewing needs of the students and take into account varying skills, interests, abilities and backgrounds.

Once developed, the collection development policy should be used regularly as the basis for the evaluation and selection of materials. It should be reviewed and revised at least every three years.

Sources of Potential Complaints

Questions about school library media materials can be expected, based on individual as well as organized group concerns. While many may view with alarm any question which arises, every question is not necessarily an effort to censor. Every person has the right to query public school officials regarding the materials that are made available for student use. Providing an understanding of the selection process and the principles upon which libraries exist may go far in answering questions that may be asked. Letting a questioner know that a concern is respectfully received is another another way to respond constructively. Calls for censorship may come from any source, whether conservative or liberal.

A national study in secondary school library media centers (Hopkins, 1991) examined reasons for challenges to materials. Subject areas which formed the basis for such challenges were consistent with most previous studies. Primary grounds for complaints were: sexuality, profanity, obscenity, and morality. Other concerns included: witchcraft and the occult, immaturity of possible student users, nudity, material inconsistent with family values, and violence.

In recent years, a primary basis for challenges from conservative groups, especially religious right groups, has been the belief that public school students are being indoctrinated in the "religions" of secular humanism, New Age, and globalism. Secular humanism is a difficult term to define. It suggests a Christianless force operating in the public schools. Called a religion by some conservative groups, secular humanism is depicted as being responsible for the destruction of God-based family values.

In a similar way, the view of New Age as a religion is also difficult to define, although its focus includes the belief that there are efforts to control the world through a one-world religion and a one-world government. The focus of groups that claim that the "religions" of secular humanism, New Age, and globalism are being promoted in the public schools is broad and includes the total school environment, including the curriculum, textbooks, and library media center materials.

Effectively Dealing with Challenges to Materials

A 1991 national study by Hopkins provided insights into the nature of challenges to materials, and factors that made a difference in whether challenged materials were retained, restricted, or removed. The study focused on public secondary school challenges to library media materials which occurred during a three year period. The findings were based on a 70 percent response from school library media specialists participating in the study, who focused on the most recent, resolved challenge.

Among the factors influencing whether challenged materials were retained or not were the following:

existence and use of the collection development policy during the challenge process;

internal and external support received by the library media specialist during the challenge process, including the support of the principal and teachers;

challenge in writing rather than oral.

The study suggests that the library media specialists who seek consistent implementation of the collection development policy, seek support during the challenge process, and require that challenges to library materials are written have a higher rate of success in retaining challenged materials.

Promotion of Intellectual Freedom

Intellectual freedom must be promoted within the school as well as in the community. Selection of library media center materials, while coordinated by the library media specialist, should actively involve teachers, administrators, and students. Discussions and in-service programs about the philosophy of libraries in general, purpose and objectives of the library media center, and the criteria used in selections should be ongoing, not only for new faculty, but for all faculty. These programs should include building as well as district level staff. School board members also should actively participate. In addition, up-to-date information on a continuing basis will be valuable to the school community.

School personnel must be aggressive in regularly communicating information about the district's educational objectives, the purposes the school library media centers fulfill, and in introducing information about selected materials themselves. The communication can be accomplished through such means as school newsletters, community newspapers and other information media, and parent workshops or presentations on topics such as the place of realism in children's and young adult literature. Communication must be facilitated both inside and outside the district.

An important part of the promotion of intellectual freedom is through example. School board members, administrators, teachers, and library media specialists should demonstrate their support for intellectual freedom. Negative demonstrations that are not supportive of intellectual freedom include: (1) immediate removal of materials when a complaint or challenge first occurs regardless of the policy; (2) full discussion of a complaint in a school board meeting when complaining individuals have not followed established procedures or when such discussion is not on the agenda; (3) precensorship, which is the decision not to select material for the collection because of its perceived potential for controversy; (4) elimination of potentially controversial materials in the collection under the guise of ongoing evaluation; (5) limiting access to a collection by imposing such barriers as restricted shelving or parental permission requirements because the restricted material is potentially controversial. Whether the above acts are conducted openly or in secret, the climate for open access and availability of information directly affects the students who are served.

Conclusion

Intellectual freedom in schools demands the commitment of library media specialists who:

> are active supporters of intellectual freedom committees, coalitions, and associations at all levels (i.e., local, state, regional, national);
>
> practice the selection of materials on the basis of sound educational criteria unbiased by personal, political, social, or religious views;
>
> promote an understanding of the value of information to the young, which includes diverse viewpoints and relevance to today's world;
>
> invite the active participation of teachers in the selection of materials;
>
> encourage and instruct students in gaining further access to information beyond the walls of the school library media center through interlibrary loan and computer networks;
>
> communicate the importance of intellectual freedom in an ongoing manner to principals and teachers;
>
> promote the use of the collection development policy for the selection or reconsideration of materials;
>
> seek support when a challenge to library media center materials occurs.

Intellectual freedom requires that all who are responsible for the education of the young—school board members, administrators, teachers, and library media specialists—work together continually to assure that First Amendment rights and intellectual freedom are a reality for children and young adults.

References

Hopkins, Dianne McAfee. "Challenges to Materials in Secondary School Library Media Centers: Results of a National Study," *Journal of Youth Services in Libraries*, vol. 4, no. 2, (Winter, 1991): p 131–40.

_____. *Factors Influencing the Outcome of Challenges to Materials in Secondary School Libraries: Report of a National Study*. Madison, Wisconsin: School of Library and Information Studies, 1991.

_____. "Toward a Conceptual Model of Factors Influencing the Outcome of Challenges to Library Materials in School Settings." *Library and Information Science Research*, vol. 11, no. 3, (July–September, 1989): 247–271.

McDonald, Frances M. "Information Access for Youth: Issues and Concerns," *Library Trends*, vol. 37, no. 1, (Summer, 1988): 28–42.

Selected Interpretations of the Library Bill of Rights

Access to Resources and Services in the School Library Media Program
Challenged Materials
Evaluating Library Collections
Expurgation of Library Materials
Regulations, Policies, and Procedures Affecting Access to Library Resources and Services
Statement on Labeling

4

Academic Libraries and Intellectual Freedom

Paul B. Cors

Since the function of the academic library is to support the teaching and research programs of the college or university of which it forms a part, the degree to which the library enjoys intellectual freedom will be largely determined by the parent institution's commitment to academic freedom. If the institution is firmly committed to freedom of inquiry in all areas of knowledge, and this commitment has been made formal policy by its governing body, the library should be able to defend itself successfully against external censorship attempts. While it is true that academic libraries are much less frequently the censors' targets than school and public libraries (one would like to believe that this is because the principle of academic freedom enjoys general acceptance, though it may in fact be that academic libraries are not seen as sufficiently influential to merit the censors' attention), this should not cause academic librarians to become complacent; censorship controversies can and will arise, and the library's first line of defense must be the commitment of the college or university itself to academic freedom.

The library, of course, accepts an equally strong obligation to be certain that neither its formal policies nor the conscious or unconscious biases of its staff violate the intellectual freedom of its constituency. Regrettably, there appears to be good reason to believe that in academic libraries, as in all others, the greatest dangers to intellectual freedom are more often internal than external. Even if the parent institution is not wholly committed to academic freedom, the library should still attempt to practice intellectual freedom principles to the extent that it can. While it must be con-

---

Paul B. Cors is a catalog librarian at the University of Wyoming Library, Laramie.

ceded that the library in a college operated by a religious organization, for example, may have to function within doctrinal limits imposed by that organization, the library still has an obligation to provide the most diversified collection possible within those limits; it also has an obligation to inform both its patrons and employees of exactly what those limits are.

Every academic library needs to have a written collection development policy incorporating the principles of the Library Bill of Rights. This policy should be drafted by the Library staff, preferably in cooperation with the faculty library committee if such a group exists, and ratified by the appropriate administrative body of the institution. One common problem can be prevented if the policy states clearly to what extent the library will acquire materials of general interest, including recreational reading, for student use. Copies of the policy should be freely available to students and faculty.

The collection development policy should include a clearly outlined procedure for handling complaints about the presence—or absence—of specific titles or subject areas. All staff members should be thoroughly familiar with both policy and procedure. Standard library complaint forms may need to be adapted for use in academic libraries to include provisions for requests to add materials as well as remove them, since experience suggests that students' complaints are usually of the former type.

The library's cataloging/processing manual should specify that the organization of the collection must not be used as a tool of censorship. If the collection is basically open-stack, definitions of material to be housed in restricted access areas must be carefully drawn.[1] Classifications and subject headings should accurately reflect content (which may mean that decisions to use standard subject headings lists without

---

1. ALA policy on Restricted Access to Library Materials, as revised at the 1991 Annual Conference, is quite clear on this point:
> Libraries are a traditional forum for the open exchange of information. Attempts to restrict access to library materials violate the basic tenets of the Library Bill of Rights.

Recognizing the many historical reasons for restricting access, the revised policy limits acceptable reasons to only those necessary to protect library materials, "for reasons of physical preservation including protection from theft or mutilation," adding the caveat that "[a]ny such policies must be carefully formulated and administered with extreme attention to the principles of intellectual freedom. . ."

Restrictions resulting from donor agreements or contracts for special collections also must be narrowly tailored to respect intellectual freedom. The policy concludes, stating that "[p]ermanent exclusions are not acceptable. The overriding impetus must be to work for free and unfettered access to all documentary heritage."

modification will have to be questioned), and all material in the collection should be listed in the public records of the library.[2]

Unlike public libraries, it is in the area of services—not collections—that academic libraries are more likely to fall short in their devotion to intellectual freedom. In part, this is due to conditions which the library cannot alter: the academic community is a socially stratified one, and this stratification will affect the library. Nevertheless, one of the basic principles of the Library Bill of Rights is equality of access, and the library should strive to follow that principle. It is necessary, therefore, that certain traditional policies followed by many—if not most—academic libraries be reexamined. It is of little merit to develop an excellent collection and then place insurmountable obstacles in the path of those who wish to use that collection.

The primary constituency of the academic library is the students, faculty, and staff of the parent college or university. While most academic libraries provide some service beyond the campus (through interlibrary loan, if nothing else), such service, unless mandated by the charter of a public institution or agreed to by contract, is always a courtesy, not a right; academic libraries do not violate intellectual freedom if off-campus patrons are not given equal treatment with the libraries' prime constituency. Fairness, however, demands that the policies in this area be clearly enunciated and administered evenhandedly.

Circulation policies should be uniform for all patrons and should aim at providing adequate time for the use of material without allowing anyone to monopolize an item at the expense of others. Restrictions on the circulation of materials such as reference books, current journals, or rare books are not inherently in violation of intellectual freedom, provided that they apply equally to all. Reference staffs should respond

---

2. Classification of materials must not include judgments on the content of materials. As stated in the revised (1990) Statement on Labeling:

A variety of private organizations promulgate rating systems and/or review materials as a means of advising either their members or the general public concerning their opinions of the contents and suitability or appropriate age for use of certain books, films, recordings, or other materials. For the library to adopt or enforce any of these private systems, to attach such ratings to library materials, to include them in bibliographic records, library catalogs, or other finding aids, or otherwise to endorse them would violate the Library Bill of Rights.

Publishers, industry groups, and distributors sometimes add ratings to material or include them as part of their packaging. Librarians should not endorse such practices. However, removing or obliterating such ratings—if placed there by or with permission of the copyright holder—could constitute expurgation, which is also unacceptable.

to all requests for assistance with equal diligence, making no distinction based on the "importance" of the patron.

A most difficult question is posed by interlibrary loan. The present general practice of denying this service to undergraduates is incompatible with the Library Bill of Rights. The rationale for this limitation is not altogether indefensible, because faculty and graduate research often does require access to a wider range of materials than undergraduates normally need or any one library can supply. However, libraries should attempt to find some means of meeting the genuine interlibrary loan needs of undergraduates.

A similar problem is limited access to stacks, although again the reasons for the practice have some validity. Still, policies which provide some users with more direct access to the collection than others do not conform to the Library Bill of Rights. Security measures, designed to protect collections from theft, should be applied equally to all patrons, regardless of their status within the academic community.

The widespread replacement of printed information sources with online or compact disc databases can present some special problems. These tools commonly require special training to be used effectively and academic libraries often require fees for their use; both circumstances may create barriers to access. The library must be prepared to provide adequate training for users and do everything possible to provide services without additional cost to the users. The ALA asserts, in section 50.4 of the ALA Policy Manual, that "the charging of fees and levies for information services, including those services utilizing the latest information technology, is discriminatory in publicly supported institutions providing library and information services." Although it may be unrealistic to expect that all fees for database searching be eliminated, all libraries must strive to limit fees and find alternative means to pay for advanced technology.

Any other specialized services which the library provides (for example, photocopying or document delivery) should be available equally to everybody in its primary constituency.

The academic library has the same obligation to respect the privacy of its users as do other types of libraries. Circulation and interlibrary loan files, reference and database searching requests, journal routing lists and similar records are confidential; access to them should be limited to those staff who must use these records to perform their jobs. If such records are sought as evidence in an administrative or judicial hearing, due process must be rigorously followed in making them available to a third party, even in situations (suspected plagiarism, for example) where the integrity of the institution is at stake. Staff must be aware that gossip about library users' interests is not acceptable, however harmless it may seem.

New technologies greatly complicate the issue of confidentiality, and their impact must be carefully considered. Files maintained online, especially in a central computer facility that is used for other purposes by many campus units, may be deliberately or inadvertently invaded without the library's knowledge, so it is essential to maintain the best security system possible. Given the well-publicized cases of computer hackers gaining access to inadequately protected databases and the large body of skilled computer users on most college campuses, the security requirements of an academic library should be carefully established and rigorously fulfilled. Obsolete records such as completed circulation transactions should be purged from the file immediately; any permanent records needed for statistical purposes should not include the names of individuals.

The internal administrative procedures of the library, including its personnel policies, should foster a spirit of intellectual freedom among all staff members. Whether this is best done informally or through a structured program of in-service training will depend upon the size and character of the staff. In either case, it is especially important to include some instruction in the principles of intellectual freedom in the training given to student assistants and other temporary employees, who in most cases are not planning on a library career and are unlikely to be aware of the ethical commitments of the profession. They must also be assured that they will be fully supported by their supervisors when they put these principles into practice.

Finally, the more clearly the library administration exemplifies its own commitment to intellectual freedom, the more likely intellectual freedom will become the foundation for all library programs.

5

Federal Libraries and Intellectual Freedom

Bernadine Abbot Hoduski

The federal library community is composed of a variety of libraries comparable in type to those in the library community as a whole. Federal libraries range from the one-of-a-kind Library of Congress to small school libraries on Native American reservations and to specialized libraries serving executive agencies.

Federal libraries have censorship programs just like other libraries, but these are seldom brought to the attention of the library profession or the public. Many federal librarians feel there is no problem with censorship in government libraries. Others do not agree. Most of them do agree that positive steps should be taken to help prevent possible censorship situations.

Even though federal libraries differ in many respects, they do have some things in common: (1) They must function according to a number of federal laws and regulations; (2) Their mission is usually dictated by the agency to which they belong; (3) Since they are supported by federal taxes they are answerable, directly or indirectly, to all U.S. citizens.

Federal libraries can prevent many problems, including censorship, by following some simple procedures:

1. With the assistance of the agency's lawyer, it should be determined which laws and regulations govern the agency and the library because regulations differ from one agency to the next.

2. An order describing the purpose, functions, and policies of the library should be written, thus officially establishing and protecting the

Bernadine Abbott Hoduski is Professional Staff Member for Library and Distribution Services, Congress of the United States, Joint Committee on Printing, and was the founder of the Government Documents Round Table of the American Library Association.

existence of the library. This order should be signed and distributed by the administrator of the agency.

3. Librarians should take every opportunity to educate the agency administrator, the staff, and the public as to the policies of the Library.

4. Federal libraries should cooperate with each other, comparing policies on book selection, circulation, and other issues. Such comparisons can be used as examples in educating the staff.

5. Library directors should determine whether and how the Freedom of Information Act affects the library. Some federal libraries serve as the agency's public reading room in order to fulfill the requirements of the law, which states that the public must have reasonable access to documents issued by an agency. If the library is the official repository for agency documents, these have to be accessible to the public. If the library keeps classified and unclassified documents, some provision will have to be made to keep these separate. This should be done in consultation with the agency's attorney.

6. If possible, a library committee representing all elements of the agency should be established so materials selection, circulation policies, and other practices will be fair to all. In turn, the library committee can help educate the rest of the agency employees and support library policies.

7. The library should have a written circulation policy, not favoring one department or group in an agency over another. If the library circulates material to the public, it should do so for everyone, not just for a select few. Libraries may decide to loan through another library rather than to individuals. If so, this decision should be publicized. Some agencies have regulations which do not allow those outside the agency to use their library.

8. The library should maintain a written materials selection policy. Even though the subject area is often determined by the mission of the agency, the diversity of views in that subject area must be guarded. An obvious example of censorship would be refusal to buy publications critical of an agency.

9. Finally, the library should develop and implement a policy protecting the confidentiality of library users. Records associating individuals with the materials they borrow should never be released to others—whether requested by employers or colleagues—without the written consent of individual in question.

Because federal libraries are important information links in the decision-making process of the U.S. government, they must be protected from censorship.

6

State Library Agencies and Intellectual Freedom

Bruce E. Daniels

James Madison wrote: "A popular government, without popular information, or the means of acquiring it, is but a Prologue to a Farce or a Tragedy; or perhaps both. Knowledge will forever govern ignorance; and a people who mean to be their own Governors must arm themselves with the power which knowledge gives." Today, more than ever before, information is crucial to the functioning of a democratic society. Information provided by libraries can help citizens and public officials anticipate, keep abreast of, and understand issues confronting our society.

Although the state library agency, as an institution, varies from state to state, every state library agency has responsibility for promoting library development and coordinating interlibrary cooperation. In some states, it is responsible for maintaining a collection, either to serve state government or to serve the residents of the state. Whatever the state library structure may be, it must actively assume the responsibility of fostering the free exchange of information and ideas. In carrying out this responsibility, the state library agency can use a number of techniques in promoting intellectual freedom principles as embodied in the Library Bill of Rights.

Library standards or performance measures are a means by which libraries are evaluated and held accountable. In developing such standards or measures, the state library agency needs to base them upon the philosophy that every individual should have equal access to information and that the citizens of the state should have the opportunity to access library services as envisioned in the Library Bill of Rights. For example, a standard on services for children and young adults might

Bruce E. Daniels is the director, Onondaga County Public Library, Syracuse, New York.

read: "In accordance with the American Library Association's policy statement Free Access to Libraries for Minors, the library shall provide children and young adults access to all materials and services."[1]

Serving as a catalyst, the state library agency must provide support and assistance in creating an environment that provides citizens with access to information. In working with library staffs and trustees, state agency staff should serve as change agents. Boards of Trustees and library administrators should be encouraged to regularly examine the library's policies and programs. The results should lead to policies and practices that support the fundamental tenets of intellectual freedom.

When a local library is faced with a censorship challenge, the state library agency needs to provide support. Advice can be provided on how to handle the situation. The local library may only need a sympathetic listener, or the statewide intellectual freedom network may need to be activated. Whatever is required, the state library agency must insure that the necessary assistance is available.

Continuing education and staff development are key components of library development. The state library agency should offer library staffs and trustees opportunities to explore intellectual freedom issues and to examine what their respective roles are. In addition, library staffs and trustees need training not only in how to handle censorship challenges, but also in what to do to minimize the negative effects of such challenges. Through continuing education activities, the state library agency also provides library staffs and trustees with the opportunity to meet and to share information with their counterparts from other parts of the state. From these activities a support network can grow.

In its leadership capacity, the state library agency must assume legislative leadership and coordination roles at both the state and federal levels. It is critical for the state library agency to monitor state and federal legislation as well as legal opinions. Librarians, trustees, and other interested individuals need to be kept informed about legislative efforts that have an impact on intellectual freedom. In every state there are a number of library advocacy groups—library associations, friends of libraries, trustee organizations—that work for the advancement of library services. State library agencies need to work closely with these organizations and be able to rally them when needed in the legislative arena.

---

1. Rhode Island Department of State Library Services. *Minimum Standards for Rhode Island Public Libraries*. Rhode Island Department of State Library Services, 1983.

As a component of state government, the state library agencies are in a unique position to influence state law and policy. State library administrators are informed about the philosophies of government leaders and knowledgeable about the decision-making processes. Of particular importance is the state library agency's leadership role in guaranteeing the citizens' "right to know." First and foremost, the general public and government officials need to be kept aware of the importance of the free flow of government information. The state library agency needs to monitor the policy and procedure development and implementation relating to the flow of both state and federal government information. If policies and procedures, adverse to the free flow of information, are formulated, the state library agency needs to exert its leadership in changing them.

Technology has provided the means for states to develop sophisticated networks. Since the operation of these networks is costly, there is a tendency to question the seriousness of any user's request. In addition, many libraries charge user fees. It is imperative that state library agencies strongly encourage libraries to provide equal access to information resources for all library users regardless of socioeconomic status.

In many states, the state library agency maintains a collection that is used for government research or as a research library for state residents. It should serve as a model for the rest of the state. The collection should be developed from a selection policy that embodies the principles of the Library Bill of Rights. Additionally, the policies governing the use of the collection should be reflective of intellectual freedom principles.

The state library agency in any state plays a pivotal role in the development of library services. A significant part of that role is to ensure that citizens have the best possible access to information. This access will, in turn, help preserve our democratic society as we now know it and will allow citizens to participate fully in the society.

PART IV

Intellectual Freedom
and the Law

1

School Library Censorship and the Courts: Before Hazelwood

William D. North

During the 1970s, librarians, parents, teachers, and students, often supported by the Freedom to Read Foundation, began to challenge in court the censorious removal of books from school libraries. The results of such litigation efforts, by and large, were promising, although the courts, including the U.S. Supreme Court, offered conflicting interpretations of the issues presented, leaving the legal foundation to challenges to book removal uncertain. As of this writing, by far the most important case was *Board of Education, Island Trees (New York) Union Free School District 26, v. Pico*, which was decided by the U.S. Supreme Court on June 25, 1982. But that decision, far from resolving the thorny legal questions raised by book removal, did little more than establish that these issues are unlikely to be resolved by the Supreme Court, at least as constituted in 1982, under any rationale commanding even a majority of the justices, let alone a consensus.

The *Pico* case, even though it did not produce a majority opinion, is, however, one of the most significant first amendment decisions to be rendered by the Supreme Court since its obscenity decisions of June 1973. Like the obscenity decisions, *Pico* reflects the continuing and fundamental schism existing between two factions of the Court concerning the scope and application of the First Amendment.

The issue presented by *Pico* was whether "the First Amendment imposes limitations upon the exercise by a local school board of its discretion to remove library books from high school and junior school libraries." The case involved the right of one junior high school and four

William D. North served as Freedom to Read Foundation General Counsel, 1969-1980; Vice-President, 1980-81; and President, 1981-1984. This chapter is a revised version of an article, "Pico and the Challenge to Books in Schools," which appeared in the November 1982 *Newsletter on Intellectual Freedom*.

high school students to challenge as unconstitutional the removal by the Island Trees Union Free School District board of all copies of nine books from the school libraries under the board's control. The board removed the books because they were, in the board's view, "anti-American, anti-Christian, anti-Semitic, and just plain filthy." The board justified the removal on the ground of its "duty, or moral obligation, to protect the children in our schools from this moral danger as surely as from physical and medical dangers."

Five of the books were removed despite the report of a Book Review Committee appointed by the board itself that recommended their retention under standards of "educational suitability," "good taste," "relevance," and appropriateness to age and grade level. The board gave no reasons for rejecting the recommendation of the committee it had appointed.

The district court granted summary judgment in favor of the Board of Education holding that

> While removal of such books from a school library may . . . reflect a misguided educational philosophy, it does not constitute a sharp and direct infringement of any first amendment right.

On appeal to a three-judge panel of the United States Court of Appeals for the Second Circuit, the judgment of the district court was reversed by a two-to-one majority and the case remanded for trial.

On *certiorari* to the Supreme Court, the decision of the Second Circuit was affirmed by a vote of 5 to 4, with Justice Brennan writing the plurality opinion, in which Justices Marshall and Stevens joined and in which Justice Blackmun joined with the judgment and concurred in part in a separate opinion. Justice White concurred in the judgment, thereby constituting the majority, while Chief Justice Burger and Justices Powell, Rehnquist, and O'Connor dissented in four separate opinions, with Justices Powell, Rehnquist, and O'Connor joining in Chief Justice Burger's dissent and the Chief Justice and Justice Powell joining in Justice Rehnquist's dissent.

Although Justice White clearly opposed the grant of *certiorari*, the issue presented by *Pico* was preeminently ripe for consideration by the Supreme Court. Starting in 1971 and continuing throughout the decade of the 1970s, courts were encountering with increasing frequency cases in which school boards were accused of, and even admitted to, removing books from their school libraries, not because of obsolescence, lack of shelf space, or lack of relevance, but rather because the books were deemed inconsistent or contrary to the "value inculcation" objectives of the curriculum. As in the *Pico* case, these cases consistently involved the removal of a library work previously identified as worthy of acquisition under accepted book selection criteria. Likewise, they involved books which were elective reading and not part of the required curriculum. Moreover, they were invariably removed without regard for established procedures for "culling" or "winnowing" works no longer deemed appropriate for retention.

The earliest of the school library book suppression opinions was the Second Circuit's 1972 decision in *Presidents Council District 25* v. *Community School Board No. 25*. There, the court upheld the removal of *Down These Mean Streets* by Piri Thomas from the library over the objection of parents, teachers, the local PTA, librarians, and students, as well as the principal of a junior high school in the district. The court declined "to review either the wisdom or the efficacy of the determination of the Board" on the ground that it was precluded by the Supreme Court's decision in *Epperson* v. *Arkansas* from intervening "in the resolution of conflicts which arise in the daily operation of school systems and which do not directly and sharply implicate basic constitutional values."

In *Presidents Council* the court did not perceive the elimination of the book as involving an effort to aid or oppose religion as did the state statute prohibiting texts teaching evolution which *Epperson* condemned. Nor did the court perceive the elimination of the book from the library as analogous to the ban on nondisruptive silent speech which the Supreme Court condemned in *Tinker* v. *Des Moines Independent Community School District*.

In 1976, the Court of Appeals for the Sixth Circuit was confronted, in *Minarcini* v. *Strongsville City School District*, with a challenge to the school district's removal of Joseph Heller's *Catch 22* and Kurt Vonnegut's *Cat's Cradle* and *God Bless You, Mr. Rosewater* from its school library. The court found that the "Board removed the books because it found them objectionable in content and because it felt it had the power, unfettered by the First Amendment, to censor the school library for subject matter which the Board members found distasteful."

In contrast to the Second Circuit, the Sixth Circuit held that "[t]he removal of books from a school library is a much more serious burden upon freedom of classroom discussion than the action found unconstitutional in *Tinker* v. *Des Moines Independent Community School District*. . . ." It based this holding first, on its perception that "[a] library is a mighty resource in the free marketplace of ideas, and second, on its understanding that the First Amendment protects the "right to know," because as Justice Blackmun stated in *Virginia State Board of Pharmacy* v. *Virginia Citizens Consumers Council, Inc.*, "where a speaker exists . . . the protection afforded is to the communication, to its source and to its recipients both."

Relying on the *Minarcini* rationale, in 1978, the Massachusetts federal district court required a Chelsea school committee to return to the high school library an anthology entitled *Male and Female under 18*, which included a poem the committee found "objectionable," "obnoxious," "filthy," "vile and offensive garbage." (*Right to Read Defense Committee* v. *School Committee of the City of Chelsea*) The *Chelsea* Court found that the poem was "tough but not obscene" and "no substantial governmental interest was served by cutting off students access to 'Male and Female' in the library." As in *Minarcini*, the court distinguished between the school board's power to control curriculum content and its power to control library collections. It also distinguished between the school board's power to select books for the library and its power to remove books, once selected.

Adopting the *Chelsea* analysis, the Federal District Court for New Hampshire, in *Salvail* v. *Nashua Board of Education*, required the Nashua Board of Education to return to its high school library copies of *Ms.* magazine which had been removed because they allegedly "contained advertisements for 'vibrators, contraceptives, materials dealing with lesbianism and witchcraft and gay material' as well as advertisements for trips to Cuba, records by communist folk singers, and a procommunist newspaper." The *Nashua* Court found that the board had failed "to demonstrate a substantial and legitimate government interest sufficient to warrant the removal of *Ms.* magazine from the Nashua High School Library."

The 1980s opened with two Circuits presented with three cases challenging the removal of materials from high school libraries. In two of these cases the challenge was rejected. The third case was *Pico*.

The Seventh Circuit rejected the challenge in *Zykan* v. *Warsaw Community School Corporation*. There, the school board ordered the removal of several books from the high school library, including *Growing Up Female in America*, *Go Ask Alice*, *The Bell Jar*, and *The Stepford Wives*.

The uncontroverted record in *Zykan* showed that the school board turned the "offending" books over to complaining citizens who caused them to be publicly burned. While the court condemned this ceremony as "contemptible," it nevertheless concluded that the complaint failed to state a cause of action. The court held that

> two factors tend to limit the relevance of "academic freedom" at the secondary school level. First, the student's right to and need for such freedom is bounded by the level of his or her intellectual development. . . . Second, the importance of secondary schools in the development of intellectual faculties is only one part of a broad formative role encompassing the encouragement and nurturing of

those fundamental social, political, and moral values that will permit a student to take his place in the community.

By the operation of these factors, the court concluded that

complaints filed by secondary school students to contest the educational decisions of local authorities are sometimes cognizable but generally must cross a relatively high threshold before entering upon the field of a constitutional claim suitable for federal court litigation.

While the Seventh Circuit was deciding *Zykan,* the Second Circuit was presented with two opportunities to reconsider its 1972 *Presidents Council* opinion. The first was the *Pico* case and the second was *Bicknell* v. *Vergennes Union High School Board of Directors.* Decided the same day, by the same panel, both *Pico* and *Bicknell* involved the removal of books of considerable literary reputation from the school library. The dismissal of the complaint in *Vergennes* was affirmed and the dismissal of the complaint in *Pico* was reversed, both by two-to-one majorities. In each case, one judge saw both cases as an unconstitutional effort to purge the school library of ideas deemed inconsistent with the value inculcation objectives of the curriculum. Also, in each case, one judge saw both cases as an appropriate and constitutionally proper exercise of the value inculcation function traditionally assigned secondary education. The deciding judge in each case distinguished between *Bicknell* and *Pico* on the basis of the board's motive for removal. In *Bicknell* he found the motive to be the books' "vulgar and indecent language," which justified removal, while in *Pico* he found the motive to be the books' "ideas" or content, apart from vulgar or indecent language, which did not justify removal.

While all of these cases, including *Pico,* arose in the context of First Amendment challenges to the removal of books from school libraries, they all turned on differences in judicial perceptions of the proper role of school officials in the educational process. As a consequence, the primary effect of the Supreme Court's consideration in *Pico* was to identify what must be characterized as a fundamental philosophical dispute over the nature and function of elementary and secondary education in America. This dispute, revealed most graphically in the *Pico* opinions, has divided the Court into two substantially equal and determined factions.

One faction, led by Chief Justice Burger, clearly perceives elementary and secondary education to be "indoctrinative" or "prescriptive" in purpose. The other faction, led by Justice Brennan, clearly perceives such education to involve an "analytic" objective which cannot constitutionally be subordinated to or frustrated by the indoctrinative function.

Under the indoctrinative or prescriptive concept of education, information and accepted truths are furnished to a theoretically passive, absorbent student. The function of teacher, school, and educational materials is to convey these truths, rather than create new wisdom. On the other hand, the analytic educational concept contemplates the examination of data and values in a way that involves the teacher, school, and students in a search for truth.

The self-evident source of Justice Brennan's concern with Chief Justice Burger's perception of schools as "vehicles for 'inculcating fundamental values necessary to the maintenance of a democratic political system'" is that, so used, students will become nothing more than "closed circuit recipients of only that which the State chooses to communicate."

Justice Brennan's concern with laws, official conduct, and policies which "cast a pall of orthodoxy over the classroom" has been a consistent, recurrent, and intensifying theme in opinions he has written in First Amendment cases since he first expressed it in *Keyishian* v. *Board of Regents*. There he contended that, "the classroom is peculiarly the 'marketplace of ideas,'" and that "the Nation's future depends upon leaders trained through wide exposure to that robust exchange of ideas which discovers truth 'out of a multitude of tongues, [rather] than through any kind of authoritative selection.'"

Justice Brennan, in his dissent in *Paris Adult Theatre I* v. *Slaton*, revealed, perhaps most clearly, the source and nature of his fear of the "value inculcation" model of education. There he quoted the following language from the Court's 1923 decision in *Meyer* v. *Nebraska*:

> In order to submerge the individual and develop ideal citizens, Sparta assembled the males at seven into barracks and entrusted their subsequent education and training to official guardians. Although such measures have been deliberately approved by men of great genius, their ideas touching the relations between individual and State were wholly different from those upon which our institutions rest.

Justice Brennan's insistence that schools function as "marketplaces" of ideas as well as a means of "promoting respect for authority and traditional values be they social, moral, or political," reveals his doubt about the ability of a political majority to resist imposing its orthodoxy at the expense of individual inquiry and intellectual freedom.

As Justice Brennan's First Amendment opinions consistently reflect his abiding concern for individual freedom of inquiry, Justice Burger's First Amendment opinions, in *Pico* and other cases, reflect his equally abiding concern for the promotion and protection of the "social interest in order and morality."

Having concluded that schools may legitimately be used for inculcating "fundamental values," Chief Justice Burger has no hesitation in granting school authorities "broad discretion to fulfill that obligation," including the right to make "content based decisions about the appropriateness of retaining materials in the school library and curriculum." Justice Burger's concern with the conduct of school authorities is not that they may impose orthodoxy in the classroom, but rather that they may impose an orthodoxy that does not accurately reflect community values. This risk, however, Chief Justice Burger dismisses summarily on the basis of the following syllogism: "[L]ocal control of education involves democracy in a microcosm" because "in most public schools in the United States the parents have a large voice in the school," and, therefore, "through participation in the election of school board members, parents influence, if not control, the direction of their children's education." And because "a school board is not a giant bureaucracy far removed from accountability for its actions; it is truly 'of the people and by the people,' " it follows that "a school board reflects its constituency in a very real sense and thus could not long exercise unchecked discretion in its choice to acquire or remove books." Therefore, "if parents disagree with the educational decisions of the school board, they can take steps to remove the board members from office."

The empirical basis for this model of parent-teacher-student-school board relationships is, however, not readily identifiable. Less than twenty percent of the voters are parents of elementary and secondary school children. The six-year average term of a school board member nationwide makes change in board composition and orientation a process requiring years. In most communities the school system, governed by the school board, is larger in terms of bureaucracy, budget, and manpower than any other government activity.

Total reliance on participative political solutions to controversies involving value inculcation is difficult to reconcile with the highly charged circumstances which almost invariably surround the removal of library materials. In *Zykan*, the removal was demanded not by parents, but by an organization of senior citizens which then burned the books. In *Chelsea*, the offending book was removed on the complaint of a single parent and over the objection of many. The celebrated Kanawha County, West Virginia, textbook controversy prompted death threats, school boycotts, attacks on school buses, and bombing of schools. Even in *Pico*, the books were banned from the library, not on the basis of a complaint from a local parent, but on the basis of an "objectionable book list" prepared by an organization called Concerned Citizens and Taxpayers for Decent School Books of Baton Rouge, Louisiana, and distributed to three members of the Island Trees School Board at a meeting of a "conservative" organization in Watkins Glen, New York.

Chief Justice Burger's solution to the failure of a school board to reflect correctly the community values to be inculcated by the secondary school appears philosophically consistent with his solution for those whose values are not represented in the curricular orthodoxy. "They," says Chief Justice Burger, "have alternative sources to the same end. Books may be acquired from book stores, public libraries, or other alternative sources unconnected with the unique environment of the local public schools."

Justice Rehnquist, in his *Pico* dissent, joined by the Chief Justice, expressed the same perception in these words:

> When it acts as an educator, at least at the elementary and secondary school level, the government is engaged in inculcating social values and knowledge in relatively impressionable young people. . . . In short, actions by the government as educator do not raise the same First Amendment concerns as actions by the government as sovereign.

The willingness of no fewer than four justices of the Supreme Court to accept and endorse this view of the First Amendment's application to secondary education is a significant indication of the philosophical change which has occurred on the Court since 1943, when it held, in *West Virginia State Board of Education* v. *Barnette*, that "the Fourteenth Amendment, as now applied to the States, protects the citizens against the State itself and all of its creatures—Boards of Education not excepted."

But even more to the point is Justice Jackson's observation in *Barnette* that

> Probably no deeper division of our people could proceed from any provocation than from finding it necessary to choose what doctrine and whose program public educational officials may compel youth to unite in embracing. . . . the First Amendment to our Constitution was designed to avoid these ends by avoiding these beginnings.

The concept that secondary school can, consistent with the First Amendment, be reduced to a purely indoctrinative function serving the will of any transient political majority which might gain control of the system appears as a repudiation of the very purpose for which this amendment was adopted. That purpose was not to protect the rights *of* the majority, but rather to protect the rights of the minority *from* the majority. As Justice Jackson put it in *Thomas* v. *Collins*:

> This liberty was not protected because the forefathers expected its use would always be agreeable to those in authority or that its exercise always would be wise, temperate, or useful to society. As I read their intentions, this liberty was protected because they knew of no other way by which free men could conduct representative democracy.

The concept that the secondary school can constitutionally be restricted to a value inculcating mechanism is affirmatively counterproductive to the society and the people in at least three fundamental respects: first, the concept absolutely guarantees that secondary schools will become political and ideological battlegrounds. It assures the "winner" of the competition for control of the school system, for the time he can remain in control, the right, not only to control curriculum content, but also to purge the school library of competing ideas. This is an opportunity no demagogue or ideologue can or will resist, and the Kanawha County chaos will be the norm, not the exception.

Second, the concept is in direct opposition to the objective of educational integration recognized by the Supreme Court as a constitutional mandate since *Brown* v. *Board of Education*. The success of such integration is a function of, and is measured by, not merely the numerical mix of races, religions, and nationalities in a school, but also in the capacity of the school to accommodate a variety of cultural, social, economic, and political perspectives and values. Educational parochialism is a fountainhead of bigotry and such parochialism is promoted, not deterred, by an indoctrinative mechanism which brooks no opposing viewpoints and values. Indeed, the very utility of the school as an "assimilative force" in our society is frustrated if the values which it inculcates are mere functions of the accident of geography, school district boundary or school board composition at any point in time.

Finally, and perhaps most inconsistent philosophically with the "values on which our society rests," is the concept that the secondary public school, unlike the institution of higher learning, can be restricted to a narrow indoctrinative function. This constitutes nothing more nor less than constitutionally protected "educational elitism." The distinction which Justice Rehnquist makes in *Pico* between the application of the First Amendment to secondary schools and its application to institutions of higher education is implicitly based on the factually unsupportable conclusions of the seventh circuit in *Zykan* that "high school students lack . . . intellectual skills necessary for taking full advantage of the marketplace of ideas . . . ," and that the student's need for academic freedom "is bounded by the level of his or her intellectual development."

This theory that access to the "marketplace of ideas" is reserved only to those who have the financial, physical, or mental capacity or the personal or professional interest to enter what the *Zykan* court described as "the rarefied atmosphere of the college or university" seems fundamentally at variance with the great tradition of American public education. Of particular concern is the notion that the "need" for access to the marketplace of ideas is a function of intellectual development, when most educators recognize such access as "indispensable" to intellectual development.

The plurality opinion in *Pico* rejects the concept that there are no limits to the measures or means which secondary school authorities may employ to inculcate values in their students. It does so by recognizing a constitutional "right to receive information." Although such right is condemned by Justices Burger, Rehnquist, and Powell as having simply "no application to the one public institution which, by its very nature, is a place for the selective conveyance of ideas," even they do not deny that the "right to receive information" has long been recognized by the Court as an indispensable and constitutionally protected corollary to the rights of free speech and press. As James Madison expressed it, "A popular Government, without popular information, or the means of acquiring it, is but a Prologue to a Farce or a Tragedy, or perhaps both."

Specific recognition of the "right to receive information" is of paramount importance to what has now become a "knowledge society." Knowledge is power and access to all our society has to offer. The existence of the "right to receive information" does not negate the indoctrinative function of secondary schools. It merely requires that such function be performed by persuasion and example, by focus and emphasis, and by selection and presentation, rather than by suppression and excision.

The judicial recognition in *Pico* of a "right to receive information" and of the special role played by the school library in implementing this right, however limited in its support among the Justices, offers a significant line of legal defense against censorship. The judicial debate over the nature and role of public education and over the applicability of the First Amendment to public schools will continue. But the hope which the largely positive outcome of the *Pico* case represents for the cause of intellectual freedom could not be more timely. Historic institutions, values, and traditions are being buffeted by winds of change. But, as President Kennedy observed, "freedom and security are but opposite sides of the same coin—and the free expression of ideas is not more expendable but far more essential in a period of challenge and crisis."

2

School Library Censorship and the Courts: After Hazelwood

Robert S. Peck

Parents often agonize over what they will allow their children to do. Now that the kids are eight and ten, how late should they be allowed to stay up? Are they watching too much television? Are there certain magazines or books that they should not be allowed to read? These are difficult questions for which there are no right answers that serve all families. Still, parents hold a unique position of authority. Their decisions, at least in the home and to the extent they can exercise control, are unappealable. The only reason a parent need give is: "because I say so."

Although the same temptations to control youthful expression and access to material are present in the classroom, the same finality does not necessarily appy to decisions made by educational authorities, particularly when the suitability of books for children is involved. School officials must comply with the right of free expression, guaranteed by the First Amendment. Just how the First Amendment applies to the school book issue and what violates that constitutional mandate remains ill-defined under current judicial precedents.

Courts have had particular difficulty in ruling on these issues. The dilemma the courts face in these cases arise from two seemingly conflicting legal principles: freedom of expression and judicial restraint. The courts have interpreted the free-speech guarantee to disable a public school official from claiming parent-like authority to make arbitrary and unappealable decisions about the books available to students. In an important 1982 U.S. Supreme Court case, *Island Trees Union*

Robert S. Peck, an attorney, is the Legislative Counsel of the American Civil Liberties Union, Washington, District Columbia, and author of several books in the field of constitutional law. He served as a member of the Freedom to Read Fountation Board of Trustees 1987–91 and as president of the Board 1988–90.

Free School District No. 26 v. *Pico*,[1] several students brought a lawsuit seeking the return of nine books that had been removed by the board of education from the school library's shelves. The school officials justified the books' removal on the grounds that the banished publications were "anti-American, anti-Christian, anti-Semitic, and just plain filthy."[2] In upholding the students' right to sue in this case, a clear majority of the justices agreed that school boards do not have unfettered authority to select library books and First Amendment rights are implicated when books are removed arbitrarily. An overwhelming majority of the Court also condemned politically motivated book removals.

The Court's decision, however, was a fractured one, with seven of the nine justices writing separate opinions. While the Court held that the First Amendment prevents government officials, which includes public school officials, from denying access to ideas with which they disagree, the justices strongly suggested that decisions based on educational suitability would be upheld, particularly where a regular system of review using standardized guidelines was followed. The Court's caveat about educational aptness stands as a proxy for the judicial restraint principle. It is a longstanding judicial practice to avoid interfering in areas where the courts have little expertise or license to act. In the field of education, this principle manifests itself through judicial recognition that "the education of the Nation's youth is primarily the responsibility of parents, teachers, and state and local school officials, and not of federal judges."[3] In the 1988 *Hazelwood School District* v. *Kuhlmeier*[4] decision, the Supreme Court added: "It is only when the decision to censor a school-sponsored publication, theatrical production, or other vehicle of student expression has no valid educational purpose that the First Amendment is so 'directly and sharply implicate[d],' as to require judicial intervention to protect students' constitutional rights."[5]

In *Hazelwood*, the Court found no constitutional bar to a principal's conduct when he removed two pages of a student newspaper produced as part of a high-school journalism class. The Court held that teachers, principals, and school boards may legitimately make decisions that might otherwise smack of unconstitutionality, in order to further the school's educational mission. The Court declared that school-sponsored expressive activities can be subjected to content control as long as the

---

1. *Board of Education, Island Trees Union Free School District No. 26* v. *Pico*, 457 U.S. 853, 102 S.Ct. 2799, 73 L.Ed.2d 435 (1982).

2. *Pico* at 2803, 457 U.S. 857.

3. *Hazelwood School District* v. *Kuhlmeier*, 56 U.S.L.W. 4082 (1988).

4. *Hazelwood School District* v. *Kuhlmeier*, 484 U.S. 260, 108 S.Ct. 562, 98 L.Ed.2d 592 (1988).

5. *Hazelwood*, 108 S.Ct. 562, 571 (1988).

censorious conduct is "reasonably related to legitimate pedagogical concerns."[6] Many critics have branded the *Hazelwood* decision a rogue elephant upsetting the field of established First Amendment precedents because it appears to place educationally motivated censorship beyond the ambit of First Amendment inquiry. The Court, however, has always been enamored of the notion that legitimate educational purposes can justify some infringement of free expression. In a 1969 landmark decision, *Tinker* v. *Des Moines Independent Community School District*,[7] the Court held that neither "students [n]or teachers shed their constitutional rights to freedom of speech or expression at the schoolhouse gate."[8] Yet, in the same case, the Court also recognized school officials could suppress speech when "necessary to avoid material and substantial interference with school work or discipline . . . or the rights of others."[9]

When the issue is the removal of school library books, justifications based on educational suitability and interference with the learning environment require courts to answer a number of related questions: when is a decision to remove books actually based on legitimate educational reasons, and when is it based on constitutionally impermissible ones? How can the litigants prove what was in the mind of the censor in order to demonstrate his or her true motivation? When someone dislikes the viewpoint a book advocates, cannot a rationale based on plausible educational objections insulate an unconstitutionally motivated book banning from judicial inquiry?

These are questions likely to be confronted over a period of time. As yet, they remain unsettled. Still, one pattern is already discernable. The most plausible "educational reason," in the eyes of the courts, for removing a book is because it is vulgar or indecent. Vulgarity or indecency, of course, are not constitutionally justifiable reasons for banning a work from a public library. Only a higher standard, obscenity, can. "The special characteristics of the school environment," however, allow the age of the likely audience to be a constitutionally permissible deciding factor, according to recent court decisions. In virtually every instance where the censorship act has been upheld, it has been over the sexual content of the work. Thus, in *Seyfried* v. *Walton* (1981),[10] the U.S. Court of Appeals for the Third Circuit sided with a school superintendent who canceled the play *Pippin*, because even an edited version of it had too much sexual content. In underground newspaper cases,

---

6. *Hazelwood*, 108 S.Ct. 562, 571 (1988).

7. *Tinker* v. *Des Moines School District*, 393 U.S. 503, 89 S.Ct. 733, 21 L.Ed.2d 731 (1969).

8. *Tinker*, 89 S.Ct. 736.

9. *Tinker*, 89 S.Ct. 739.

10. *Seyfried* v. *Walton*, 572 F. Supp. 235 (D. Del. 1981).

federal courts have approved of school guidelines that limit the distribution of publications on campus if they are "obscene to minors," "libelous," "pervasively indecent or vulgar," or likely to cause "a material and substantial disruption of the proper and orderly operation of the school or school activities." Overwhelmingly, the issue has remained indecency and vulgarity.

The strongly offending nature of speech that contains a high degree of sexual reference was a critical factor in the Supreme Court's decision in *Bethel School District No. 403* v. *Fraser* (1986).[11] Matthew Fraser, a high school student, was suspended from school for making sexually suggestive remarks in a student-government assembly. Fraser challenged his suspension unsuccessfully. The Supreme Court, in an opinion written by Chief Justice Warren Burger, a dissenter in the *Island Trees* case, held that "[i]t does not follow . . . that simply because the use of an offensive form of expression may not be prohibited to adults making what the speaker considers a political point, that the same latitude must be permitted to children in a public school."[12] Chief Justice Burger went on to declare, "[t]he undoubted freedom to advocate unpopular and controversial views in schools and classrooms must be balanced against the society's countervailing interest in teaching students the boundaries of socially appropriate behavior."[13]

Applying the Supreme Court's approach in *Hazelwood*, the Eleventh Circuit upheld a school board's removal of a previously approved class textbook because of the material's perceived vulgarity and sexual explicitness. In *Virgil* v. *School Board of Columbia County* (1989),[14] the book's banishment to locked storage was occasioned by selections from *Lysistrata*, written around 411 B.C. by Aristophanes, and *The Miller's Tale*, written around 1385 by Geoffrey Chaucer. For judicial purposes, the classical nature of the material was irrelevant. Although the court upheld the school board's censorship action, the judges felt compelled to "seriously question how young persons just below the age of majority can be harmed by these masterpieces of Western literature."[15] Instead, the court focused on the fact that these were materials used within the curriculum and thus bearing the imprimatur of school approval. It then found that the reason for the textbook's removal from the curriculum was the passages' "explicit sexuality and excessively vulgar language,"[16] which it held to be a legitimate pedagogical con-

---

11. *Bethel School District No. 403* v. *Fraser*, 478 U.S. 675, 106 S.Ct. 3159, 92 L.Ed. 549 (1986).

12. *Bethel*, 478 U.S. 682, 106 S.Ct. 3164.

13. *Bethel*, 478 U.S. 681, 106 S.Ct. 3163.

14. *Virgil* v. *School Board of Columbia County*, 862 F.2d 1517 (11th Cir. 1989).

15. *Id.*

16. *Id.*

cern. Ironically, the court found the school board's action reasonable because the textbook, as well as other versions of the disputed selections, remained available in the school library, thereby suggesting that yet a different standard of analysis would be apropos to the removal of a book from a school library. That same approach, differentiating between curricular activity and other activities within the school environment, was adopted by a federal court in New York in the case of *Romano* v. *Harrington* (1989),[17] where a faculty advisor's responsibility for supervising the content of an extracurricular student newspaper was at issue. These cases, building on the Supreme Court's *Hazelwood* decision, appear to establish that there are different levels of constitutional protection for books and other publications depending on whether the material is removed from a public library, a school library, or a classroom.

In contrast to the cases where there is evidence of indecency or obscenity, other educational purposes justifying censorship have been more difficult to prove. In *Pratt* v. *Independent School District No. 831* (1982),[18] the U.S. Court of Appeals for the Eighth Circuit found the removal of a film version of "The Lottery" and a related film trailer from the curriculum unconstitutional. The films had been part of the curriculum for five years, but were excised after parents and other citizens complained about the story's violence and its impact on students' religious and family values. The court declared that the film was eliminated because of its "ideological content" in contravention of the First Amendment.

It may seem difficult to conceive how a description of violence or an assault on traditional values may be protected by the First Amendment, while mere sexual innuendo may not. The explanation is more cultural than legal. A society that values intellectual freedom can oppose controversial notions, but, at the same time, proudly defend the right of anyone to express those insidious ideas. That is the essence of a free society—to allow ideas to compete with each other for majority approval. Yet, sex is a different category of expression. That is why the Supreme Court has repeatedly held that obscenity falls outside the bounds of protected free speech. (The Oregon Supreme Court ruled in 1987 that obscenity comes within the free speech protections of that state's constitution and has done so without bringing about the moral downfall of the state). Society's sexual taboos explain why violent movies and television programs are often accessible to minors, but those with "adult content" are not. If there is a societal consensus on any free speech issues, it is that children should not be exposed to sexual con-

17. *Romano* v. *Harrington*, 725 F.Supp. 687 (D.N.Y. 1989).
18. *Pratt* v. *Independent School District*, 670 F.2d 771 (8th Cir. 1982).

tent. If this means that children's free expression rights are less than adults', society does not appear to mind.

This means that the books most likely to be the successful targets of censors are those with a degree of sexuality that some educational authority considers harmful to minors or disruptive to the educational mission of the school. Those committed to intellectual freedom must be prepared to challenge that rationale, especially when it is actually a subterfuge for ideological objections.

Still, sex is not the only target of censors. Religious fundamentalists have been the instigators of an increasing number of censorship incidents. They have been more successful in influencing local school policies than they have been in winning legal victories.

Many of these deeply religious individuals see the books used in schools and the ideas contained in them as assaults on their fundamentalist views, attacks aimed at leading their children away from the parents' religion. Their counterattacks on books are a means of self-defense, but also an indication of their intolerance for other viewpoints.

In 1985, more than 130 textbook censorship incidents took place, spread over 44 states. The numbers show no sign of diminishing. Three recent cases gained a certain notoriety. In Hawkins County, Tennessee, *The Diary of Anne Frank* and *The Wizard of Oz* were among the books accused of being "anti-Christian." *Anne Frank*, the fundamentalists claimed, suggested that all religions were the same in a passage that indicated that any religious belief could serve as a source of strength in trying times. The statement was antithetical to the objecting parents' fundamentalist tenets that held there is only one true religion. *Oz* promoted witchcraft and self-reliance at the expense of trust in God, according to its detractors. Other books were objected to for promoting feminism and other philosophies that the claimants found heretical. Although the fundamentalists were ultimately unsuccessful in their lawsuit, *Mozert* v. *Hawkins County Board of Education* (1987),[19] controversies such as these have ripple effects that chill the vitality of intellectual freedom. Rather than face further objections from the fundamentalist parents behind the lawsuit, the school involved denied a group of students permission to stage *Anne Frank* as a play. In this incident, no one came out the winner. The religious fundamentalists lost their lawsuit, but the school was cowed into playing it safe and avoiding controversy because of the high cost in emotional energy, time, and dollars in standing up for First Amendment values. Unfortunately, the cause of intellectual freedom is only served when people are willing to fight. Liberty erodes when controversy is avoided, rather than confronted.

---

19. *Mozert* v. *Hawkins County Board of Education*, 827 F.2d 1058 (6th Cir. 1987).

In Mobile, Alabama, the issue was whether the school was attempting to foist a religion called "secular humanism" on the children. Seeking changes in the curriculum and the removal of some 45 textbooks, a lawsuit, *Smith* v. *Board of School Commissioners* (1987)[20] was brought by 624 Christian Evangelicals. At the heart of their complaint was a claim that textbook publishers and classroom teachers were denying any role to religion in American society out of a misplaced fear of breaching the constitutional separation of church and state. In its place, their theory stated, secular humanism, an antireligious "religion," was being promoted and this, in fact, violated the concept of separation. While many could agree with the first part of their claim—that mention of religion had been so removed from the curriculum as to become an educational disservice—their solution, censorship of existing materials, violated free expression, as the U.S. Court of Appeals for the Eleventh Circuit held in the case. The answer was not less speech, but more. Like the attraction of the proverbial better mousetrap, the publication of better textbooks—with an appropriately balanced treatment of the role of religion in American society—would naturally supplant the watered-down texts then in use as schools beat a path to the publisher of the improved texts.

The third case, *Edwards* v. *Aguillard* (1987),[21] was the latest chapter in the continuing battle over Darwinian evolution that dates back to the 1925 "monkey trial" of John T. Scopes. Seeking "equal time" for the biblical story of Genesis, a 1981 Louisiana law outlawed the teaching of evolution in the public schools unless "creation science" was also taught. In its decision, the Supreme Court overturned the law as an unconstitutional attempt to inject a particular religious belief into the public schools.

Challenges to our First Amendment freedoms are continuous, often variations on themes that have come before. There are no final victories. Ultimately, it is not the courts, but the people who must take a stand to protect their liberty. Despite the protection afforded us by the existence of the First Amendment, our precious freedoms remain only when people are knowledgeable about the challenges to our free expression rights and participate in resolving the issues. Intellectual freedom is, as Andrew Hamilton said in defense of colonial printer John Peter Zenger, "the best Cause."

---

20. *Smith* v. *Board of School Commissioners of Mobile (Ala.) County*, 827 F.2d 684 (11th Cir. 1987).

21. *Edwards* v. *Aguillard*, 107 S.Ct. 2573, 96 L.Ed.2d 510 (1987).

3

The Buckley Amendment: Student Privacy *v.* Parents' Right to Know

Andréa Gambino and Anne E. Levinson

The *Family Educational and Privacy Rights Act of 1974*—commonly referred to as the Buckley Amendment after it's sponsor, Senator James Buckley of New York—was designed to protect student records against access by third parties without the knowledge or consent of the student; if he or she is over 18, or of the student's legal guardian, in the case of minors. Concurrently, the law gave legal guardians of minor students and individuals over the age of 18 years the right to know the number and content of student records kept by an educational institution or agency. In addition, legal guardians and individuals 18 years or older were accorded the right to a hearing for the purposes of challenging any inaccurate, misleading, or false information contained in the file.

The extent to which this law applies to school library records and the precise definition of a school record have been the subject of much debate. These issues are particularly problematic for school librarians who must determine whether or not they are bound by law to release otherwise confidential information about students to their parents or guardians. The language of the law and the Department of Education's interpretation of it are broad and inclusive, suggesting that all records containing personally identifiable information about a student are covered, with only three exceptions:

> 1. Private notes and other materials created by instructional, supervisory, administrative, and educational personnel which are in the sole possession of the maker and which are not accessible or revealed to any other person except a substitute;

Andréa Gambino was a consultant to the Office for Intellectual Freedom, and is a law student at Northwestern University School of Law. Anne E. Levinson is Assistant Director of the Office for Intellectual Freedom.

2. Records and documents maintained solely for law enforcement purposes and not made available to persons other than law enforcement officials of the same jurisdiction;

3. Records of a student who is 18 years of age or older which are created or maintained by a physician, psychiatrist, psychologist, or other recognized professional or paraprofessional and which are created, maintained, or used only in connection with the provision of treatment to the student, and are not available to anyone other than persons providing such treatment. Such records can be personally reviewed by a physician or other appropriate professional of the student's choice.

In keeping with the broad Department of Education interpretation of the law, some state library confidentiality laws include a specific exemption for the records of minors, allowing parents or legal guardians access to these records.

Free expression advocates, proponents of children's rights, and the ALA's Office for Intellectual Freedom, oppose the application of this law to library records. In view of the fact that library circulation and registration records are maintained solely for administrative purposes and are not accessible to anyone other than library staff, the first *Buckley Amendment* exception (see above) arguably should apply to school library records, prohibiting access—even by the legal guardian of a minor patron. Though this interpretation of the status of school library records has never been tested directly in court, the theory is bolstered by a 1991 federal court decision in *Bauer* v. *Kincaid*,[1] which defined school records narrowly to include only those ". . . records relating to individual student academic performance, financial aid, or scholastic probation which are kept in individual student files." (Slip op. at 38–39) This definition could be interpreted to support the exclusion of library records from the provisions of the Buckley Amendment. Although the decision is not binding outside the district for which it was issued, it sets a valuable precedent for any future cases and provides another basis from which to argue for protection of confidentiality for the library records of children and young adults.

Although no absolute recommendations are possible due to the murky state of the law surrounding confidentiality as regards minor patrons, the Office for Intellectual Freedom advocates according the same confidentiality protection to minors as to adult patrons. Using the following factors, a strong case can be made *against* the right of parents to have access to the library records of their children and *for*

---

1. *Bauer* v. *Kincaid*, U.S. District Court for Western District of Missouri, Judge Russell G. Clark presiding, March 13, 1991. As of this writing this case had not been appealed. A law librarian can provide an update on the status of the case.

librarians' responsibility to protect the privacy rights of all patrons, including minors and young adults:

The Supreme Court has recognized children as persons under the constitution.

The Library Bill of Rights guarantees protection from discrimination in library service based on age.

The ALA has an explicit Policy on the Confidentiality of Library Records of *all* patrons.

The first exemption listed in the Buckley Amendment may be applicable to school library records.

The recent federal court decision in *Bauer* v. *Kincaid* narrows the definition of school records in a way which may exclude library records.

The ALA believes that parents *not* librarians must be responsible for guiding their own—and only their own—child's reading.

Children and young adults will not learn to exercise their own intellectual freedom if they are taught that the guarantees of the Constitution do not apply to them. Protecting their right to read freely and use library resources is critically important, if we wish to raise new generations to be active First Amendment advocates and protectors of the Constitution which provides the basis for government by and for *all* the people.

4

Librarians and Their Legislators

Eileen D. Cooke

Librarians are more qualified than many other citizens to work productively with their legislators at local, state, and national levels. Legislators do respond to pressures. These may be the pressures of numbers—the almost irresistible force of massive public opinion opposing or supporting a measure. But legislators also respond—and to a greater degree than many realize—to the pressures of facts, logical reasoning, and intangible factors. Pressures like these are qualitative, yet no less effective. One good argument, one well-documented presentation, one staunch friend in a strategic position can accomplish more than great numbers on the other side of the question.

As a result, although librarians are not numerous, they can be and often are strikingly successful in their participation in the legislative process. They are accustomed to marshaling information, which is half the battle in a legislative contest. Their dedication to the public good is generally unquestioned, so that their support of or opposition to a measure is accepted by most legislators as soundly motivated, not for personal advantage. Moreover, librarians have many friends and allies, who are more numerous than themselves and hence count for more in the political scales. Librarians can work with groups representing educators and educational institutions, for example, or with groups representing children or parents or scholars—all groups that share or can be persuaded to share a legislative goal in common with librarians. The very nature and diversity of their work and contacts make librarians highly capable coalition builders.

Eileen D. Cooke is director of the American Library Association Washington Office. For more information on lobbying for intellectual freedom, *see also* Lobbying for Intellectual Freedom in part VII.

Specific Facts about the Legislative Situation

The first step, once a legislative committee or subcommittee has been organized, is to inform leaders and membership alike of the specific facts regarding the legislative situation. With respect to the U.S. Congress, this is accomplished by close attention to the *ALA Washington Newsletter* and other communications from the ALA Washington Office appearing, for example, in *American Libraries*. The task is much more difficult at state or local levels, for what is needed is not the sort of general information reported in newspapers but much more detailed reports. The Office for Intellectual Freedom is a principal source of news relating specifically to activities in this area. Accurate and timely information about a proposal is essential if an individual or organization is to take effective action:

> Who is sponsoring what measures? (More must be known about the sponsor than name and hometown.)
> What committee is the sponsor on?
> What is the sponsor's political situation?
> What are the sponsor's views?
> To whom does the sponsor respond?
> What is the sponsor's background?

It may be, for example, that a legislator will appreciate the implications of a pending measure much more readily if these are explained in terms of law libraries rather than in terms of public or school libraries. This is the sort of information that must be collected and collated and made easily available with respect to as many legislators as possible.

As the measure itself, a thorough analysis must be made. If it involves First Amendment issues, the analysis must obviously be made by someone qualified to comment on this aspect. If it is a proposed appropriation, the analysis must indicate the probable effects of enactment—what services would be affected by a reduction of funds or what services could be expanded with an increase? The analysis will suggest potential allies to join the effort to enact or to defeat the measure. It will also suggest the best arguments in favor of or against the measure.

Legislative Strategy and Timing

Next there is the question of legislative strategy and timing. Here one must rely on friends in the legislation. They will know the many other factors that are involved with the fate of the bill of concern:

> What is the workload of the committee to which it has been referred?

When can the committee turn its attention to your measure?

What is the sentiment of the chair of the committee with respect to this bill?

What is the sentiment of the committee as a whole?

Some of this information can be obtained through previously established contacts with the legislators, but other information is best obtained firsthand by the legislators themselves. Thousands of bills are introduced each year; however, relatively few are enacted into law.

Only a few legislators will take a strong interest in library legislation, some because they have a personal interest, perhaps because of a concerned relative or friend, and others because they are on the committee handling bills of this type. These members will not only advise the library of the prospect of its bill, but will also offer counsel regarding the strategy to be adopted, the position to be taken in hearings, the nature of the testimony to be presented, the kind of witnesses to be secured, and the like. This advice is invaluable and should be heeded.

Contact between Librarians and Legislators

It is implicit in all that has been said thus far that considerable contact between librarians and legislators is essential during this process. All persons who are active in legislative affairs will be seeing legislators frequently and, in time, they will know many of them well as individuals. Ideally, one should visit legislators when they are "at home," that is, in their district rather than at the state capital or in Washington. One should be familiar with their home office and should be acquainted with their home office staff. All members of Congress maintain at least one office in their district, and the staffs of these offices can reveal when their boss will be at that office and available to citizens.

To meet with a legislator, a librarian should make an appointment, then leave little to chance. Plan what to say, be well-versed on the bill being discussed, and, if possible, prepare a brief memorandum, preferably only one page, covering the relevant points. (A copy should be left with the legislator.) A fact sheet on the library, listing its strengths, its problems, and its prospects would also be valuable. During the meeting, the librarian should give the legislator ample opportunity for questioning, ask which member of the staff to keep in touch with when the legislator is unavailable, and request to be put on a mailing list to keep abreast of legislative activities. Similarly, it is important that the library keep legislators informed of the library's activities, invite them to functions or special activities when this is appropriate, or ask them to join a board or advisory group if this is feasible.

Meetings with legislators need not be frequent. Usually one meeting before a legislative session begins, preferably in the district, and perhaps one more meeting during the legislative session when an important measure is at a decisive point, will be sufficient. Of course, at each session of the legislature there are new members, and these should be visited to ascertain their viewpoint, their interests, and their potential position vis-à-vis the legislation that concerns you.

Personal contacts with legislators should precede letters and other less personal communications whenever possible. Letters will prove much more effective if they are read by a legislator who has met the sender. Ideally, each legislator should have a flow of contacts with one or more librarians from the home district or state, a few letters each year, and at least one visit, during each legislative session.

From time to time, members of the U.S. House of Representatives pass on tips to their constituents on "Writing Your Congressman." These suggestions apply just as well to state and local lawmakers. The main message is that frequently a single, thoughtful, factually persuasive letter has changed a legislator's mind or caused him or her to review an issue based on helpful letters from well-informed constituents. Letters should be timely and constructive as well as accurate, brief, and clear (*see* figure 1).

Remember that legislators are human; they like to get letters thanking them for the positions they have taken. They don't like letters threatening or berating them, nor those that demand a commitment to a position before all sides have been heard or before the pending bill has been modified, as most are before a final vote.

Bipartisanship

Neither party should be neglected, of course. Today's minority in the legislature may be tomorrow's majority. It is rare, indeed, that all one's foes or friends will be found in one party. Therefore, librarians will want to cultivate legislators of both parties. Surprisingly, few librarians have met their representatives, senators, or state legislators. Even fewer have developed a continuing correspondence or series of visits with their legislators. Yet, these are the people who will have much to say and do about the future of nearly every library.

Network Approach

A network approach is required to bring maximum constituent effort to bear upon the Congress, the state legislatures, the national and state administrations, and appropriate regulatory agencies in support of library services. Proponents of library-related legislation must develop

Figure 1. How to Write to Members of Congress and Other Legislators

The most frequently used, correct forms of address are:

To your Senator:	To your Representative:
The Honorable (full name)	The Honorable (full name)
United States Senate	U.S. House of Representatives
Washington, D.C. 20510	Washington, D.C. 20515

"Sincerely yours" is in good taste as a complimentary close. Remember to sign your given name and surname. If you use a title in your signature, be sure to enclose it in parentheses.

Forms similar to the above, addressed to your state capital, are appropriate for your state representatives and senators.

Where possible use your official letterhead. If this is not in order, and you write as an individual, use plain white bond paper, and give your official title following your signature as a means of identification and to indicate your competency to speak on the subject.

DO's

1. Your Legislators like to hear opinions from home and want to be kept informed of conditions in the district. Base your letter on your own pertinent experiences and observations.

2. If writing about a specific bill, describe it by number or its popular name. Your Legislators have thousands of bills before them in the course of a year, and cannot always take time to figure out to which one you are referring.

3. They appreciate intelligent, well-thought-out letters which present a definite position, even if they do not agree.

4. Even more important and valuable to them is a concrete statement of the reasons for your position— particularly if you are writing about a field in which you have specialized knowledge. Representatives have to vote on many matters with which they have had little or no firsthand experience. Some of the most valuable information they receive comes from facts presented in letters from people who have knowledge in the field.

5. Short letters are almost always best. Members of Congress receive many, many letters each day, and a long one may not get as prompt a reading as a brief statement.

6. Letters should be timed to arrive while the issue is alive. Members of the committee considering the bill will appreciate having your views while the bill is ripe for study and action.

7. Don't forget to follow through with a thank-you letter.

DON'Ts

1. Avoid letters that merely demand or insist on votes for or against a certain bill; or that say what vote you want but not why. A letter with no reasoning, good or bad, is not very influential.

2. Threats of defeat at the next election are not effective.

3. Boasts of how influential the writer is are not helpful.

4. Do not ask for a vote commitment on a particular bill before the committee in charge of the subject has had a chance to hear the evidence and make its report.

5. Form letters or letters which include excerpts from other letters on the same subject are not as influential as a simple letter drawing on your own experience.

6. Congressional courtesy require Legislators to refer letters from non-constituents to the proper offices, so you should generally confine your letter-writing to members of your state's delegation or members of the committee specifically considering the bill.

7. Do not engage in letter-writing overkill. Quality, not quantity, is what counts.

clear lines of communication and action, and avoid duplication of effort. This means strengthening ALA's working relationships with other national associations and with state chapters; strengthening state chapters' relationships with each other; and integrating activities aimed at federal, state, and local legislation. For example, a state legislative "watchdog"—the person (or persons) who keeps track of all legislation introduced—is imperative, particularly in regard to intellectual freedom. Many bills affecting this area of concern are nonlibrary measures, and too often librarians learn of them only after the fact. Someone else in each state should be responsible for keeping track of face-to-face contacts with legislators. Contacts should be reported, albeit informally, with some indication of the legislator's response to the position or concern conveyed. These reports will indicate which members must still be visited as well as which ones require other, perhaps more persuasive, visits by librarians. Some legislators may respond to a visit from a representative of their alma mater, others, to a visit by a large group or to a request to address a meeting of librarians and their friends. Knowledge about the proposed measure, followed by individual attention and treatment of legislators, is the way to success.

Coalition

As librarians become more active in the processes discussed above, they will find that other groups either share their objectives or can be persuaded to do so. These actual or potential allies should be sought and worked with. They may be education organizations, other professional societies, trade associations, or civic groups. Chapters of the American Civil Liberties Union and state and local intellectual freedom units of other national organizations are obvious allies. They may work with the library on all the measures of concern, or their interest in its legislative objectives may be limited to one bill alone. In any event, the library should make contact and keep in touch with the leadership and the legislative activists of these organizations.

It should be recognized that American politics is coalition politics, for the most part, rather than confrontation politics. Candidates strive to satisfy as many elements of their constituency as possible. Each party seeks the support of as many segments of the electorate as possible. It is therefore very helpful to demonstrate to legislators that many other organizations are joining or supporting the library's efforts. If the library takes a position on a bill, it is helpful if the statement of position is signed by many other organizations. Obviously, these relationships, too, must be seeded and nurtured.

Public opinion should not be overlooked. In addition to letters to legislators, there should be timely, concise, and cogent letters to newspapers and other publications. This is another instance in which the library's public relations program can bear fruit. If an editorial or columnist calls for lower government expenditures, a letter should point out the effects of a cutback on the library's users. If a pending legislative measure is endorsed, or opposed, a letter should present the librarian's position on the issue. Letters should be directed, in particular, to the publications of greatest influence in the area. With a strong working relationship developed with the press, the chances of having the library's materials published are much stronger. If they are published, a wide audience will be reached. Even if they are unpublished, it is sure that they were read and perhaps remembered in the editorial offices.

Persistence, Persuasion, and Planning

Each step in the process of achieving rapport with legislators is simple in itself; the power of these efforts is in their cumulative impact and their multiplication when performed by many others. In this process, each participant is significant. The story of the lobbying once endured by former Senator Mike Monroney of Oklahoma is instructive with respect to this point. Years ago Senator Monroney sponsored a bill that was favored by the oil industry. Mrs. Monroney, however, was personally opposed to the bill, believing it to be detrimental to the consumer. For weeks she tried to persuade her husband to withdraw his support for the bill. He remained unpersuaded, however, and in the end the bill was enacted by Congress.

Nevertheless, Mrs. Monroney had the last word. Convinced that she was right and her husband wrong, she contacted her friend, Bess Truman, and asked the First Lady to lobby her husband. Persuaded, Mrs. Truman agreed to speak to the president about the bill. She did, and that is said to have been a major reason for President Truman's veto of Senator Monroney's bill.

In the legislative process, as in so many other matters, where there is a will, there is always a way. Persuasion plays an important role in the political process, but planning and persistence are equally essential for substantial success. Politics is called the art of the possible, and that is the art of compromise. Progress often comes one step at a time.

PART V

Before the Censor Comes: Essential Preparations

1

Before the Censor Comes: Essential Preparations

Many challenges to the principles of intellectual freedom go unchecked or are mishandled simply because preparations for an effective response have not been made. An arsenal of defenses must be available at the moment the librarian is confronted by the would-be censor. And if these preparations are to be ready at a moment's notice, they must be in writing and a part of the library's procedures manual.

Why is written policy stressed? First, it encourages stability and continuity in the library's operations. Library staff members may come and go but the procedures manual, kept up-to-date, of course, will help assure smooth transitions when organization or staff changes occur. Second, ambiguity and confusion are far less likely to result if a library's procedures are set down in writing.

Additional and convincing reasons for maintaining written procedures can be outlined:

1. They show everyone that the library is running a businesslike operation.

2. They inform everyone about the library's intent, goals, and aspirations and circumvent ambiguity, confusion, and trouble.

3. They give credence to library actions; people respect what is in writing even though they may not agree with every jot and title in the library's procedures manual.

4. They are impersonal; they make whimsical administration difficult.

5. They give the public a means to evaluate library performance; publicly pronounced policy statements prove that the library is willing to be held accountable for its decisions.

6. They contribute to the library's efficiency; many routine decisions can be incorporated into written procedures.

7. They help disarm potential censors; unfounded accusations seldom prevail when the library's operations are based on clear-cut and timely written procedures that reflect thorough research, sound judgment, and careful planning.

If such written procedures are later adopted by the library's governing body, so much the better. But regardless of whether or not the governing body adopts them as policy, four procedures, at least, are vital for the good of the library and the defense of intellectual freedom.

In the following sections the four most essential preparations—developing a materials selection program, a procedure for handling complaints, developing a confidentiality policy, and a public relations program—are described in depth and practical guidelines are provided. These guidelines derive from and expand upon the basic outline of procedures offered in the document Dealing with Concerns about Library Resources, which should be reviewed in conjunction with the following chapters. Such preparations are important on a day-to-day basis. If they also have the endorsement of the library's governing body, they provide an even firmer foundation for supporting intellectual freedom in the event of a censorship dispute.

2

Development of a
Materials Selection Program

The primary purpose of a materials selection or collection development program is to promote the development of a collection based on institutional goals and user needs. A secondary purpose is service in defending the principles of intellectual freedom.

The basis of a sound selection program is a materials selection statement. Although a majority of professional librarians believe a materials selection statement is desirable, in too many instances the belief does not become reality. Many reasons for not writing such a statement are given, but often two unmentioned reasons are the most important: lack of knowledge about how to prepare one, and lack of confidence in one's abilities to do so. Regardless of past failures and existing difficulties, however, there is an absolute need for the firm foundation that a selection statement provides.

In virtually every case, it will be the librarian's task to prepare the materials selection statement. Although approval or official adoption of the statement rests with the institution's legally responsible governing body, it is the librarian who has the expertise and practical knowledge of the day-to-day activities of the library.

A materials selection statement must relate to concrete practices. It should, in effect, provide guidelines for strengthening and adding to the library's collection. Furthermore, if the statement is to fulfill its secondary purpose, that of defending intellectual freedom, it must be a viable, working document which relates to the library's day-to-day operations. In the case of very large libraries or even medium-sized institutions with highly sophisticated holdings, the librarian may prefer to separate the policy statement from procedural considerations. Thus, the materials selection statement would reflect institutional policies, while a separate procedures manual would deal with the day-to-day applications of those policies.

207

A strong collection and intellectual freedom go hand in hand. It is less likely that problems will remain unresolved if the collection reflects the logical, coherent, and explicit statement from which it grows. In developing a materials selection statement, four basic factors must be considered: (1) service policy, (2) environmental characteristics, (3) collection specifications, and (4) current selection needs.

Service Policy

A service policy will provide practical operational guidelines to govern future collection development in accordance with the needs of the library's users and the goals of the library. In order to establish a service policy, it is necessary to determine what groups the library is striving to serve and what purposes it is attempting to achieve. To do so will entail a study of user-group characteristics and institutional objectives.

I. User groups. A materials selection statement must reflect the needs of the people the library will serve in trying to fulfill its objectives. To establish guidelines for collection development and related library activities, it is necessary to gather detailed information on various user groups.

A questionnaire to establish basic data could be prepared and completed by each staff member working with the public. Or, such informaton could be compiled on the basis of institutional statistics and records. After the library staff has been surveyed, users can be given questionnaires on their purposes in using the library, their library activities, and the like. It should be noted that certain sections of the prepared form can be used to determine the desired state of affairs as well.

A. Population characteristics

1. Age
2. Education
3. Employment level
4. Others

B. Size of each user group
C. Primary purpose of each group in using the library
D. Kinds of material used in accomplishing these purposes
E. Kinds of activities engaged in during the accomplishment of these purposes

II. Institutional objectives. The materials selection statement should define the library's goals and reason for existing. There are at least two sources from which institutional goals can be determined.

A. Statements of objectives are ideally available in a public document designed to inform all concerned persons.

    1. General need(s) the library is designated to fulfill
    2. Activities or standards most valued
    3. Distinction in some field of endeavor

B. Public documents and records, in lieu of a statement of objectives, may outline the institution's objectives and supplement statements of objectives.

    1. Annual reports of the institution
    2. Charter of the institution
    3. Published history of the institution
    4. Records of the governing body
    5. Budget (because preparation of a budget usually demands a resolution of difficult questions of priorities in order to allocate scarce resources, this item should not be overlooked).

Environmental Characteristics

The librarian should determine all aspects of the environment surrounding the institution that could possibly influence the development of the library collection and the library's related activities. A few such environmental factors and their implications are the following:

ENVIRONMENTAL FACTORS	PROVISIONS AFFECTED
Relative geographical isolation	Materials related to the cultural/ recreational needs of users
Economic structure	Materials related to specific educational needs
Presence/absence of library resources external to the institution	Degree of self-sufficiency or completeness of materials
Presence/absence of postsecondary learning institutions	Scholarly/technical works
Relationship to local industries	Technical reports and business materials
Relationship to local professional/ cultural groups	Specialized subcollections

Collection Specifications

Specifications should be established for each subject area or area of concern. (The data gathered to determine service policy and environmental characteristics will show, in large measure, what the library requires.) For this section of the selection statement, each subject area should be carefully reviewed in order to determine the types of materials to be acquired in each and the depth in which materials are to be sought. Such a review is especially important in smaller libraries where funds are severely limited and the needs of the users potentially great.

If possible, the following data should be collected for each area:

Number of library materials currently held
Total number of relevant materials available
Percent of total materials held
Distribution of current holdings by publication date.

In addition, holdings should be rated by subject area in terms of specific user purposes:

Recreation
Self-help
Continuing education
Business.

Finally, a desired acquisition level should be specified for each area.

The section of the selection statement dealing with collection specifications will no doubt be the largest and most detailed of all. It will specify the criteria to be used in selecting and reevaluating materials in terms of (1) users' age groups; (2) users' special needs by virtue of occupation, cultural interest, etc.; and (3) types of materials (books, periodicals, newspapers, government publications, maps, records, films, etc.). This section will also specify policies to be used in handling such matters as gifts and special bequests.

Current Selection Needs

Current selection needs can be determined by the difference between the present collection and the collection specifications. In deciding what is currently needed, the desired state of affairs that may have been detailed under service policy should also be consulted. Once current needs are determined, other considerations come into play. Most prominent among these is the library's budget. Regardless of the amount of money available, the selection statement should indicate in as clear a manner as possible which materials are to be bought and which are not.

Components of a Selection Policy

After full consideration of the above four factors: service policy, environmental characteristics, collection specifications, and current collection needs, the next step is to prepare a final draft of the selection (or collection development) statement itself for submission to the library's governing body. Taking into account the factors discussed above, the statement should relate to and include all materials and services offered by the library.

A good policy statement will first discuss the library's *objectives* in acquiring materials and maintaining services. It will state in succinct terms what the library is trying to accomplish in its program of services, and the specific objectives in given areas of service.

The policy should be derived from the Library's Mission Statement. It is helpful if the role of the library in society (or in the parent institution) is spelled out in the policy and related to the objectives of selection, collection development, and maintenance. The overarching goal may be expressed in the broadest terms. For example, a policy for a public library should include reference to the traditional function of the library in the marketplace of ideas. It could include language like the following: "The library serves a traditional role as a public forum for the receipt of information and for access to the full range of recorded information within the marketplace of ideas. Collection development shall be content neutral so that the library represents significant viewpoints on subjects of interest and does not favor any particular viewpoint."

A school library may declare that its main objective is "to make available to faculty and students a collection of materials that will enrich and support the curriculum and meet the educational needs of the students and faculty served." This may then be broken down to more specific objectives, such as to provide background materials to supplement classroom instruction, to provide access to classics of American and world literature, or to provide a broad range of materials on current issues of controversy to help students develop critical analytic skills.

The policy will precisely define *responsibility* for selection of all types of library materials. It will name by professional position those persons responsible in each area of selection. While selection of materials will, of course, involve many people other than professionally trained librarians, ultimate responsibility should be delegated by the library's governing body to the professional staff. A public library's statement of responsibility might read: "The elected Library Board shall delegate to the Head Librarian the authority and responsibility for selection of all print and nonprint materials. Responsibilities for actual selection shall rest with appropriate professionally trained personnel who shall discharge this obligation consistent with the Board's adopted selection criteria and procedures." Depending upon the size and purpose of the library, the statement might continue by elaborating on any specialized selection responsibilities, the role of user input, and the like.

In terms of subject matter covered, the policy will include *criteria*, and the application of criteria, relevant to the library's stated objectives. These will include artistic or literary excellence, appropriateness to level of user, authenticity, interest, cost, and circumstances of use. Technical criteria, such as clarity of sound in audio materials, can be included as well. To guide the professional staff with responsibility for selection, criteria should be spelled out as specifically as possible. Bibliographies, reviewing journals, and other selection aids to be consulted should be listed. Special criteria to be applied in exceptional cases should be clearly stated. So, for example, a public library which regularly purchases all books on the *New York Times* best-seller list, even if these titles do not always meet other criteria, should state this clearly in the policy.

The policy should directly address problems associated with the acquisition of *controversial materials*. The document should include here a statement on intellectual freedom and its importance to librarianship as well as an affirmation of the Library Bill of Rights. Some libraries also include the text of the First Amendment to the U.S. Constitution. A statement on intellectual freedom might read: "The library subscribes in principle to the statements of policy on library philosophy as expressed in the American Library Association Library Bill of Rights, a copy of which is appended to and made an integral part of this policy." The statement can also include the text of the Freedom to Read statement and the ALA Policy on Confidentiality of Library Records, which states that circulation records and other records identifying the names of library users are considered confidential in nature.

The library's selection *procedures* should be described step by step from initial screening to final selection. The procedures should provide for coordination among departments and professional staff, for handling recommendations from library users, and for review of existing material. Any special procedures pertinent to collection developement should be spelled out precisely in the materials selection statement. Some items to consider for treatment in the statement are gifts, sponsored materials, expensive materials, ephemeral materials, jobbers and salespersons, locked case, distribution of free materials, and handling of special collections. The document should review procedures for *collection maintenance*.

Finally, occasional objections to materials will be made despite the quality of the selection process. The procedure for *review of challenged materials* in response to concerns of library users should be stated clearly. The procedure should establish a fair framework for registering complaints, while defending the principles of intellectual freedom, the library user's right of access, and professional responsibility and integrity. Each specific step to be taken when a request for reconsideration is made, and all possible avenues of appeal, should be listed.

The final format and organization of the materials selection statement will depend, of course, on the particularities of the library concerned. One possible table of contents, however, might look like this:

Part 1: Selection of Library Materials

    I. Statement of Policy

    II. Objectives of Selection

    III. Responsibility for Selection

        A. Delegation of Responsibility to Professional Staff
        B. Particular Responsibilities of Staff Members

    IV. Selection Criteria

        A. General Selection Criteria
        B. Specific Selection Criteria

    V. Policy on Controversial Materials

        A. General Statement
        B. Library Bill of Rights
        C. Freedom to Read

Part 2: Procedures for Selection of Library Materials

    I. Procedures for Implementation

        A. Selection Aids
        B. Outside Recommendation Procedures
        C. Gifts
        D. Special Collections and Concerns

    II. Collection Maintenance: Evaluation and Review of Existing Materials

    III. Procedures for Dealing With Challenged Materials

        A. Request for Informal Review
        B. Request for Formal Review
        C. The Review Committee
        D. Resolution and Appeal.

It hardly needs to be said that preparation of a complete statement requires work—a great amount of it. And the work must be done before the censorship problem arises. Unfortunately, there are no shortcuts. The materials in this manual, including the texts of current ALA intellectual freedom policies, will be of some assistance. For school libraries, the American Association of School Librarians distributes a document entitled "Policies and Procedures for Selection of Instructional Materials." OIF distributes a "Workbook for Selection Policy Writing," with specific suggestions and examples of how to write a school library policy, the basic principles of which are also help-ful in formulating policies for other libraries. The OIF and many state intellectual freedom committees have also collected sample selection statements which can serve as examples. It is, however, impossible to simply borrow a statement based on another institution's goals and needs. Above all, the statement must be a working document, a hand-book for daily activities reflecting the needs of those who are to use it.

3

Procedures for Handling Complaints*

All librarians must be aware that at some time there will be complaints about library service—and sometimes these complaints will center around a particular book, magazine, or other item which the library distributes. What should one do when a complaint of this kind is made? As in handling any type of complaint about library operations, a courteous and calm approach is essential. Above all, complainants must know that their objections will be given serious consideration and that interest in the library is welcome. Complainants who come by in person or telephone, should be listened to courteously and invited to file a complaint in writing, if the problem cannot be resolved through informal discussion. If the complaint comes by letter, it should be acknowledged promptly. In either case, the complainant should be offered a prepared questionnaire in order that a formal complaint may be submitted. In addition, the rationale for having a formal complaint procedure should be explained.

Having a prepared form is not just an additional piece of record keeping. There are a number of advantages in having a complaint procedure available. First, knowing that a response is ready and that there is a procedure to be followed, the librarian will be relieved of much of the initial panic which inevitably strikes when confronted by an outspoken and perhaps irate library patron. Also important, the complaint form asks complainants to state their objections in logical, unemotional terms, thereby allowing the librarian to evaluate the merits of the objections. In addition, the form benefits the complainant. When citizens with complaints are asked to follow an established procedure for lodging their objections, they feel assured they are being properly heard and that their objections will be considered.

---

* *See also* Dealing with Concerns about Library Resources 2.14 in Part I.

The accompanying sample complaint form, entitled Statement of Concern about Library/Media Center Resources (figure 2), was adapted by the Intellectual Freedom Committee. Libraries and librarians should feel free to reproduce and use it, although alternative forms may certainly be devised to reflect the specifics of a given library situation.

As soon as the complaint has been filed, the objections should be reviewed. The review should consist of specific steps, although the number will vary somewhat according to the individual library involved. Simultaneous with the review, the governing body (that is, board of trustees, school board, etc.) should be routinely notified that a formal complaint has been made.

First, the person or committee that selected the item, or an ad hoc committee, should evaluate the original reasons for the purchase. The objections should be considered in terms of the library's materials selection statement, the principles of the Library Bill of Rights, and the opinions of the various reviewing sources used in materials selection. If the materials selection statement is sufficiently detailed to function as a guide for selection decisions, it should not be difficult to make a logical, strong response to the objections.

Second, the objections and the response should be forwarded to the librarian who has final responsibility for ordering materials, and who, in turn, should review the response and either add relevant comments or return the response to the individual or committee for further clarification. At this point, then, either the order librarian or the selection committee can make a written response to the complainant.

It is critical that the review process be as objective as possible. If the challenged item does not meet the library's own criteria for selection (assuming, of course, that these criteria themselves are consistent with the principles of intellectual freedom), the library must be ready to acknowledge that the material is indeed unsuitable and withdraw it from the collection. If, on the other hand, as is most often the case, the material does meet the selection criteria and is deemed suitable for the collection, it is the responsibility of the library staff to respond to the complaint clearly and precisely. This response should also inform the complainant how to pursue the matter further. If the complainant is not satisfied, then the head administrator of the library (the person to whom the governing body has given authority) can serve as the person to whom an initial appeal is made. The complainant should be contacted promptly, explained the decision of the library, and advised that further discussions are welcome.

If the complainant still feels that the problem has been dealt with inadequately, a final appeal (within the structure of the library) to the governing body of the institution can be made. This body will in turn

Figure 2. Sample Complaint Form

STATEMENT OF CONCERN ABOUT
LIBRARY/MEDIA CENTER RESOURCES

This is where you identify who in your own structure has authorized use of this form—
Director, Board of Trustees, Board of Education, etc.—and to whom to return form.

Name _____   Date _____

Address _____

City _____ State _____ Zip _____   Phone # _____

1. Resource on which you are commenting:

   _____ Book   _____ Audiovisual Resource

   _____ Magazine   _____ Content of Library Program

   _____ Newspaper   _____ Other

   Title _____

   Author/Producer _____

2. What brought this title to your attention?

3. Please comment on the resource as a whole as well as being specific on those
   matters which concern you. (Use other side if needed.) Comment:

Optional:

4. What resource(s) do you suggest to provide additional information on this topic?

Revised by the ALA Intellectual Freedom Committee, January 12, 1983 decide upon an appropriate course of action—for example, a public hearing. It must be emphasized, however, that requests for action from the governing body should not be routine; such requests are best avoided by an adequate initial response to the complaint.

At each step of this process the utmost courtesy toward and respect for the complainant should be maintained. There is no reason for a librarian to become defensive or jealous of professional privilege when a complaint is made. Not only is this counterproductive, but it runs counter to library efforts to encourage user involvement. Most complainants are sincere in their concerns and frequently can be prevailed upon to see the censorious implications of their actions. It should be recognized that many library users are intimidated by the librarian's authority and expertise, and for many patrons the decision to complain may be an act of admirable personal courage and a reaffirmation of their democratic right to involvement, from which all may benefit.

The review procedure, including the written questionnaire, should be designed not only as a defense against potential censors, but also as a means to facilitate constructive dialogue. While these procedures do offer the library a defense against arbitrary attacks, they should never be permitted to degenerate into a bureaucratic smokescreen. In a word, the library should welcome constructive input even as it maintains firm barriers to censorship.

Conducting a Challenge Hearing

Challenges to materials only occasionally reach the stage of a full-blown administrative hearing; often they are resolved at an earlier step in the challenge resolution process. When a hearing is necessary, however, certain important do's and don'ts should be observed. A number of battles have been lost because the challenge hearing has been poorly organized. Even though procedures have been followed to the letter up to this point, the handling of the challenge hearing may be the weak link in the process.

The challenge process begins when someone objects to materials in a library collection. At this point, providing (1) an explanation of selection procedures, (2) a copy of the selection policy, or (3) a copy of the reconsideration or complaint form, will often resolve the concern. A complainant sometimes may not return the reconsideration form, because he or she sees the logic of the selection process that emphasizes intellectual freedom and due process. The complainant tends to be satisfied in registering a concern and knowing the library is taking the concern seriously.

There are some, however, who will wish to follow through on the procedures established in the selection policy approved by the governing authority for handling complaints. To activate the reconsideration procedure, a complaint should be in writing. In fact, the written and approved selection policy should state that anonymous phone calls, rumors, or voiced concerns are not honored; action occurs only when the reconsideration or complaint form has been returned. When a written complaint is filed, the reconsideration committee, usually comprised of representatives of all library users and the librarian (often, all are library staff—the actual composition of the committee is up to the individual institution), is formed. The committee should then undertake the following:

1. Read, view or listen to the challenged material in its entirety;

2. Review the selection process and the criteria for selection;

3. Check reviews and recommended lists to determine recommendations by the experts and critics;

4. Meet to discuss the challenge; and

5. Make a recommendation to the administrator on removal, retention, or replacement.

Before the Hearing

After a formal, written request for reconsideration has been submitted and reviewed, and a recommendation for retention or removal has been made, the complainant should be notified of the committee's decision. At the same time, the procedure for appealing the decision also should be provided. The appeal may involve a hearing by a school board, a board of trustees, or a city or county board of commissioners or council. (The selection policy should clearly identify the chain of command.) The appeal also must be in writing in order for the chair of the governing authority to place it on the agenda for the next meeting. The librarian should follow up on this step to make certain the presiding officer is aware of the policies and procedures that should be followed, including open meetings laws and the agenda. Normally, the board conducts a challenge hearing which provides the forum for the complainant to air his or her objections to the title in the collection and the recommendation of the reconsideration committee.

A hearing on challenged material is serious and often lengthy. Such a hearing may be the only item on the agenda; indeed, best results are most often achieved this way.

Decide in advance on a length of time for the entire hearing. Have a definite beginning and ending time. Guard against overlong meetings when decisions may be made by small groups in the late hours. This has spelled disaster in some instances.

Never attempt to stage a hearing quietly. The entire community should be aware of the meeting and what has transpired up to this point. The hearing should be announced well in advance. Publicity is very important to assure good attendance at the meeting. Make the time and place very clear. Indicate in an announcement or news release that an open hearing is being held and that the public is invited. Try to obtain full coverage by the local press, radio, and television. Prepare a news release for each of these groups to make certain they have the facts correct. Deliver copies of the media center's or library's selection policies to them, along with a copy of the Library Bill of Rights. These policies, of course, should include procedures for handling complaints.

Seek help and advice from your state intellectual freedom committee, local and state colleges and universities, educational groups, teachers' professional organizations and coalitions, and the ALA Office for Intellectual Freedom. Many nonlibrary groups have committees on intellectual freedom, freedom of speech, and/or academic freedom. Even when representatives from these groups are not present at the hearing, solicited resolutions in written form sometimes help in supporting your philosophy.

Find people who will be willing to speak in support of the freedom to read, view, and listen. This pool of speakers should be contacted well in advance of the hearing. In fact, many librarians have lists of persons they have contacted previously and who are library supporters. The best spokespersons in hearings tend to be attorneys, ministers, people from the news media, educators, and, of course, librarians. Response to persons from the local community is usually more favorable than to people brought in from outside. Student speakers are also effective. They speak from the heart and have no vested interest other than maintaining their freedom of choice guaranteed by the Constitution.

Attempt to estimate in advance the size of the gathering for the hearing. Make certain the meeting place is large enough to prevent postponing the meeting or changing locations at the last minute. A late site change may result in losing part of the group attending.

Long before a hearing, members of your advisory board, your reconsideration committee, and governing board should have become well-schooled in intellectual freedom principles and procedures. It is the responsibility of the librarian to accomplish this and it will ensure board support when a challenge hearing is necessary. All those selected to testify should be reminded they are defending a principle more than an individual title. The actual title in question should play a secondary role. It is very difficult to disagree with the freedom to read, view, and listen in a democratic society.

The Hearing

As people arrive for the hearing, they should be given a copy of the selection policy. The policy should include the following elements, among others: a statement of the philosophy of materials selection; a statement that the governing board has the final responsibility for selection of materials; a statement detailing the delegation of this responsibility to the professional library personnel; criteria for selection of materials; and a section on procedures for handling challenged materials. If the Library Bill of Rights is not a formal part of the policy, it should be duplicated and distributed as well.

One or more persons should be stationed at the entrance to sign in people wishing to speak. Request that they identify the side on which they will be speaking. If at all possible, attempt to ensure that there will be a balanced number of speakers on both sides.

Begin the hearing on time. The chair of the governing board should preside, as at any other business meeting. After calling the meeting to order, he or she should review the procedures to be followed at the meeting, and the process followed up to this point for reconsideration of the material. The board should announce at the beginning of the hearing that it will issue its decision at the next regularly scheduled meeting, and that the meeting is simply to hear all sides of the issue. Speakers should be allowed to speak in the order they signed in. Limit each speaker to a specific amount of time, e.g., three or four minutes, and appoint a timekeeper in advance. No participant should be allowed to speak a second time until everyone registered has been heard once. It is extremely important to adhere strictly both to the time limits and to the order of the speakers.

Through the whole process, it is crucial to follow the traditional advice of remaining calm. Remember to practice what you preach and ensure due process. Listen carefully and courteously to everyone. By using good communication skills, you will help people understand your logic in ensuring diversity in library collections.

After the Hearing

The Board should announce its decision publicly at its next regularly scheduled meeting. The agenda should include an item showing that the board will announce its decision (but not the decision itself). The usual notices and publication of the agenda will alert the public; news releases may also be used to ensure coverage and attendance at the meeting if desired. Whatever the board's decision, the principles of the Library Bill of Rights should be reiterated and how the decision is in accordance with those principles, should be explained. A *very* brief statement of the reason for the decision should also be made, e.g., "we have concluded that the material meets our selection criteria, and will be retained without restriction."

Keep your governing authority up-to-date on all events and incidents. Examine your personal philosophy of intellectual freedom on a regular basis. Meet all negative pressure with positive pressures, such as emphasizing intellectual freedom rather than the perils of censorship.

By following this advice, you will be able to conduct a successful challenge hearing and improve your image in the process.

4

Developing a Confidentiality Policy

Recent years have seen an increase in the number and frequency of challenges to the confidentiality of library records across the United States, and a new dimension has been added to confidentiality concerns. Throughout the 1980s, the Office for Intellectual Freedom (OIF) received queries from individual librarians who had been pressured by the FBI or local law enforcement agencies for information about library users, or who were afraid of being held liable for a patron's acts after providing information on such topics as bomb construction, weapons, or satanism. Some of these librarians were tempted to maintain special files on patrons who seemed "suspicious" or who made "unusual" requests. These queries revealed a lack of confidence in confidentiality procedures or a misunderstanding of the important links between confidentiality, intellectual freedom, and librarians' professional and legal obligations to uphold the privacy rights of patrons.

Why is Confidentiality Crucial to Freedom of Inquiry?

Inquiries about patron reading habits raise serious questions for librarians and patrons. For example, are *you* what you read? Would you want others to make decisions affecting your life based on their opinion of the books you read, the music you listen to, or the films you view? How would library use change if patrons thought their reading records and other information about their lives would be open for scrutiny? How widely would people read knowing their choices might prejudice others against them? If libraries are to survive as centers for the free and uninhibited access to information so necessary to a democratic society, librarians must vigilantly guard their patron's privacy and freedom of inquiry.

To support librarians in their role as defenders of the right to read, in 1971 the IFC proposed, and the ALA Council adopted, the Policy on Confidentiality of Liberty Records (revised in 1975). This important addition to the IFC's expanding inventory of tools for defending intellectual freedom was initiated in response to U.S. Treasury Department efforts to identify potentially "subversive" individuals based on their choice of reading material. Looking for the names of those who had borrowed or read books about the construction of explosives, treasury agents conducted inquiries in libraries in Ohio, California, Georgia, and Wisconsin. Librarians sounded the alarm over these apparent "fishing expeditions" and the department ceased its inquiries, but not before some librarians had handed over their records.

Firmly committed to the freedom to read as a necessary corollary to freedom of expression, the IFC encouraged librarians to resist such open-ended government inquiries. One cannot exercise the right to read if the possible consequences include damage to one's reputation, ostracism from the community or workplace, or criminal penalties. Choice requires both a varied selection and the assurance that one's choice is not monitored. In the case of criminal investigations or other government inquiries, it is especially critical that a librarian preserve the patron's confidentiality since the consequences of releasing information about the individual(s) under investigation may be dire, and the potential for abuse of information about a person's reading habits is great.

A case in Decatur, Texas, dramatically illustrates this danger. Early in 1990, the Wise County District Attorney's office, investigating a child abandonment case, subpoenaed the records of the Decatur Public Library, requesting the names, addresses, and telephone numbers of all individuals who had checked out books on childbirth within the previous nine months, the titles they borrowed, and the dates the materials were checked out and returned. The police had no evidence indicating that the person who abandoned the child might have borrowed library books or otherwise used the library. Lacking any other leads, police were simply conducting a "fishing expedition."

The director of the Decatur Public Library refused to release the records. Instead, she chose to respond, with the help of the city attorney, by filing a motion to quash the subpoena, filed on behalf of the library's patrons. On May 9, 1990, Texas District Court Judge John R. Lindsey ruled in favor of the library and quashed the subpoena. The library director in this case was successful in defending her patrons, but imagine the consequences if she had failed: all patrons who had borrowed books on childbirth might have been subjected to police interrogation based solely upon their choice of reading materials. Thanks to this librarian's courageous implementation of the library confidentiality policy, patrons were not subject to such unjust and humiliating proceedings.[1]

Threats to confidentiality arise within the library from loosely managed information or circulation systems, library staff or board members who are unaware of their responsibilities under existing confidentiality policy or state law, or from lack of any policy at all on the issue. Librarians or their staff may be asked for confidential information by patrons, journalists, students, or professors who wish to check on the reading habits of their students, or parents of young children who must pay overdue fines or who wish to monitor their children's reading preferences. Finally, many of the most difficult and complicated challenges do come from local or federal law enforcement officials investigating criminal activities, or from feuding litigants in civil cases. While these situations are relatively infrequent, they can be the most intimidating if a librarian, staff, and governing board are inadequately prepared to respond.

In 1989, responding to an increase in external threats and the clear need for further education on intellectual freedom and confidentiality for all librarians, the ALA Intellectual Freedom Committee (IFC) initiated Confidentiality in Libraries: An Intellectual Freedom Modular Education Program. Concurrently, the ALA Council requested a new and more specific policy to address the problem of confidentiality in the context of law enforcement inquiries, a trend sparked by the FBI Library Awareness Program and emulated by law enforcement agencies at all levels across the country—from county sheriffs to urban detectives. The IFC developed a new policy, and Council adopted it at the June 1991 Annual Meeting (see Policy Concerning Confidentiality of Personally Identifiable Information About Library Users, p. 133).

Confidentiality and the Law

Although librarians' main concern has been the potential chilling effect a violation of confidentiality could have on the exercise of First Amendment rights, a growing body of law exists that protects individual privacy rights and the confidentiality of library records, raising concerns of librarian liability when confidentiality is breached. The right to privacy is not among the rights enumerated in the Bill of Rights, but legal scholars and U.S. Supreme Court interpretations of the Constitution have found an implied right of privacy or zones of privacy surrounding the First Amendment freedom of expression,[2] the Fifth Amendment

---

1. From the files of the ALA Office for Intellectual Freedom.

2. *Griswold* v. *Connecticut*, 381 U.S. 479,483 (1965). Justice Douglas stated that "the First Amendment has a penumbra where privacy is protected from governmental intrusion."

privilege against self-incrimination, the Fourteenth Amendment provision for due process and, above all, the Fourth Amendment protection against unreasonable search and seizure.

The Supreme Court, in two decisions, laid the foundation for recognizing a right to privacy in one's choice of reading materials and in so doing has also given support to the idea of a First Amendment right to read concomitant with the right to freedom of expression. In *Lamont* v. *Postmaster General*[3], the Court affirmed the right of an individual to receive controversial political materials through the U.S. mail. Later, in *Stanley* v. *Georgia*[4], the Court made explicit the right of individual privacy in controversial reading material, holding that an individual may read as he/she chooses—even material alleged to be obscene, as was the case in *Stanley*—within the privacy of his/her home. In 1990, however, this right suffered a setback in *Osborne* v. *Ohio*[5], when the Supreme Court upheld an Ohio law banning the possession of child pornography, arguing for a narrow interpretation of *Stanley*, and stating that "the interests underlying child pornography prohibitions far exceed the interests justifying the Georgia law at issue in *Stanley*. Every court to address the issue has so concluded."[6]

Early Supreme Court interpretations of the Fourth Amendment sought to protect private property against government intrusion. This protection was expanded by later Court decisions, in cases such as *NAACP* v. *Alabama*[7] and *Griswold* v. *Connecticut*[8], to protect a person and personal information, as opposed to a particular place or property. In the NAACP case, the Court recognized the "chilling effect on First Amendment Rights of unauthorized disclosure of member lists." A 1967 ruling in *Katz* v. *United States*[9] took this recognition further, setting forth a standard for constitutionally protected zones of privacy. In this case, the individual's expectation of privacy was weighed against the government's interest in searching or invading that privacy. Based on *Katz* and preceding cases, the Court has interpreted the Fourth Amendment and the Bill of Rights as a whole to protect an individual's property, communications, personality, politics, and thoughts.

Although some Supreme Court decisions had favored the right to privacy, there remained a need for more explicit protections for individuals in an age of computer-based information systems. Seeking to

---

3. *Lamont* v. *U.S. Postmaster General*, 381 U.S. 301 (1965).
4. *Stanley* v. *Georgia*, 394 U.S. 557 (1969).
5. *Clyde Osborne v. Ohio*, 109 L.Ed. 2d (1990).
6. *Clyde Osborne v. Ohio*, 109 L.Ed. 2d (1990) at 108.
7. *NAACP* v. *Alabama*, 357 U.S. 449 (1958).
8. *Griswold* v. *Connecticut*, 381 U.S. 479 (1965).
9. *Katz* v. *United States*, 389 U.S. 347 (1967).

address this need, Congress passed the Privacy Act of 1974,[10] prohibiting the maintenance of secret data files, ensuring the right of individuals to know what files are kept and what information they contain, and outlining a process by which individuals can correct false or misleading information found in records maintained about them.

The Act was amended in 1988[11] to prevent the establishment of a national data bank, merging information on individuals maintained in systems of records by other federal agencies; the direct linking of computerized systems of records; the computer matching of records not otherwise authorized by law; and the disclosure of records for computer matching except to a federal, state, or local government agency. This attempt to legislate a right to privacy has had mixed success in the courts and has suffered some setbacks. To compensate for its inadequacies, nearly all states now recognize the right to privacy in their statutory law.

State Law Protection of Library Records

Forty-four states and the District of Columbia also have laws that provide for the confidentiality of library records. This protection usually takes one of two basic forms: affirmative protection of a patron's privacy rights; or, exceptions to open public record or state freedom of information acts, exempting library records from scrutiny. Direct protection is preferable, of course, because this format often provides for punitive action and redress if the law is broken; and exemption from an open public records act is not as easily enforced. Laws which do not specifically *forbid* revealing the information contained in library records are subject to varying interpretations and manipulation that might allow law enforcement agents easier access to privileged information. As of this writing, only six states are without legislative protection of the confidentiality of library records: Kentucky, Hawaii, Mississippi, Ohio, Texas, and Utah. Of these states, Kentucky and Texas have official opinions from their attorneys general, affirming the right of privacy in regard to library patron records.[12]

It is imperative for librarians to know their legal rights and responsibilities and to create or revise confidentiality policies to conform with the law. Without taking these steps, the librarian may risk civil liability for harm suffered by a patron because the individual's library

---

10. 5. U.S.C. §552(a).

11. The "Computer Matching and Privacy Protection Act of 1988," P.L. 100-503. 5 U.S.C. §552(a).

12. 81 Op. Att'y. Gen. Ky. 81-159 (1981); and, Att'y. Gen Tex. Open Records Decision No. 100, at 2 (July 10, 1975).

records were revealed to law enforcement agents, government officials, or others. Librarians also may be subjected to the penalties provided in state laws in the event that confidential records are revealed.

What is a Librarian to Do?

Although questions of confidentiality can be complicated and have potentially serious consequences, they are exceedingly manageable and may be responded to in a way which protects both librarians and patrons. As all politics are local so, too, are most attempts at censorship local in origin. Victories for the First Amendment are won (or lost) case by case and usually without fanfare, through the conviction and dedication (or lack thereof) of individuals who stand up for the freedom of expression, regardless of the alleged offensiveness of content or the good cause of the person requesting or demanding confidential information. This means that every librarian must understand the importance of maintaining confidentiality and be prepared to educate people with a wide range of interests and expertise about the role of confidentiality in protecting the intellectual freedom of all library users.

This critical responsibility is best managed by choosing to be proactive and take the initiative, rather than waiting for a crisis to develop. Protecting confidentiality requires a rapid and well-orchestrated defense, beginning with a library policy on confidentiality.

Writing a Policy

The basis in policy and law for the protection of confidentiality can be found in the following documents:

1. Library Bill of Rights and its interpretations.
2. Statement on Professional Ethics
3. ALA Policy on Confidentiality of Library Records
4. First, Fourth, Fifth, and Fourteenth Amendments to the United States Constitution
5. Privacy Act of 1974, amended
6. State confidentiality of library records laws

An effective policy should include the following sections:

Objective: Who or what is to be protected? From whom or what? Why is the policy necessary?

Responsibility: Who is responsible for implementing the policy? Who will enforce it? Who has a right to know? A need to know?

Criteria: Which information will be protected? How will this be determined?

Procedures: What steps are to be taken by staff in identifying situations where the policy applies? How will the policy be implemented in response to such situations? How will the policy be adopted, amended, repealed? How will it be incorporated into the training of new staff, and what specific steps must staff follow under the policy? What provisions will there be for making the policy known to patrons and the public at large?
Circumstances, if any, under which records will be released.

Librarians will find it useful to append supporting documents (chosen from those listed above) to their policy. With these resources close at hand, librarians can prove formidable opponents for anyone who seeks access to confidential information.

Adopting a Policy

A policy stands a much better chance of being adopted if key board members have participated in the policy's development. This may involve consultation by phone calls or even a special meeting to explain the need for policy and seek board members' input. This step, while perhaps cumbersome or inconvenient, will help smooth the way for board adoption of the final document.

Before the meeting at which the policy will be considered, copies of the draft should be sent to all board members along with the agenda and other enclosures. Enlisting supportive board members to "lobby" their colleagues in advance is a valuable aid to the process.

Enlisting the most persuasive and supportive board member to present the policy to the entire board may prove useful. In addition, library directors may want to invite the library's counsel to be present and support the policy from a legal perspective. If opposition to the policy is anticipated, the presenter should be ready to use data on other libraries in the state or region which already have confidentiality policies and on "real-life" examples of horrendous situations which can and do arise in the absence of such a policy.

Implementing a Policy

Once the policy has been successfully adopted by the governing board, the *real* work begins. Every member of the staff should be responsible for knowing the policy and his/her role in its implementation. This is important, even, and especially, for those who have no direct role to play. When initial attempts to obtain information through proper channels have been unsuccessful, determined and harried law enforcement officials, snoopy journalists, and irate patrons have been known to try prying the information they seek from staff members who appear more easily intimidated than their supervisors.

The new policy should be incorporated into all training manuals and procedure books, especially those sections which involve the use of patron information: circulation, registration, and information services.

The governing board and legal counsel also must be familiar with the policy and the roles they will be expected to play when the library is faced with a challenge to the confidentiality of patron information. If board members and counsel have been involved in the policy process from the beginning, this aspect of the task will take care of itself.

5

Public Relations and the Library

Marion L. Simmons

Public relations, some say, is ninety percent performance and ten percent interpretation. This remark gives a good description of the amount of effort required to achieve results in creating the desired image to be projected by the institution. In other words, public relations is doing a good job and telling people about it. But what is said is considerably less important than what is done.

Public relations is not a project designed to meet a specific situation like a censorship problem. It is an ongoing and continuing part of the management function of the library. Policies designed to meet established goals and considered in terms of their effect upon the people served form the basis for the public relations program. If the library is large enough to suport a public relations officer, that person should meet with the group that recommends policies for the institution.

The first responsibility of the policy-making group is to know the community served, whether it is a university or a small college campus and its surrounding community, a high school and the area from which it draws students, a great metropolis, or a wide geographical area. There must be enough research and enough listening to learn the needs of the various publics served. Circles of interest, organizations and their key people, opinion leaders, political figures—all must be identified. This information will also be invaluable later when it is time to interpret the policies and the library's program.

The listening may be done on a person-to-person basis in the library, in the faculty dining room, and at meetings of community groups which staff should be encouraged to join. Formal research and survey methods require special skills and are costly. They should be under-

---

Marion L. Simmons has served as chief of the Public Relations Office of the New York Public Library and is a public relations consultant for libraries.

taken only with the assistance of professional researchers who may be found within the library's publics. Librarians, as information specialists, can gather much data by careful reading and clipping of local papers and from a variety of reports and directories.

Based on the knowledge gleaned through listening and research, a program of service is designed to implement the policies. The listening process continues as a part of evaluating results in light of long-range goals. But that is ahead of the story.

There should be an effective organization of the public relations function within the library structure. Budgetary support is essential to provide materials and staff, including clerical assistance. There should be continuity of aims and operations. A public relations program cannot be limited to an annual report and celebration of National Library Week. Responsibility for the program must be allocated to one person who coordinates efforts and resources. This person is responsible for planning and programming for both limited and long-range objectives.

No matter where the responsibility for the public relations function lies, at some time each employee is "the library" to someone. The clerk at the desk, the telephone operator, and the reference assistant will sooner or later be interpreting library policy to their own circle of friends, if not to library users. Public relations is everybody's job. A prime responsibility, therefore, is to realize that the staff is one of the most important publics and should be well informed on policies and goals.

Only with all of this preparation through goals, policies, and services which implement policies, is the library ready for the ten percent which is interpretation. Great care should be taken in the selection and use of public relations techniques for communicating with users, community agencies, opinion leaders, and the general public. The choice will be guided by available resources in budget, staff, and facilities.

Since whatever resources exist never seem to be adequate, the library needs to seek all the help it can find to get the job done. Friends of the Library groups are a natural focus for communicating library information in a widening circle. Providing programs of films, speakers, and story tellers for local groups means reaching an already established audience with known interests. Volunteers may require time-consuming training to be useful to the library, but such training results in a new group of well-informed "natural allies."

Certain individuals are well worth the effort of developing them into "natural allies" through special techniques. Just as the university librarian may notify a faculty member of new acquisitions in his field, interest profiles on the president, the chancellor, or the controller could be kept and appropriate material sent them to prove the library's usefulness. The school librarian can use the same technique. The public librarian might send books or copies of articles to the mayor, the budget director, the councilman, the county legislator, or the heads of other city departments with a note suggesting that they or members of their staffs might find the attached information of value. A complaint from a reader, in fact, provides an opportunity to make a new friend and potential active supporter of the library and the patron's response may either clarify a misunderstanding or elicit a new idea on how to provide better service.

Apart from reaching groups and individuals, mass media are the obvious way of keeping people aware of the library. Regularly submitted news stories are vital to any library's community relations. Their effects, like those of all good library service, can build the desired image: the library is progressive and forward looking. It is a useful institution staffed by skilled people who are also newsworthy. It is a credit to the community. It continually expands to keep up with contemporary needs.

Librarians should establish good relations with news editors. They probably agree with the library's objectives and would like to help, but their job is to print news, not propaganda. Appointments to see them should be made and the library program discussed with them. Their deadlines should be learned and observed. Editors will of course expect copy in proper format—a typed, double-spaced original on the library letterhead with the telephone number and name of the public relations person and the release date. Standard newspaper style with accurate names, dates, addresses, spellings, and times should be used.

Radio news editors should receive news releases of activities which may fit into their programming scope. As with television, the proportion of their time available for local news is limited. Programming for the electronic media is demanding, and ideas for programs should be presented to the person who handles public service programming for the station.

Live copy to be read by an announcer (with a slide for television) should be discussed with news editors. They may be set up to use nothing but tapes or films which need to be prepared on a highly professional scale. This is another case in which it is advisable to seek professional help; a library can be much more successful by cooperating with others. (For further suggestions on working with the media for intellectual freedom *see* Promoting Intellectual Freedom in part VII.)

There are times when the media will seek information from the library. When that happens, the ALA Public Information Office suggests the following:

1. Ask questions. Determine the name of the publication or the network. Find out what the story is about, the reporter's angle, when the deadline is. If you do not feel qualified to address the question or

are uncomfortable with the approach, say so. Suggest other angles, other sources of information.

2. Be clear about who you are representing—yourself, your library, your state Library Association, etc.

3. Beware of manipulation. Some reporters may ask leading questions, something like "Would you say" followed by an idea for your agreement. Make your own statement.

4. Think first. Think about the subject, your audience and what message you want to convey. Do not be pressured into responding. If you need more time, tell the reporter you'll call back.

5. Be prepared to answer the standard "Who-What-When-Where-How and Why" questions. Have supporting facts and examples available.

6. Pause before answering questions to think about what you want to say and the best way to say it.

7. Keep your answers brief, to the point. This is even more important with broadcast media when you may have only 20 seconds to respond. Too much information can be confusing.

8. Don't be afraid to admit you don't know. "I don't know" is a legitimate answer. Reporters do not want incorrect information. Tell them you'll get the information and call back.

Publications and exhibits can be used to extend the usefulness of the library and interpret it both internally and externally. Pains should be taken to accomplish these with taste and skill. Here again is a case in which professional assistance is valuable. It may be sought among friends of the library or volunteers if the budget does not provide for this kind of skill.

In the development of the public relations program, as with other library activities, assistance from consultants at the state library level should be sought. They serve as a clearinghouse of ideas for effective policies and programs and can give much sound advice. Also, librarians sometimes forget to use their own collections and seek materials on all of these ideas in their shelves and files.

All of the activities above are directed toward building a firm base of support that will stand by the library when a campaign for expansion is mounted, when salary schedules need upgrading, or when the library comes under attack for any reason. As for intellectual freedom, if the library has devoted ninety percent of its efforts to good performance and the remaining ten percent to effective interpretation, it should be able to meet the challenges which come its way with a well-understood materials selection policy based on sound principles, a planned response to complaints, and the support of many allies.

6

The Censor: Motives and Tactics

The term "censor" often evokes the mental picture of an irrational, belligerent individual. Such a picture, however, is misleading. In most cases, the one to bring a complaint to the library is a concerned parent or a citizen sincerely interested in the future well-being of the community. Although complainants may not have a broad knowledge of literature or of the principles of freedom of expression, their motives in questioning a book or other library material are seldom unusual. Any number of reasons are given for recommending that certain material be removed from the library. Complainants may believe that the materials will corrupt children and adolescents, offend the sensitive or unwary reader, or undermine basic vaues and beliefs. Sometimes, because of these reasons, they may argue that the materials are of no interest or value to the community.

Although an attempt to stereotype the censor would be unfair, one generalization can be made: Regardless of specific motives, all would-be censors share one belief—that they can recognize "evil" and that other people must be protected from it. Censors do not necessarily believe their own morals should be protected, but they do feel compelled to save their fellows.

Why Censorship?

In general, there are four basic motivational factors which may lie behind a censor's actions. The four motivations are by no means mutually exclusive; indeed, they often merge, both in outward appearance and in the censor's mind.

Family values. In some cases, the censor may feel threatened by changes in the accepted, traditional way of life. Changes in attitudes toward the family and related customs are naturally reflected in library materials. Explicitly sexual works in particular are often viewed as obvious causes of repeated deviation from the norm. Because they challenge values, censors may want to protect children from exposure to works dealing frankly with sexual topics and themes.

Political views. Changes in the political structure can be equally threatening. The censor may view a work that advocates radical change as subversive. (The fact that such works have been seen as attacking basic values is confirmed by the number of attempts to label library materials with such broad terms as "communistic," "un-American," or "ungodly.") If these works also contain less than polite language, it will not be difficult for the censor to formulate an attack on the grounds of obscenity in addition to—and sometimes to cover up—objections on political grounds.

Religion. The censor may also view explicitly sexual works and politically unorthodox ideas as attacks on religious faith. Antireligious works, or materials that the censor considers damaging to religious beliefs, cause concern about a society many see as becoming more and more hostile to religious training, and buttress beliefs about society's steady disintegration.

Minority rights. Of course, not all censors are interested in preserving traditional values. The conservative censor has been joined by groups who want their own special group values recognized. For example, ethnic minorities and women struggling against long-established stereotypes are anxious to reject anything that represents a countervalue. And these groups, too, may use the devices of the censor.

Whatever the censor's motives, attempts to suppress certain library materials may also stem from a confused understanding of the role of the library and of the rights of other library users. The censor's concern about library materials is based upon a view of the library as an important social institution. But the censor may fail to see that the library fulfills its obligations to the community it serves by providing materials presenting all points of view, and that it is not the function of the library to screen materials according to arbitrary standards of acceptability. Would-be censors may think that it is the role of the library to support certain values or causes, which are, of course, their values and their causes.

In the United States, under the First Amendment, no citizen and no librarian can properly assume the duty or right to restrict or suppress legally protected expressions of ideas. The censor may not understand that a request that certain works be labeled or restricted, if fulfilled, would lead to an abridgment of the rights of other library users.

The Censor in Action

A censorship incident usually begins with a library user's complaint about specific library materials. In general, the immediate aim of the complainant is to inform the library that the materials in question are unacceptable. In some cases, the complainant may asume that the library will immediately agree that the materials are not appropriate and should not be in the library.

The censor may want to state publicly that he has found "objectionable" materials in the library and may attend a meeting of the library board to announce his "discovery." Those sections of the work that are considered especially offensive may be read aloud or distributed in writing to the library board, the local press, and the public. The censor may also go one step further and organize an ad hoc censorship organization. Even if an ad hoc group is loosely organized, the censors could use it effectively to promote a statement of purposes among other community groups, to conduct a letter-to-the-editor campaign, and to circulate petitions. The organization could also influence public funding, the appointment of the library director, and the appointment or election of library board members.

Although most censorship incidents begin with an objection to a specific work, if the censors are unsuccessful in getting the item banned they may turn their efforts to library policy. If they cannot bring about a change in the library's policy on materials selection and distribution, they may then ask that the library establish a closed shelf or adopt a policy of restricted access.

Opposing the Censor

Well in advance of the appearance of the censor, a materials selection program, a procedure for handling complaints, and a public relations program will, of course, have been established. After the censor comes, censorship of library materials can be resisted by informing a number of key support sources: (1) community leaders and community organizations who would support the position of the library; (2) local news media whose editorial support would be valuable; (3) other librarians in the community and state whose support could then be available if needed; (4) the publisher of the challenged work who may have on file all its reviews and also may be interested in the legal questions raised by such practices as labeling and restricted access; (5) all library staff members and the governing board; (6) library's counsel; (7) the state library association's intellectual freedom committee; and (8) ALA's Office for Intellectual Freedom.

A censorship attempt presents the library with a good opportunity to explain the philosophy of intellectual freedom which underlies library service in the United States. For example, the library should prepare an article for local newspapers explaining the role of the library and its commitment to the Library Bill of Rights. The article can emphasize the importance of the freedom to read as established by the First Amendment.

It is important to keep in mind that not every attempt to resist censorship will be successful; in many instances, developments will take a discouraging turn. However, it is certain that if the library is not prepared to offer any resistance, no battle will be won. And every battle won will contribute to establishing the library as an institution for free citizens in an open society.

PART VI

Assistance from ALA

1

What ALA Can Do to Help
Librarians Combat Censorship

The American Library Association maintains a broadly based program for the promotion and defense of intellectual freedom. The program is composed of the Intellectual Freedom Committee; the Office for Intellectual Freedom; the Intellectual Freedom Round Table; the Freedom to Read Foundation; and the LeRoy C. Merritt Humanitarian Fund.

Establishment of Policy

According to its revised statement of responsibility, approved by the Council in 1970, the purpose of the Intellectual Freedom Committee, a committee of the Council, is "to recommend such steps as may be necessary to safeguard the rights of library users, libraries, and librarians, in accordance with the First Amendment to the United States Constitution and the Library Bill of Rights as adopted by the ALA Council; to work closely with the Office for Intellectual Freedom and with other units and officers of the Association in matters touching intellectual freedom and censorship."[1]

The first part of this responsibility is discharged in large measure through the recommendation of policies concerning intellectual freedom to the ALA Council. The Council approved policy statements on such matters as free access to libraries for minors, labeling of library materials, censorship of library materials because of alleged racism or sexism, and the like, not only provide the front-line librarian with concrete guidelines for establishing policy, but also establish a professional code to whose defense the Association is committed. It is on the basis of such policy statements that the Association can come to the aid of a

---

1. *American Libraries* 3, no.10:1048 (Nov. 1972).

librarian whose professional conduct in defense of the principles of intellectual freedom is challenged.

Educational and Professional Support

The basic program of the Intellectual Freedom Committee is educational in nature. The most effective safeguards for the rights of library users and librarians are an informed public and a library profession aware of repressive activities and how to combat them. Toward this end, the administrative arm of the Intellectual Freedom Committee, the Office for Intellectual Freedom, attempts to implement ALA policies on intellectual freedom and to educate librarians to the importance of the concept. The Office for Intellectual Freedom maintains a wideranging program of educational and informational publications, projects, and services.

The *Newsletter on Intellectual Freedom*, the official bimonthly publication of the Intellectual Freedom Committee, was initiated in 1952 and has been edited and produced by the OIF staff since 1970. The *Newsletter* is addressed to both librarians and members of the general public concerned about intellectual freedom. Its main purpose is to provide a comprehensive, national picture of censorship efforts, court cases, legislation, and current readings on the subject. Through original and reprinted articles, the *Newsletter* offers a forum for expressing varying views about intellectual freedom, while providing a means for reporting activities of the Intellectual Freedom Committee, the Office for Intellectual Freedom, and the Freedom to Read Foundation. In 1982, noted civil liberties authority Nat Hentoff named the *Newsletter* "the best small publication in America." It is available by subscription from the Office for Intellectual Freedom.

The *OIF Memorandum*, a somewhat different publication, is a brief, informal monthly communication designed for the chairs and members of state library association intellectual freedom committees. It is also circulated to ALA chapter councillors and is available by subscription to others. The *Memorandum* provides information pertinent to state intellectual freedom committees, such as legislative news and information on Supreme Court decisions. It is also used by the Office for Intellectual Freedom to disseminate new materials and information which may assist in the promotion and defense of intellectual freedom, and to give suggestions for new programs and project ideas.

The Office for Intellectual Freedom also distributes documents, articles, and ALA policies concerning intellectual freedom to both librarians and the general public, including: *Banned Books Week Kit; Bicentennial of the Bill of Rights: A Resource Book;* Confidentiality in Libraries: An Intellectual Freedom Modular Education Program; and

Censorship and Selection: Issues and Answers for Schools, by Henry Reichman. As special circumstances require, materials regularly distributed by the Office are augmented. During nationwide controversies concerning individual titles, press clippings, editorials, and public statements detailing the ways various libraries around the country handled requests to remove specific materials are compiled and sent out to others with problems. The Office also seeks to make the library profession's support and concern for intellectual freedom known to the general public through the mass media and other forums. The Office has produced three audiovisual products: *Censorship or Selection: Choosing Books for Public Schools, The Speaker . . . A Film about Freedom,* and a sound filmstrip entitled *Freedom in America: The Two-Century Record.* Both the Intellectual Freedom Committee and the office for Intellectual Freedom cooperate with other national organizations, such as the Association of American Publishers, in activities which support free expression.

One of the most often used and least heard about functions of the Office is its provision of advice and consultation to individuals (whether librarians or others) in the throes of potential or actual censorship controversies. Rarely does a day go by without a request by phone or letter asking for advice about a specific book which has drawn the censorious attention of an individual or group. In these cases, every effort is made to provide information or give any other assistance. Sometimes this takes the form of a written position statement defending the principles of intellectual freedom in materials selection. other times it requires names of persons available to offer testimony or support before library boards. In extreme cases, it demands a visit to the community to view the problem firsthand and provide moral and professional support for the defenders of First Amendment principles. The alternative(s) chosen is always the prerogative of the individual requesting assistance. If a censorship problem arises, librarians should contact the Office for Intellectual Freedom (50 East Huron Street, Chicago, Illinois 60611; phone 312-944-6780).

In 1990, the Office for Intellectual Freedom established a censorship database to record and, eventually, produce statistics on challenges to library materials across the country. The database will become a useful tool for identifying trends in types of censorship cases and for documenting responses and solutions to these cases. The long term utility of this project depends on the active participation of ALA members across the country. All librarians are encouraged to document and report challenges—successful and unsuccessful—to the Office for Intellectual Freedom. Information about the institution, its location, and the parties involved are kept confidential until—and only if—the information is published elsewhere.

Figure 3. ALA Office for Intellectual Freedom Censorship Database Form

ALA OFFICE FOR INTELLECTUAL FREEDOM--CENSORSHIP DATABASE FORM

OIF USE ONLY
OIF Record No.:   -   Date of Report: Filed by:

I. OBJECT OF CHALLENGE:

Title: Copyright/Issue Date:

Author/Performer(s):
(last, first name)
Publisher/Producer:

Print: ___ Book ___ Textbk ___ Mag. ___ Nwsppr. ___ Pamph. ___ Play ___ Student Publn.
Non-Print: ___ Artwork ___ Film ___ Photo ___ Sound Recording ___ Video
Or: ___ Collection ___ Exhibit ___ Performance ___ Speech ___Other:

Grounds For Challenge: (check all applicable)

1. Cultural	2. Sexual	3. Values	4. Social Issues
___ Anti-Ethnic	___ Homosexuality	___ Anti-Family	___ Abortion
___ Insensitivity	___ Nudity	___ Offensive Language	___ Drugs
___ Racism	___ Sex Education	___ Political Viewpoint	___ Occult/Satanism
___ Sexism	___ Sexually Explicit	___ Religious Viewpoint	___ Suicide
5. ___ OTHER:		___ Unsuited to Age Group	___ Violence

II. INITIATOR OF CHALLENGE:

Individual: ___ Administrator ___ Bd Member ___ Clergy ___ Parent ___ Teacher ___ Patron
   Group: ___ Government ___ Pressure Group ___ Religious Orgn. ___ Other
Organizations Supporting Challenge:

III. INSTITUTION BEING CHALLENGED:
Name:
City: State:

School-Related: ___ School or ___ School Library: Grade Level ___ to ___
Other Library: ___ Academic ___ Public ___ Prison ___ Special
         Or: ___ Community Group ___ Museum/Gallery ___ Publisher
             ___ Student Group ___ Theatre ___ Other:

Person Reporting (optional):   Title:

Address (if different from above):

PLEASE NOTE: THIS INFORMATION IS FOR STATISTICAL USE ONLY; NAMES OF
INDIVIDUALS AND INSTITUTIONS WILL BE KEPT CONFIDENTIAL.
Feel free to attach news clippings or other supporting material. Return to:
Office for Intellectual Freedom, 50 East Huron Street, Chicago, IL 60611

The Office for Intellectual welcomes reports in the form of clips, cards, and letters in addition to the standard reporting form shown in figure 3.*

Combating Repressive Legislation

Repressive legislation on such matters as obscenity and material deemed harmful to minors can severely restrict the activities of the librarian who strives to provide service in accordance with the principles of the Library Bill of Rights. Therefore, the ALA, through the Intellectual Freedom Committee and the Office for Intellectual Freedom, as well as the Freedom to Read Foundation, often supplies testimony, either singly or jointly, supporting or opposing proposed legislation affecting the principles of intellectual freedom as applied to library service. pending legislation in the United States Congress is frequently brought to the attention of these groups by the ALA Washington Office. With the assistance of legal counsel, the Office for Intellectual Freedom will analyze any proposed state or local statute affecting intellectual freedom brought to its attention.

In furtherance of its purpose "to support the right of libraries to include in their collections and to make available to the public any creative work which they may legally acquire," the Freedom to Read Foundation combats through the courts statutes in force that limit or make illegal application of the principles of intellectual freedom. Librarians affected by repressive statutes in force should contact the Freedom to Read Foundation.

Financial and Legal Assistance

According to its constitution, one purpose of the Freedom to Read Foundation, which is formally independent of ALA, but closely linked to it, is "to supply legal counsel, which counsel may or may not be directly employed by the Foundation, and otherwise to provide support to such libraries and librarians as are suffering legal injustices by reason of their defense of freedom of speech and freedom of the press as guaranteed by law against efforts to subvert such freedoms through suppression or censorship. . . ." Librarians whose professional positions and personal well-being are endangered because of their defense of intellectual freedom, and library boards, librarians, and library em-

---

* *Note*: This form is subject to periodic revisions which may be required to facilitate data entry and correspond to changes in technology or software. Contact the Office for Intellectual Freedom for current copies of this form.

ployees threatened with legal action on such grounds, should contact the Foundation.

Librarians requiring immediate financial aid should contact the Le-Roy C. Merritt Humanitarian Fund. The Merritt Fund was established in recognition of the need for support at the moment an individual is in jeopardy or is fired in the cause of intellectual freedom. This special fund not only assists librarians who have been victims of discrimination, it also allows for immediate assistance even prior to the establishment of all pertinent facts in a particular case. Depending on the situation, grants can be made prior to establishment of claims that intellectual freedom is involved. Both the Foundation and the Merritt Fund are administered through the Office for Intellectual Freedom.

Mediation and Arbitration

In June 1971, the ALA Council approved the Program of Action for Mediation, Arbitration, and Inquiry, thus establishing a means for ALA to gather facts regarding violations of ALA policies concerning status, tenure, due process, fair employment practices, ethical considerations, and, certainly, the principles of intellectual freedom. When it receives a complaint, the Staff Committee on Mediation, Arbitration, and Inquiry attempts various means by which to effect a just resolution to the problem. If these efforts fail, a fact-finding team may be appointed and its reports reviewed by the staff committee. The staff committee may then recommend to the ALA Executive Board, which determines the final disposition of cases, one of the following actions:

> 1. Publication of a report that includes a statement of censure, indicating the strong disapproval of ALA because of a violation of one or more of the policies to which [the] Program of Action relates.
>
> 2. Suspension or expulsion from membership in ALA.
>
> 3. Listing of parties under censure in *American Libraries* as a warning to persons considering employment in an institution under censure that its practices and policies are in conflict with ALA policies concerning tenure, status, fair employment practices, due process, ethical practices, and/or the principles of intellectual freedom. On the same page with such listings of censured libraries shall appear the following statement:
>
>> The fact that the name of an institution appears on the censured list of administrations does not establish a boycott of a library, nor does it visit censure on the staff. There is no obligation for ALA members to refrain from accepting appointment in censured libraries. The ALA advises only that librarians, before ac-

cepting appointments, seek information on present conditions from the Staff Committee on Mediation, Arbitration, and Inquiry at Headquarters.[2]

The ALA Executive Board determines the final disposition of cases handled by the Staff Committee.

In June 1990, in response to the recommendations of a SCMAI review committee, SCMAI was replaced by the Standing Committee on Review, Inquiry, and Mediation (SCRIM). The new committee was to be responsible for the basic mandate of the previous one, but would be composed of ALA members (instead of staff) with a staff liaison and two ex officio members from the ALA staff: the Director of the Office of Library Personnel Resources and the Director of the Office for Intellectual Freedom. The procedures to be followed by SCRIM were more clearly defined than those of SCMAI and included the following: instructions to become proactive in the litigation arena, providing "expert witnesses" or filing *amicus curiae* briefs in instances where it is clear that Association policies or professional principles are at stake; to decline to function as an arbitrator and refer parties to professional arbitrators instead; to increase the level of publicity and public relations activity about the committee; and to revise the confidentiality policy of the former committee.

SCRIM had barely begun to implement its new mandate when it fell victim to ALA's budgetary woes. As of the 1992 fiscal year, SCRIM activities have been suspended until further notice.

Without the other programs of support, the Association's call to all librarians to commit themselves to the principles of intellectual freedom would indeed be hypocrisy. Thus the Association makes every effort to maintain these principles and includes them among its highest priorities.

Membership Involvement

ALA encourages its members to become actively involved in the defense of intellectual freedom. The Intellectual Freedom Round Table, established in 1974, is a membership organization within the American Library Association. Participation in the Round Table allows members of the Association close contact with ALA's overall intellectual freedom program.

The Round Table is what its members make of it; all officers are elected by the members. In the past, the Round Table has sponsored

2. From "Program of Action for Mediation, Arbitration, and Inquiry," adopted January 11, 1979, by the ALA Council, amended July 3, 1980.

programs on various intellectual freedom-related subjects, circulated its own newsletter, and coordinated exchanges of experience among state library association intellectual freedom committees. The Round Table, and individual Round Table members are available to assist the IFC, the OIF, and the Freedom to Read Foundation in various joint activities.

Not the least of the Round Table's functions is to contribute funds to special intellectual freedom projects which cannot be funded out of the general ALA budget. The Round Table also administers the annual John Phillip Immroth Memorial Award for Intellectual Freedom. Since 1984, the Round Table has presented the state Program Award, an annual award to the state intellectual freedom committee that has implemented the most successful and creative state project during the preceding year.

Many avenues of activism in support of intellectual freedom are also open to ALA members on the state and local levels. The Library Bill of Rights calls on libraries to "cooperate with all persons and groups concerned with resisting abridgment of free expression and free access to ideas." Such groups and individuals exist in virtually every community, and very often it is the formal and informal ties established by individual ALA members which enable ALA to cooperate with them.

Of special importance, of course, are the state library association intellectual freedom committees. The extent and nature of the activities of these committees vary from state to state. Some groups are more active than others. In some states, the committees have worked with other organizations to build impressive state coalitions in defense of intellectual and academic freedom. Elsewhere they have concentrated on compiling and developing educational materials. The relationship of the ALA Intellectual Freedom Committee and the Office with the state committees is one of mutual cooperation and assistance. Through the monthly *Memorandum* and other mechanisms the Office supports the work at the state level with information, coordination, and ideas. On their part, the state committees can be the Office's "eyes and ears" at the local level. And, of course, when incidents or other controversies arise, it is very frequently the state library association intellectual freedom committee which "mobilizes the troops" and, in cooperation with ALA, provides embattled librarians with "on the spot" assistance.

PART VII

Working for Intellectual Freedom

1

Your State Intellectual Freedom Committee

Over several decades, ALA and the library community as a whole have built an impressive network of support for intellectual freedom. But the foundation of this network remains the too often unacknowledged efforts of volunteer librarians, library trustees, and library users at the state and local levels. Such people have contributed and continue to contribute to the cause of intellectual freedom in many ways and through many organizational forms. The most basic and common outlet for intellectual activism, however, is the state library association intellectual freedom committee.

These committees exist under differing conditions and take on varied organizational forms. But one thing is everywhere the same: it is impossible to separate intellectual freedom concerns from other concerns of library associations. State intellectual freedom committees must work closely not only with ALA's Office for Intellectual Freedom and other intellectual freedom and civil liberties groups, but with the entire state library association. The committees should maintain close and regular contact with the officers and executive bodies of their associations. Where the state library association also has a legislation committee and/or a public relations committee, liaisons should be established, the committee chairs should meet on a regular basis, and, where possible, the full committees should meet jointly each year.

The following pages offer materials to help orient members of state intellectual freedom committees and other individuals working for intellectual freedom in libraries on the state and local levels. The articles included were prepared with the participation of Lee Brawner, J. Dennis Day, Martha Gould, and Susan Heath, all members of the 1981-1982 ALA Intellectual Freedom Committee. These pages are not, however, the definitive organizational guide to intellectual freedom activism. Conditions and problems vary from locality to locality. In the final analysis, it will be the enthusiasm and imagination of committee members themselves which will both define and determine the success or failure of the committee's work.

While this part of the *Manual* is aimed chiefly at those who are active—or interested in becoming active—in intellectual freedom work, individual libraries and librarians will benefit as well from the materials included. Much of what has been said in previous chapters about how individual libraries can prepare to face challenges to intellectual freedom is equally relevant to similar efforts by state associations and other groups. And the additional suggestions made in this section on working with the media, lobbying, coalition work, and responding to major censorship incidents can certainly be applied by many individual libraries. Again, promotion of intellectual freedom and promotion of libraries are inseparable.

2

Promoting Intellectual Freedom

Promoting library services and promoting intellectual freedom mean reaching out to the public. But such promotion is a two-way street. To be an effective advocate of intellectual freedom, just as to be an effective promoter of library services, one must first know the people one seeks to reach. Promotion efforts begin by identifying library users. What are their needs? What "competition" do libraries face? It is important to remember that each library exists to serve *all* of its users.

With respect to intellectual freedom, it is essential to know what attitudes and forces exist in a given community or state and how these relate to national trends. Those working for intellectual freedom must do their homework. Who are the people with influence? What are their views? Which political, social, religious, business, and labor groups are potential allies? Which are potential supporters of censorship? What are their principal concerns? State intellectual freedom committees should strive to keep themselves and librarians in their state informed of the activities and ideas of potentially censorious organizations and individuals, both local and nationwide. The more that is known about the philosophies and beliefs held by potential censors, as well as their organizational goals and concerns, the better prepared librarians will be to engage them in meaningful dialogue when the time comes to do so.

In gathering information on potential censors, however, there is the danger of opposing censorship with the tactics of the censors themselves. The American Library Association opposes all practices which involve the prejudgment and labeling of groups and individuals as censors—libraries do not blacklist. Those involved in the defense of intellectual freedom should work hard to avoid developing an adversary relationship with individuals or groups who are been involved in censorship activity. It is much more productive to work toward developing relationships based on mutual respect. The more librarians and their supporters understand about the feelings and beliefs of would-be censors, the easier it will be to relate to them as individuals with serious concerns. Building an image of receptivity, openness, fairness, and friendliness toward the *entire* community can only enhance the standing of libraries and the concept of intellectual freedom.

Working with the Media

Promotion of intellectual freedom through the mass media must be understood within the context of the overall commitment of the libraries to public relations (*see* Public Relations and the Library in part V). State intellectual freedom committees should thus coordinate all media work with the state library association public relations committee. But media treatment of questions relevant to intellectual freedom in libraries has its particularities, which should be thoroughly understood.

In general, members of the mass media are among the best potential allies in the promotion of intellectual freedom. Much has already been done to make the national media aware of censorship problems. Just about every major television network, every major newspaper, and many national magazines have carried feature stories on challenges to the public's right of access to certain materials in libraries. Usually, the more nationally oriented the media, the more likely they are to be sympathetic. Such sympathy, however, does not mean that the case for intellectual freedom must not be presented as forcefully and as skillfully as possible at all times.

The media seek out conflict. Hence, they are far more likely to cover a censorship story when there is data to prove a marked increase or change in direction of censorship pressures, when a case is pending in the courts, or when there is a local incident. At moments of controversy, members of state committees and local librarians may find media attention thrust upon them. But such attentions will be extensive and better focused if at all times regular contact is maintained with appropriate media figures.

The media are always looking for local people who can be quoted with authority regarding specific issues, including intellectual freedom. Where appropriate, members of state intellectual freedom committees can make themselves known to the media as such a resource, or they may inform the media of the presence in the community or state of other authorities, including figures of national reputation. To do this, write the feature and city editors of local newspapers and send along pertinent background. A brief letter could simply say that "intellectual freedom issues are much in the news, and if you are interested in a local point of view, I would be happy to help." Provide a short biography.

The same approach can be used with radio and television programs by writing the producer of these shows.

One also need not wait to be called by reporters or television producers. Some techniques for getting coverage include:

Letters to the editor. Don't write long letters; stick to the point; and write them well. A letter has a better chance of getting printed if it is tied into something the paper has featured.

Guest columnist. Many newspapers provide for guest columnists on certain days of the week.

Columns and editorials. Many newspapers carry locally originated columns, and nearly all run editorials. Writing a potentially sympathetic columnist with an idea, or a phone call to determine who writes the editorials and a conversation about the subject might prove fruitful.

Talk shows. Listen to the various stations in your area and make a list of those with talk shows. Call the station and get the name of the producer and either write or call about doing a show on intellectual freedom. Be prepared to offer both a rationale for the show (perhaps a local "hook") and to suggest potential guests, including perhaps someone from the "other side."

Situations will arise when those working for intellectual freedom will be the focus of a story or will be sought for an interview. When a local incident occurs, members of the state intellectual freedom committee may be asked to comment. Or comment may be sought on a situation that has occurred elsewhere—an incident, a court decision, or a reported increase in censorship pressures. Individual librarians faced with censorship challenges may also have media attention thrust upon them; they very likely will seek advice on handling the situation from the state committee.

Regardless of the circumstances, the following general advice will be useful to those contacted by the media:

Try to get all the information possible about the story or program. Don't be afraid to ask questions.

Make sure to have the facts at hand. Avoid giving quotes or comments without first thinking through the situation. It is permissible to get the questions from a reporter and answer them at a later time, especially if the reporter has simply telephoned.

Don't offer personal opinions unless you are convinced they can really advance your cause. Stick to facts and the explication of basic principles. Be prepared to quote the Library Bill of Rights and other ALA policies.

Try not to become embroiled in particulars. Move the discussion to larger issues—the true impact of censorship and the importance of intellectual freedom.

Don't assume those you are speaking to know the background of the continuing challenge to intellectual freedom. Be prepared to go over basic principles and issues, starting with the First Amendment itself.

Don't make long speeches. Reduce your arguments to one or two pithy sentences.

Control your emotions. Angry people don't win arguments. Try to identify with your audience and speak to their concerns.

Try to think of all the questions you might be asked and prepare convincing responses in advance. A meeting with a writer or reporter, or an appearance on radio or television, no matter how brief, needs preparation.

3

Building Intellectual Freedom Coalitions

Librarians who work for intellectual freedom know that there is broad support for the concept among diverse constituencies. When would-be censors seek to deny access to library materials, a remarkable array of individuals and organizations can and do come to the library's defense. Many of these people are already active in defense of intellectual freedom elsewhere in society.

Article 4 of the Library Bill of Rights states that "Libraries should cooperate with all persons and groups concerned with resisting abridgment of free expression and free access to ideas." To facilitate such cooperation, libraries, individual librarians, and state intellectual freedom committees have joined with other groups and individuals in local, state, and regional coalitions in defense of intellectual freedom.

Such coalitions are helpful for several reasons. It is, of course, simply common sense to know, so to speak, who your friends are and how to keep in touch. But beyond this, uniting with others in coalition permits greater coordination of effort and allows supporters of intellectual freedom to reach broader audiences. Coalitions can also benefit from an expanded financial base and from the collective prestige, resources and contacts of the constituent groups. By uniting together, concerned organizations can pool resources to avoid duplications of effort and to concentrate limited funds and personnel where they are most needed. For example, groups concerned with intellectual freedom may collectively monitor legislative activity. Or they may form a joint speakers' bureau.

The task of organizing a statewide coalition for intellectual freedom may at first seem intimidating. But coalitions differ greatly from each other. Some are highly structured, full-time organizations themselves. Others are closer to an informal network of communication and support. The same coalition which may, at times of crisis, function like a well-oiled machine, may at other moments be minimally active. In short, a coalition is what its members make it. There is no coalition ideal model. The level of organization and commitment should be appropriate to the needs of those involved and no more. If a state committee's needs can be met through a structure which simply facilitates regular contact and little more, this is also fine.

The organization of statewide intellectual freedom coalitions was greatly stimulated by the formation in 1977 of the Academic Freedom Group, a national coalition initally of eight and, subsequently, ten educational organizations, including the American Library Association. Between 1978 and 1981, the Academic Freedom Group held a series of regional workshops to bring together supporters of intellectual freedom from various groups on the local level, and to encourage the building of regional and state coalitions. The first Academic Freedom Group regional workshop in Indianapolis, Indiana, in March 1978 provided delegates from Wisconsin with the necessary impetus and support to begin work. Later that year, the first, and one of the most successful, state coalitions, the Wisconsin Intellectual Freedom Coalition, was formed.

The Wisconsin experience is highly instructive. The delegates who attended the Indianapolis workshop selected a contact person and drew up a roster of names. After extensive communication, an organizational meeting was held, and the task of determining the goals and objectives of the group began. At a second meeting, four months later, a constitution and bylaws were approved, stationery designed and printed, and work on a general publicity brochure completed. Four major committees were formed to carry out the goals of the coalition: Membership; Project and Research; Legislative Monitoring; and Public Relations and Publicity. The Projects and Research Committee immediately began to organize a highly successful speakers' bureau.

In 1979, the Wisconsin Intellectual Freedom Coalition held its first annual conference, attended by over one hundred interested citizens from all parts of the state. On the basis of this success, the Coalition board decided to begin publication of a regular *WIFC Newsletter*. At the second conference in 1980, the Wisconsin coalition began to develop a statewide clearinghouse for information. A collection of newspaper clippings, books, pamphlets, magazine articles, tapes, and the like was begun. The Wisconsin group continues to offer consultation services to beleaguered librarians, administrators, and teachers. It also forwards informational materials and will send a representative to board meetings or other public forums where controversy may be brewing. Press releases are also issued, when warranted, regarding censorship issues, and the coalition has arranged television and radio interviews.

Not every state will find conditions ripe for the kind of ambitious effort undertaken in Wisconsin. But everywhere there is a need for greater cooperation and more joint efforts by various supporters of intellectual freedom. The following suggestions will be useful to state intellectual freedom committees seeking to organize a coalition in their states.

The first step in organizing a coalition is to identify those organizations in the state or region whose goals and objectives are consistent with ALA's intellectual freedom principles. Consider inviting such organizations to participate as local chapters of the American Civil Liberties Union; religious organizations; civic groups; educational organizations, including the PTA, the National Education Association, the American Federation of Teachers, and groups of school administrators; lawyers' organizations; and societies of journalists. Individuals should also be sought out and encouraged to participate, since they may be in the best position to do the kind of day-to-day coordination that will be necessary to keep the coalition functioning.

Develop a succinct letter of introduction to be sent to those invited to the organizational meeting. Spell out clearly your own committee's conception of the proposed coalition, but make it clear that the final goals and objectives, as well as the structure of the group, are to be determined democratically.

At the first meeting, the coalition should draft a statement of its principles and, if desired, a constitution and bylaws. These can be more or less formal, depending on the desires of the constituent groups. Committees with concrete goals and specific projects should be organized immediately so that the coalition does not become bogged down in sterile debate or bureaucratic busywork. Choose responsible officers who have the time and commitment to keep things going.

Some projects for the coalition to take up include: design of a public relations brochure, publication of a newsletter, legislative monitoring, organization of an information network to mobilize support during times of crisis, and organization of statewide conferences on intellectual freedom.

For further information, a publication, *Coalition Building Resource Book*, edited by Susan L. Heath of Nicolet College, Wisconsin, is available for $10 from the Office for Intellectual Freedom.

A strong state coalition in support of intellectual freedom should not and cannot replace the state library association intellectual freedom committee. But active participation in such coalitions will strengthen the committee's ability to function effectively and help the state association as a whole in its promotion not only of intellectual freedom, but of library services as well.

4

Lobbying for Intellectual Freedom*

One activity in which members of state intellectual freedom committees frequently are involved is legislative lobbying. In this work the committee should always cooperate closely with the state library association legislation committee and with any full-time lobbyists associated with the state association. Simply put, legislative lobbying is the process through which citizens seek to persuade legislators to support a given cause. Lobbying involves the joint efforts of permanent, usually professional, lobbyists and individual citizens who seek to meet with or simply to write their legislative representatives. In general, lobbying for the interests of libraries, including libraries' interest in defending intellectual freedom, is an on-going task.

There are, however, times when special efforts are demanded; when the state committee, together with the legislation committee, must go "all out" to mobilize librarians and their supporters in favor of or in opposition to a specific legislative measure which will have a significant positive or negative impact on intellectual freedom. At such times, committee members may be called upon to give testimony before legislative committees, or it may be necessary to mobilize a large group to descend upon the legislature in a major lobbying effort.

In such situations, librarians too often find themselves ill prepared and on the defensive. This need not be the case. To protect our libraries from would-be censors, librarians must learn to lobby effectively for intellectual freedom. In part IV of this *Manual*, Eileen Cooke, Direc-

---

* Employees of public libraries classified as 501(c)(3) organizations for tax purposes should review regulations governing the amount of time and funding that can be spent on lobbying. Employees of federal libraries also should become familiar with regulations restricting lobbying activities.

These regulations do not apply to persons acting as private citizens rather than in their official capacity as public or federal librarians.

tor of ALA's Washington Office, has reviewed some of the basic guidelines librarians should follow in dealing with legislators. Any state committee which becomes involved in lobbying should begin its preparation by reviewing her comments. The following suggestions offer additional guidance and ideas on how to better prepare for and more effectively conduct lobbying tasks.

Identify in advance those persons and groups who support libraries and intellectual freedom. Keep a current file of their names so they can be called upon to help when the need arises.

Identify sympathetic individuals in the local and state political structure. Keep in contact with such people on a regular basis.

Work with libraries to make sure they have written policies and procedures. Such policies and procedures help lobbying efforts because they help legislators recognize that librarians go about their work in a professional manner.

When approaching legislators, know what you are talking about. Do not make the mistake of being as emotional as those who would censor. Appeal to legislators with facts and reason.

Know enemies as well as friends. Stay alert to the moral and philosophical attitudes of candidates and officeholders. Make your concerns known early, and, where possible, get commitments in support of intellectual freedom before controversy erupts.

Maintain an active telephone tree to alert supporters when there is a problem. At the same time, be sure that a core group is ready, willing and able to speak on short notice at hearings, etc. Involve library supporters as well as librarians in this group. Public statements and testimony by official spokespersons for the library association will be strengthened if they are accompanied by statements from a broad cross section of community representatives.

When the legislature is in session, monitor all bills introduced. The legislation committee or lobbyist affiliated with your library association can work with you, and, if your committee is participating in a coalition, lobbyists for other groups may also be able to assist.

Know how the legislature works. Know the committees, their members, and where relevant legislation will be referred. Know who has power in the legislature, and who has influence on those with power. You will probably not become, or want to become, a "power broker," but such people can help you get a fair hearing.

Keep a current file on which members of the legislature support libraries and intellectual freedom, and to what extent, and which do not or are uncommitted.

Lobbying is really basically quite simple. On the most fundamental level, we all lobby for what we believe each day. In working for intellectual freedom, lobbying is a necessary extension of the broader process of promoting intellectual freedom and educating people to the dangers inherent in restrictions upon it. The most difficult part of lobbying is probably finding the time and the people willing to give of their time to do it.

5

Dealing with Censors

When libraries follow the policies and procedures outlined in this *Manual* (*see* Dealing with Concerns about Library Resources number 2.14 in part I and Before the Censor Comes: Essential Preparations number 1 in part V), the overwhelming majority of complaints will be resolved without undue controversy, very often to the mutual satisfaction of both the library and the complainant. But sometimes, despite the protections offered by a good materials selection policy and review procedure, a major censorship incident still develops. In such cases, beleaguered librarians, library trustees, or concerned library users may contact the state intellectual freedom committee directly for assistance, or they may be referred to the committee by ALA's Office for Intellectual Freedom. Sometimes the state committee will learn of an incident independently and approach those affected with an offer of assistance. It is entirely up to the affected library to decide whether to work mainly through members of the state committee, directly with OIF, or through some convenient combination thereof. The library may even choose to reject all outside assistance. In any event, the state committee should maintain close and regular contact with OIF and report all relevant information. Communications failures within the ranks of the anticensorship forces are unnecessary and can be destructive.

When a censorship incident threatens to mushroom into a crisis, everyone involved should observe two basic rules. The first is Do Not Panic! No matter how belligerent and seemingly unreasonable the complainants may become, no matter how much some local politicians, the media, or assorted independent careerists may distort the issues, the library and its librarians should strive first and foremost to maintain a calm and professional attitude. The library and the state committee should insist that established policies and procedures be upheld.

Though a careful and reasoned response should be made to all allegations, efforts should be made to keep the discussion focused on the major intellectual freedom issues. Defenders of intellectual freedom should at all times refrain from making personal attacks on their opponents, no matter how tempting this may become.

The second basic rule is that the person directly involved must always retain the final word. To the state intellectual freedom committee, a local incident may appear to be a golden opportunity to educate the public and promote the principles of intellectual freedom. But to the beleaguered librarian, it may seem like a horrible nightmare, to be resolved in a manner consistent with professional principles, to be sure, but as quickly and quietly as possible. In such instances, OIF, the Freedom to Read Foundation, and the state committees all exist to assist and support the people directly involved. The nature and extent of that assistance and support are ultimately determined by those people. If, for example, a beleaguered librarian wants to avoid statewide or national publicity, nothing should be done to attract such attention.

Although it may be tempting to immediately "pull out all the stops" in meeting a censorship challenge, this may be detrimental. Too many false alarms make it difficult to mobilize broad support when it is truly needed. Outside involvement may also force people and institutions into dogmatic positions from which they find it difficult to compromise or retreat. It is never useful to needlessly place people in positions in which they will "lose face" by backing down.

Each censorship incident has its own peculiar history. The library and its defenders must generally plot their strategy and tactics on a case-by-case basis. The following principles, however, are generally applicable:

> If the issue involves a local library, be sure that all staff members are kept fully abreast of the situation as it develops.
>
> Make sure that all members of the library's governing body are kept informed about the incident. Use this opportunity to educate or reinforce their beliefs about the principles of intellectual freedom in libraries.
>
> Confer with the president and/or the entire executive board of the state library association and keep them advised about the progress of the situation.
>
> The library's ongoing program of public education about the principles of intellectual freedom should be intensified. All library staff, governing board members, media representatives, and concerned library users should receive a copy of the Library Bill of Rights and those of its interpretations which are relevant to the issue at hand.

If national, state, or even local media become involved, all media statements should be centrally coordinated. The state library association and its intellectual freedom committee should be certain that all public statements have been cleared in principle with the affected library or librarians. In dealing with the media, it is important to stress the principles involved in the incident, to point out the implications of censorship for First Amendment freedoms, and to emphasize the library's responsibility to provide access to information for all members of the community it serves.

If radio or television talk shows or interviews are scheduled, library supporters should be alerted so that individuals may attend or even participate. The procensorship forces should not be permitted to "stack" the audience or otherwise dominate media coverage, thereby giving the false impression that they represent the majority.

Lines of communication to the complainants should always remain open, no matter how strained the situation becomes. The freedom to read is not negotiable, but an acceptable and principled solution to a crisis is better attained through dialogue than confrontation.

If legal action is threatened the library's legal counsel should be so advised at once. If the library does not have legal counsel, assistance can be obtained with the advice of the Freedom to Read Foundation. Attorneys for the Foundation are available to consult with local counsel.

When the incident is settled a responsible representative of the library and, if appropriate, the state committee should write or personally thank the media representatives, organizations, legislators, officials, board members, and other individuals who came forward in support of intellectual freedom. If the issue is unresolved, these supporters should be kept advised of the situation.

After the challenge is resolved, key members of the library staff, the governing body, members of the state committee, and others intimately involved with the incident should meet to summarize how the issue was handled and consider how the procedure may be improved in the future.

Coping with Stress

In these pages the importance of maintaining a calm approach and professional response in the face of challenges has been repeatedly emphasized. Yet this is easier said than done. A beleaguered librarian, surrounded by angry protestors who may consider the librarian a "communist pornographer" and more, may well find a professional demeanor difficult to maintain. And members of state intellectual freedom committees may find the calm handling of crises elusive when they try to respond to repeated media inquiries from sources ranging from national television networks to the *Mudville Post* and still meet all their other professional responsibilities. Working for intellectual freedom can be extremely stressful. Coping with stress is itself an important part of defending libraries and librarians against censorship.

Members of state intellectual freedom committees need not be psychologists, but in providing assistance to librarians involved in censorship incidents and in coping with the strains of activism oneself, personal concern, common sense, and knowledge of some basic facts about stress are useful. Stress may result from either positive or negative stimuli. It may take physical, emotional, psychological, or social forms, and it may be mild or severe, chronic or acute. Stress is never the product solely of external stress factors, but arises from the reaction of individual personality characteristics to environment.

Most people can recognize when they are experiencing stress, but cannot so easily identify its cause. A person in the midst of a stressful struggle against censorship may not immediately recognize that it is the demands of this involvement which lie at the root of the stress being felt. People involved in working for intellectual freedom should be aware that increased stress can be one perfectly normal and controllable byproduct of their work.

Constructive strategies for coping with stress are geared toward confronting the problem and dissipating its effects. We may not always be able to control the stress factors in our lives, but we can control how they affect us. Here are a few proven, common-sense ideas for managing stress:

Maintain good health habits, especially during times of crisis. Eat a well-balanced diet, get plenty of sleep, and exercise regularly.
Take time to get organized. Determine priorities and concentrate on them. Set reasonable demands for yourself and learn to delegate or postpone responsibilities when necessary.
Get better acquainted with yourself. Acknowledge your successes. Recognize that mistakes do not make you a failure.
Decompress. Allot time to yourself each day. Experiment with relaxation techniques and give them a chance to work.
Be creative and vary your routine.[1]

---

1. "Coping with Stress" adapted with permission from the Salt Lake City Public Library's *Orientation Program*, prepared (1980) by the Staff Development Advisory Committee in conjunction with Jed L. Erickson, ALSW, director, Salt Lake Mental Health Crisis Intervention, University Hospital, University of Utah.

Most of all, keep in mind two very important facts. First, what you are doing is right. Intellectual freedom is worth defending. The problems which arise and the mistakes you may make are secondary. Second, you are never alone. There is support out there for intellectual freedom. Not only do the great majority of Americans back the efforts of libraries to defend intellectual freedom, the library profession stands behind its commitment to intellectual freedom with a full program of support. In particular, beleaguered librarians and those working for intellectual freedom should never forget that ALA's program of assistance is always available to them.

Selected Bibliography

Bosmajian, Haig A. *The Freedom to Read: Books, Films and Plays.* New York: Neal Schuman, 1987.

———. *Freedom of Expression.* New York: Neal Schuman, 1988.

———. *Academic Freedom.* New York: Neal Schuman, 1988.

———. *The Freedom to Publish.* New York: Neal Schuman, 1990.

Brant, Irving. *The Bill of Rights: Its Origin and Meaning.* New York: New American Library, 1965.

Burress, Lee. *The Battle of the Books: Literary Censorship in the Public Schools, 1950-1985.* Metuchen, N.J.: Scarecrow, 1989.

Cornog, Martha, ed. *Libraries, Erotica and Pornography.* Phoenix: Oryx Press, 1991.

Criley, Richard. *The FBI and the First Amendment.* Los Angeles: The First Amendment Foundation, 1990.

DelFattore, Joan. *Why Johnny Shouldn't Read: Textbook Censorship in America since 1980.* New Haven, Conn.: Yale University Press, 1992.

Demac, Donna A. *Liberty Denied: The Current Rise of Censorship in America,* 2nd revised edition. New Brunswick, N.J.: Rutgers University Press, 1990.

D'Souza, Frances, ed. *Information, Freedom, and Censorship, World Report 1991, Article 19.* Chicago: American Library Association, 1991.

Downs, Robert B. and Ralph E. McCoy, eds. *The First Freedom Today: Critical Issues Relating to Censorship and Intellectual Freedom.* Chicago: American Library Association, 1984.

Emerson, Thomas I. *Toward a General Theory of the First Amendment.* New York: Vintage Books, 1966.

Emord, Jonathan W. *Freedom, Technology and the First Amendment.* San Francisco: Pacific Research Institute for Public Policy, 1991.

Foerstel, Herbert C. *Surveillance in the Stacks: The FBI's Library Awareness Program.* Westport, Conn.: Greenwood Press, 1990.

Hoffman, Frank. *Intellectual Freedom and Censorship: An Annotated Bibliography*. Metuchen, N.J.: Scarecrow, 1989.

Hull, Elizabeth. *Taking Liberties*. New York: Praeger Publishers, 1990.

Hurwitz, Leon. *Historical Dictionary of Censorship in the United States*. Westport, Conn.: Greenwood Press, 1985.

Kalven, Harry. *A Worthy Tradition: Freedom of Speech in America*. New York: Harper and Row, 1988.

Lewis, Anthony. *Make No Law: The Sullivan Case and the First Amendment*. New York: Random House, 1991.

Lurie, Alison. *Don't Tell the Grown-ups: Subversive Children's Literature*. Boston: Little, Brown, 1990.

Marsh, Dave. *50 Ways to Fight Censorship & Important Facts to Know About the Censors*. New York: Thunder's Mouth Press, 1991.

Noble, William. *Bookbanning in America: Who Bans Books?—And Why*. Middlebury, Vt.: Paul S. Eriksson, 1990.

Reichman, Henry F. *Censorship and Selection: Issues and Answers for Schools*. Chicago: American Library Association, 1988.

Index